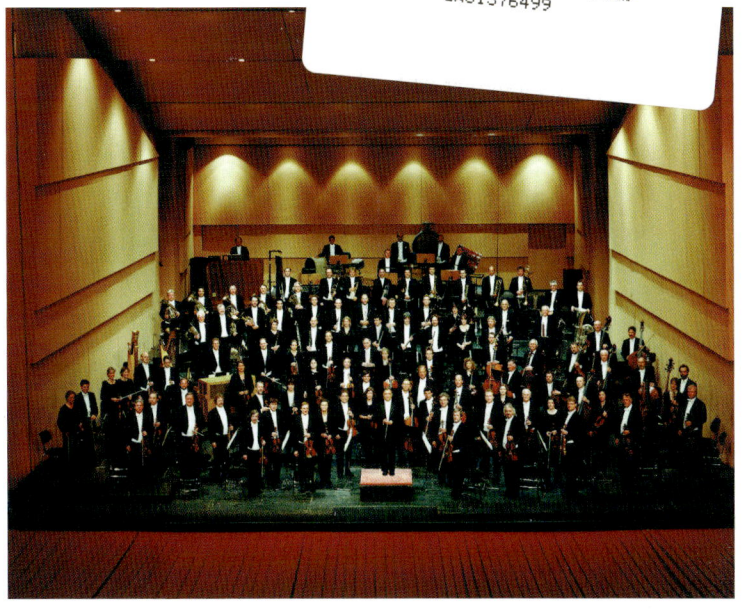

Anthem Guide to the Opera, Concert Halls and Classical Music Venues of Europe

The editors

SZU PING CHAN is a young journalist with a special interest in art and culture. In addition to her role as the main contributor on this project, she has also written for the *Guardian* and the MSN Group.

Additional research by James Proud, Mike Withey and Sarah Pett.

Anthem Guide to the Opera, Concert Halls and Classical Music Venues of Europe

Foreword by Steven Isserlis

ANTHEM PRESS
LONDON · NEW YORK · DELHI

Anthem Press
An imprint of Wimbledon Publishing Company
www.anthempress.com

This edition first published in UK and USA 2009
by ANTHEM PRESS
75-76 Blackfriars Road, London SE1 8HA, UK
or PO Box 9779, London SW19 7ZG, UK
and
244 Madison Ave. #116, New York, NY 10016, USA

Copyright © Anthem Press 2009
Foreword © Steven Isserlis 2009

The moral right of the authors has been asserted.

All rights reserved. Without limiting the rights under copyright reserved
above, no part of this publication may be reproduced, stored or introduced
into a retrieval system, or transmitted, in any form or by any means
(electronic, mechanical, photocopying, recording or otherwise),
without the prior written permission of both the copyright
owner and the above publisher of this book.

British Library Cataloguing in Publication Data
A catalogue record for this book is available from the British Library.

Library of Congress Cataloging in Publication Data
Anthem guide to the opera, concert halls and classical music venues of
Europe / edited by Anthem Press ;
foreword by Steven Isserlis.
p. cm.
Includes index.
ISBN 978-1-84331-272-7 (pbk.)
1. Music-halls—Europe—Directories. 2. Theaters—Europe—Directories.
3. Europe—Guidebooks. I. Anthem Press.
ML21.E95A68 2008
780.78'4—dc22
2007043295

ISBN-10: 1 84331 272 7 (Pbk)
ISBN-13: 978 1 84331 272 7 (Pbk)

ISBN-10: 1 84331 322 7 (Ebk)
ISBN-13: 978 1 84331 322 9 (Ebk)

1 3 5 7 9 10 8 6 4 2

Printed in India

CONTENTS

FOREWORD ix
GENERAL MAP xii–xiii

AUSTRIA
Salzburg 2
Vienna 15

BELGIUM
Antwerp 28
Bruges 30
Brussels 33
Ghent 38
Liège 40

BULGARIA
Sofia 43

CROATIA
Split 47
Zagreb 48

CZECH REPUBLIC
Prague 53

DENMARK
Aarhus 61
Copenhagen 63
Odense 68

ESTONIA
Tallinn 72

FINLAND
Helsinki 77
Lahti 79

FRANCE
Bordeaux 84
Lille 86
Lyon 88
Marseille 93
Metz 95
Montpellier 98
Nantes 101
Nice 102
Paris 105
Strasbourg 126
Toulon 128
Toulouse 129

GERMANY
Baden 133
Bayreuth 135
Berlin 137
Bonn 150
Cologne 152

Dresden	157
Duisburg	160
Düsseldorf	162
Frankfurt	164
Hamburg	169
Karlsruhe	173
Leipzig	175
Munich	180
Stuttgart	188

GREAT BRITAIN
Bath	193
Belfast	196
Birmingham	201
Brighton	205
Cardiff	207
Edinburgh	212
Glasgow	217
Glyndebourne	222
Liverpool	225
London	229
Manchester	248
Southampton	251
York	254

GREECE
Athens	258

HUNGARY
Budapest	262

ICELAND
Rejkjavik	267

IRELAND
Cork	271
Dublin	272
Wexford	277

ITALY
Bologna	280
Florence	281
Milan	283
Naples	285
Palermo	287
Parma	289
Rome	291
Turin	299
Venice	301
Verona	304

LATVIA
Riga	307

LIECHTENSTEIN
Balzers	314
Vaduz	315

LITHUANIA
Vilnius	318

MALTA
Valletta	323

MONACO
Monte Carlo	328

THE NETHERLANDS

Amsterdam	331
Rotterdam	333
Utrecht	336

NORWAY

Bergen	339
Oslo	340
Stavanger	342
Trondheim	344

POLAND

Kraków	347
Warsaw	349

PORTUGAL

Lisbon	355
Porto	359

ROMANIA

Bucharest	362

RUSSIA

Moscow	366
St Petersburg	368

SERBIA

Belgrade	378

SLOVAKIA

Bratislava	387

SLOVENIA

Ljubljana	392

SPAIN

Barcelona	397
Bilbao	402
Las Palmas	406
Madrid	408
San Sebastián	414
Seville	416
Torrent	417
Valencia	418

SWEDEN

Gothenburg	423
Stockholm	425

SWITZERLAND

Basel	435
Geneva	436
Lausanne	438
Lucerne	440
Zurich	443

TURKEY

Istanbul	449

UKRAINE

Kyiv	451
Odessa	451

PHOTO CREDITS	**453**
INDEX BY VENUE	**455**

FOREWORD BY STEVEN ISSERLIS

Welcome to this new *Guide to the Opera, Concert Halls and Classical Music Venues of Europe.* Cultural tours have come a long way since the days when the great eighteenth-century writer Dr Burney described his musical travels around Europe in much the same way that African explorers would later write about their discovery of exotic tribes. Nowadays, the world of classical music is truly international, music-lovers frequently building their holidays or business trips around visits to the world's most famous concert halls or opera houses; audiences at these venues tend to be cosmopolitan, a variety of languages filling the lobbies with excited chatter before a major musical event.

What is it that makes a great concert hall? It's a hard question to answer, because there are no hard and fast rules. Looks are important, of course – but they're not essential. I can think of a few halls which are fronted by striking exteriors, but fail to live up to their promise on the inside; conversely (and preferably, of course), there are halls which shrink apologetically off main streets, only to offer an Aladdin's cave of treasures within their portals.

Looks are really a luxury, however; one can get to love an ungainly hall, so long as it's the right shape for sound. A satisfying amount of reverberation – not too little, not too much – is far more important than visual glamour. A great acoustic should inspire both performer and audience, making it possible to produce magical tones that would never occur to either party in a lesser venue. Ideally, an artist should be able to fill the whole space with golden resonance, and then invite each member of the audience (or at least their ears) right onto the stage, to share the music's most intimate secrets.

Even acoustics, however, are for me not the most important prerequisite for greatness: even more essential are *ghosts*. They can be felt immediately as one enters a great hall: not just the memories of the major performers who have been there, but also the spirit of the people who designed and built it, those who planned all the exciting and memorable events that took place there, and – above all, perhaps – the shadows of the audiences whose lives were enriched and uplifted by the music they heard within those four walls.

Glancing through the list of places described in this book, I have to admit that not all of them could really be described as 'great' musical venues. The historic halls that have survived are almost inevitably great, otherwise they would have been long gone; it is such a struggle to keep a concert hall or opera house alive, when there would be so much more money to be made by a multi-storey car park, that any place still standing after a hundred years or more must have merited the affection of large groups of passionate devotees who will have fought for its survival as if their lives depended on it. Wars, however – particularly the second world war – have brooked no argument in their destruction of some of the world's most treasured venues. Some – such as the Leipzig Gewandhaus and the Philharmonies of Cologne and Berlin – have been worthily replaced, with a real respect for their heritage. Others, however, have left behind a vacuum that has never been adequately filled. There was a long period – far too long – after the second world war where city after city announced the opening of a brand new concert hall or opera house, inaugurated it with a feast of grand ceremonies and self-congratulations – and presented the public with a grey, soulless building that robbed the music of its magic and left audiences cold; it was understandable that music-lovers preferred to stay home of an evening and listen to recordings. Luckily, over the last fifteen years or so, that has changed: acousticians and architects have begun to work together with far more imagination and intelligence; some of the results – the halls in Gateshead, Valencia and Lucerne, for instance – have been spectacular. The fame of such places spreads immediately, adding immeasurably to the lustre of a city – and to the quality of life of its inhabitants.

This book does not attempt to make value judgements, preferring to let you make up your own mind about what is or is not a great setting for music. Its use is primarily practical: after a brief history of the venue and an overview of its principal activities, it proceeds to give you wise advice about how to obtain the best seats (and what they're likely to cost), what to do while you're in the area of the hall, and how to get there. It's all very useful stuff: despite the glories of the internet, it can be hard to obtain such information from abroad. I've been yelled at – somewhat unreasonably, I felt – by a lady from Milwaukee for the difficulties she'd faced in trying to book for a series in Britain in which I was involved. I tried to explain that playing the cello in a concert didn't also entail working as the Box Office manager, but she'd have none of it. 'If you accept an engagement from them, you should make sure they know what they're doing!' she said firmly. That silenced me. This book should be helpful to her and to others like her (except less fierce, hopefully) who enjoy musical tours within Europe. And there are many such people, despite those doom-mongers whose favourite pastime is to predict the death of classical music within the next few years. When a book like this can come out, listing well over 200 major buildings in Europe alone (and of necessity leaving out scores of other important venues), I think we can safely say that classical music is alive and well – and likely to produce several more generations' worth of ghosts!

Steven Isserlis is one of the most prominent living cellists. He is notable for his diverse repertoire, distinctive sound and total command of phrasing. He studied at Oberlin Conservatory of Music and was awarded a CBE in 1998 and the Schumann Prize 2000 by the city of Zwickau. He is also Artistic Director of the International Musicians Seminar, Prussia Cove in West Cornwall, where he both performs and teaches.

Arctic Circle
REYKJAVÍK
ICELAND
Faroes
Shetland
ATLANTIC
OCEAN
NORTH
SEA
Belfast
Edinburgh
IRELAND
DUBLIN
York
UNITED
KINGDOM
Cardff
LONDON
NETHER-
LANDS
AMSTERDAM
DENMARK
Hamburg
BRUSSELS
BELGIUM
GERMAN
Cologne
LUX.
Frankfurt
PARIS
LUXEMBOURG
Munich
FRANCE
BERN
Zürich
SWITZERLAND
Santiago de
Compostela
Bordeaux
Lyon
Bilbao
Milan
Venice
Porto
SAN
MARINO
PORTUGAL
ANDORRA
Marseille
MONACO
Florence
MADRID
LISBON
SPAIN
Barcelona
Corsica
(Fr.)
ITA
ROME
Valencia
Seville
biza
Mallorca
Sardinia
Tangier
MEDITERRAN
RABAT
Fes
Casablanca
ALGIERS
TUNIS
MOROCCO
Essaouira
Marrakesh
ALGERIA
TUNISIA

NORWAY
SWEDEN
FINLAND
HELSINKI
St Petersburg
RUSSIA
OSLO
STOCKHOLM
TALLINN
ESTONIA
Gothnburg
LATVIA
RĪGA
MOSCOW
COPENHAGEN
LITHUANIA
KALININGRAD (RUSSIA)
VILNIUS
MINSK
BELARUS
BERLIN
WARSAW
POLAND
KIEV
kraków
PRAGUE
CZECH REPUBLIC
UKRAINE
SLOVAKIA
BRATISLAVA
VIENNA
MOLDOVA
CHIŞINĂU
BUDAPEST
AUSTRIA
HUNGARY
LJUBLJANA
ZAGREB
ROMANIA
SLOVENIA
CROATIA
GEORGIA
BOSNIA-HERZEGOVINA
BELGRADE
BUCHREST
BLACK SEA
Adriatic Sea
SARAJEVO
SERBIA& MONTENEGRO
BULGARIA
SOFIA
ALBANIA
MACEDONIA
İstanbul
Naples
TIRANA
Thessaloniki
ANKARA
TURKEY
GREECE
Aegean Sea
İzmir
ATHENS
Sicily
SYRIA
MALTA
CYPRUS
LEBANON
Crete

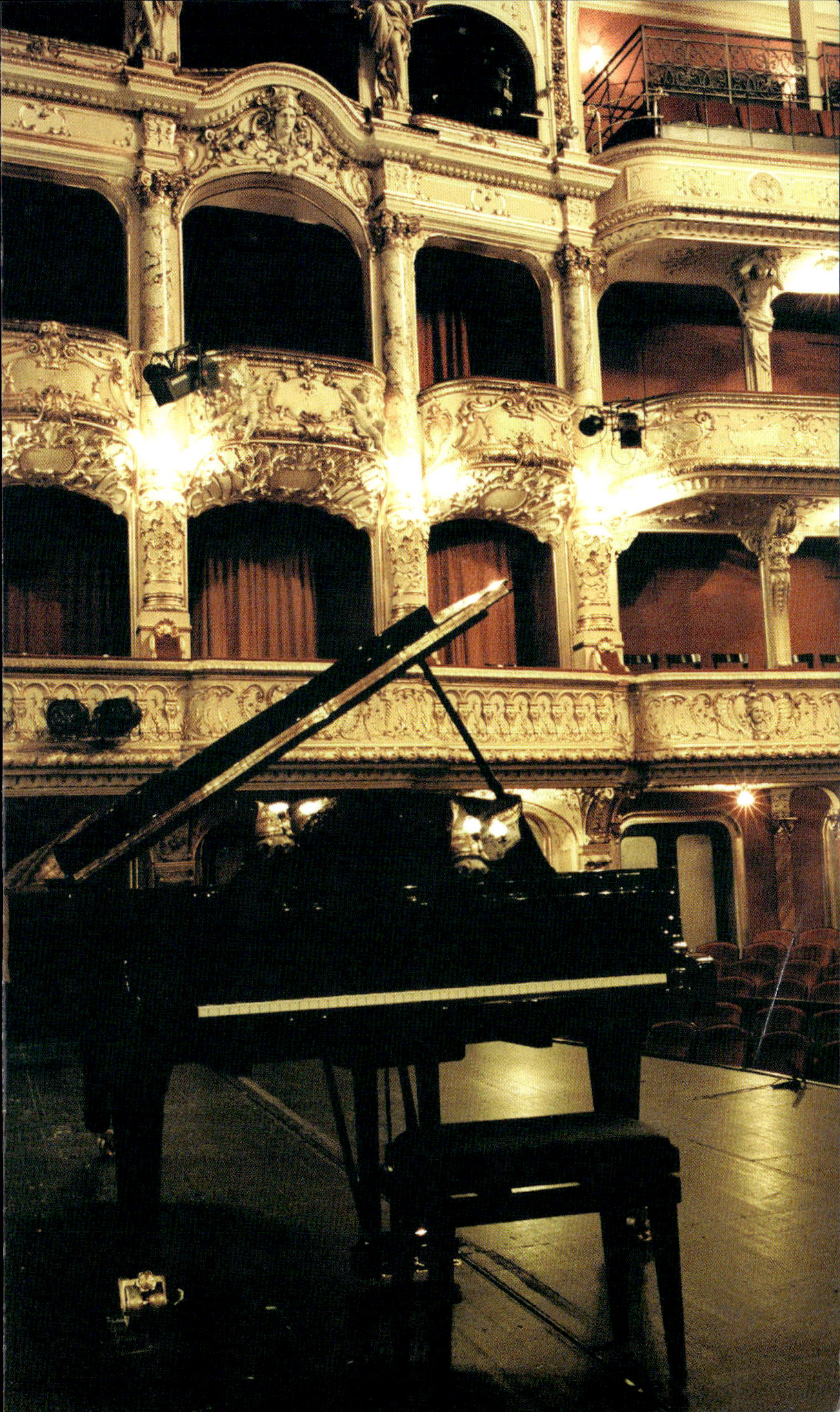

AUSTRIA

SALZBURG

Felsenreitschule

The Felsenreitschule is a dramatic open-air venue quarried out of the rock of the Mönchsberg. Today, the stage occupies an area once used for animal baiting and riding displays, hence the name 'Felsenreitschule'. Used since the first festival for open-air plays in 1948, where 'Gluck's Orfeo ed Euridice', directed by Herbert von Karajanthe was performed as the first opera. Subsequent to this, a major transformation took place during the 1960s, with the 40 metre stage enlarged by a four metre deep area created in the space beneath it. Collapsable seating for the audience and storage space for scenery underneath was added, as was a lighting gantry. To protect the stage a retractable roof was installed with a specially designed grille above it to dampen the sound of the rain, giving the Felsenreitschule a modern twist whilst managing to preserve its origins.

Hofstallgasse 1
Salzburg
A-5020
Austria
Tel: +43 (0)662 849 097
Fax: +43 (0)662 847 835
www.salzburgfestival.at

TICKETING

Advance Sales: Tickets for the Annual Festival are available from November of the previous year. For high profile concerts at the Felsenreitschule, visitors are advised to book tickets several months in advance.

Price Range: Ticket prices generally range from €40.00 to €360.00. There are no concessions available.

Box Office

The Festival Box Office is in Herbert-von-Karajan-Platz, beside all the Main Festival Buildings. The Box Office is open Monday to Friday, from 8.00 a.m. to 12.30 p.m. and from 1.00 p.m. to 4.30 p.m. Bookings can also be made by telephone, fax and online. Bookings made from Austria incur a €5.00 booking fee; for all other countries, a 20% advance booking charge and a 10% transaction charge apply. Tickets for all performances should be collected from the Box Office.
Tel: +43 (0)662 804 5500
General booking commences in April, and is open Monday to Saturday, 8.00 a.m.–5.00 p.m.
Fax: +43 (0)662 804 5555
www.salzburgfestival.at

PERFORMANCES

Events occur during Easter, Whitsun and Summer (July to August), together with occasional concerts throughout the year, such as New Year's Day concert.

Times: Times vary, but a typical concert starts at 7.30 p.m.

Resident Groups: The Berlin Philharmonic (Easter only) and the Vienna Philharmonic.

Annual Festivals/Special Events: The Felsenreitschule is involved in the world famous Salzburg Festival, which takes place every summer between July and August. The Recreation Festival also occurs on an annual basis every October.

SEATING

Capacity: 1,437

Organization: The audience is arranged in three tiers, looking out from under arches onto an open-air stage.

EDUCATION

Guided Tours

Guided tours of the venue are conducted daily, advance booking is required for groups of ten or

more. To arrange a tour, contact the venue directly.
Tel: +43 (0)662 849 097 or email: festspielshop@culturmanagement.com

Times: July to August, 9.30 a.m., 2.00 p.m. and 3.30 p.m.; June and September, 2.30 p.m.; January to May and October to December, 2.00 p.m.

Cost: €5.00. For groups of ten or more, €3.70 per person.

Concessions: Children under 12, €2.90; groups of ten or more children under 12, €2.20 per child; schoolgroups, €29.00.

HOW TO GET THERE

Bus: 1, 4, 15. A day pass costs €4.20.

Overground: Central Station

Car Parking: Parking is available in the Altstadt Garage, a large underground car park in the Monchsberg Hill. Parking costs €2.40 per hour; €14.39 per day. From one hour prior to a concert, patrons are eligible for a reduction.

Großes Festspielhaus

Opened in 1960, the Großes Festspielhaus is the modern centrepiece of the Salzburg Festival. Built in a huge cavern blasted out of the rock of the Mönchsberg mountain, the building forms a massive and opulent opera theatre. Stretching a hundred metres across, the Großes Festspielhaus boasts one of the largest stages in the world, regularly attracting the finest artists in the world. Two sculptures, representing 'music' and 'theatre' by Wander Bertoni occupy the Festpielhaus, reminding visitors of the eclectic and inspirational atmosphere within, an idea which is summed up by a Latin motto engraved on the building's façade. The motto, which reads, 'OSB: Sacra camenae domus/ concitis carmine patet/ quo attonitos/ numen ad aurus ferat' (The Muse's holy house is open to those moved by song; divine power bears us up who are inspired.) sums up perfectly the power of music, an

Hofstallgasse
Salzburg
A-5010
Austria
Tel: +43 (0)662 849 097
Fax: +43 (0)662 847 835
www.salzburgfestival.at

experience amplified ten-fold for visitors to the Großes Festspielhaus.

TICKETING

Advance Sales: Tickets for the Annual Festival are available from November of the previous year. For high profile concerts at the Großes Festspielhaus, visitors are advised to book tickets several months in advance.

Price Range: Ticket prices can range from €5.00 to €360.00. There are no concessions available.

Box Office

The Festival Box Office is located in Herbert-von-Karajan-Platz, beside the Main Festival Buildings. It is open from Monday to Friday, 8.00 a.m.–12.30 p.m. and 1.00 p.m.–4.30 p.m. Bookings can also be made by telephone, fax and online. Bookings made from Austria incur a €5.00 booking fee; for all other countries, a 20% advance booking charge and a 10% transaction charge apply. Tickets for all performances should be

collected from the Box Office.
Tel: +43 (0)662 804 5500
General booking commences in April, and is open Monday to Saturday, 8.00 a.m.–5.00 p.m.
Fax: +43 (0)662 804 5555
www.salzburgfestival.at

PERFORMANCES

Events occur during Easter, Whitsun and Summer (July to August), together with occasional concerts throughout the year, such as New Year's Day concert.

Times: Times vary, but a typical concert starts at 7.30 p.m.

Resident Groups: The Berlin Philharmonic (Easter only) and the Vienna Philharmonic.

Annual Festivals/Special Events: The Großes Festspielhaus is involved in the world famous Salzburg Festival, which takes place every summer between July and August. The Recreation Festival also occurs on an annual basis each October.

SEATING

Capacity: 2,170

Organization: There is a large parterre section on the ground floor and a balcony.

Best Seats: The best seats are at the front of the parterre section.

Good Seats on a Budget: All tickets for events in the Großes Festspielhaus are relatively expensive. The cheapest seats are at the back of the hall.

EDUCATION

Guided Tours

Guided tours of the venue are conducted daily, advance booking is required for groups of ten or more. To arrange a tour, contact the venue directly.
Tel: +43 (0)662 849 097 or email: festspielshop@culturmanagement.com

Times: July to August, 9.30 a.m., 2.00 p.m. and 3.30 p.m.; June and September, 2.30 p.m.; January to May and October to December, 2.00 p.m.

Cost: €5.00. For groups of ten or more, €3.70 per person.

Concessions: Children under 12, €2.90; groups of ten or more children under 12, €2.20 per child; schoolgroups, €29.00.

FACILITIES

Services

♿ Disabled access.

HOW TO GET THERE

Bus: 1, 4, 15. A day pass costs €4.20.

Overground: Visitors should alight at the Central Station where they can take a 15 minute walk to the venue or take a connecting bus line.

Car Parking: Parking is available in the Altstadt Garage, a large underground car park in the Monchsberg Hill with exits directly into the venue's foyer. Parking costs €2.40 per hour; €14.39 per day. From one hour prior to a concert, patrons are eligible for a reduction.

Kleines Festspielhaus

The Kleines Festspielhaus was initially erected in 1925, but has been re-modelled several times through the decades, demonstrating the development of the Großes Festspielhaus's little sister into the leading venue it is today. It was re-modelled firstly for the convenience of the Nazi regime, later undergoing several more changes to remedy many of the poor choices they made. Its latest incarnation is the Mozart House, which reopened in 2006 after a major refurbishment. As a result, there have been major improvements in capacity and comfort, with better acoustics and equipment to match the demands of modern audiences.

TICKETING

Advance Sales: Tickets for the Annual Festival are available from November of the previous year. For high profile concerts at

Hofstallgasse
Salzburg
A-5010
Austria
Tel: +43 (0)662 849 097
Fax: +43 (0)662 847 835
www.salzburgfestival.at

the Kleines Festspielhaus, visitors are advised to book tickets several months in advance.

Price Range: Tickets generally range from €8.00 to €600.00. There are no concessions available.

Box Office

The Festival Box Office is located in Herbert-von-Karajan-Platz, beside the Main Festival Buildings. It is open from Monday to Friday, 8.00 a.m.–12.30 p.m. and 1.00 p.m.–4.30 p.m. Bookings can also be made by telephone, fax and online. Bookings made from Austria incur a €5.00 booking fee; for all other countries, a 20% advance booking charge and a 10% transaction charge apply. Tickets for all performances should be collected from the Box Office.
Tel: +43 (0)662 804 5500
General booking commences in April, and is open Monday to Saturday, 8.00 a.m.–5.00 p.m.
Fax: +43 (0)662 804 5555
www.salzburgfestival.at

PERFORMANCES

Events occur during Easter, Whitsun and Summer (July to August), as well as occasional concerts throughout the year, such as New Year's Day concert.

Times: Times vary, but a typical concert starts at 7.30 p.m.

Resident Groups: The Berlin Philharmonic (Easter only) and the Vienna Philharmonic.

Annual Festivals/Special Events: The Kleines Festspielhaus is involved in the world famous Salzburg Festival, which takes place every summer between July and August. The Recreation Festival also occurs on an annual basis every October.

SEATING

Capacity: 1,650

Organization: There is a large parterre section on the ground floor and two balconies.

Good Seats on a Budget: There are cheap standing tickets available for those with good stamina.

Seats to Avoid: All seats are good, but in the parterre stalls there is very little slope to the floor, so visitors seated behind a tall person may experience restricted viewing.

EDUCATION

Guided Tours
Guided tours of the venue are conducted daily, advance booking is required for groups of ten or more. To arrange a tour, contact the venue directly.
Tel: +43 (0)662 849 097 or email: festspielshop@culturmanagement.com

Times: July to August, 9.30 a.m., 2.00 p.m. and 3.30 p.m.; June and September, 2.30 p.m.; January to May and October to December, 2.00 p.m.

Cost: €5.00. For groups of ten or more, €3.70 per person.

Concessions: Children under 12, €2.90; groups of ten or more children under 12, €2.20 per child; schoolgroups, €29.00.

HOW TO GET THERE

Bus: 1, 4, 15. A day pass costs €4.20.

Car Parking: Parking is available in the Altstadt Garage, a large underground car park in the Monchsberg Hill with exits directly into the venue's foyer. Parking costs €2.40 per hour; €14.39 per day. From one hour prior to a concert, patrons are eligible for a reduction.

Mozarteum

The International Mozarteum Foundation can trace its history back to Mozart's widow Constanza, who founded a society for the 'refinement of musical taste' in the nineteenth century. The Foundation's concert hall is a beautiful Art Nouveau building built between 1910 and 1914,

Schwarzstrasse 26
Salzburg
A-5020
Austria
Tel: +43 (0)662 889 400
Fax: +43 (0)662 889 4036
www.mozarteum.at

although the gilded auditorium dominated by a Baroque-style organ stretches back to a more distant time, allowing the building to sit harmoniously amongst the historic architecture of Salzburg. The building remains dedicated to the world-famous composer Wolfgang Amadeus Mozart, and plays homage to the musician in several areas, including a bronze statue entitled, 'Mozart as Musagète' which stands proudly in the concert hall's vestibule.

TICKETING

Advance Sales: Tickets for Mozart Week must be ordered at least 11 months in advance.

Tickets for events organized by the Mozarteum can be ordered until the end of the current season in June.

Price Range: Ticket prices generally range from €8.00 to €95.00.

Concessions: A limited number of tickets are available for all concerts organized solely by the International Mozarteum Foundation for schoolchildren, apprentices and students; tickets cost €8.00 each. Visitors with mobility impairments also qualify for this special rate.

Box Office

The Box Office is located on Theatergasse, just down the road from the Mozarteum. The Box Office is open Monday to Thursday, 9.00 a.m.–2.00 p.m. and Friday, 9.00 a.m.– 4.00 p.m. A transaction charge of €5.00 is applied to all remote bookings.
Tel: +43 (0)662 873 154
Lines are open Monday to Thursday, 9.00 a.m.–2.00 p.m. and Friday, 9.00 a.m.– 4.00 p.m.
Fax: +43 (0)662 874 454
www.mozarteum.at

PERFORMANCES

Performances take place from September to June.

Times: Most concerts start at 7.30 p.m. In addition, there are Sunday morning concerts at 11.00 a.m.

Resident Groups: The Mozarteum Orchestra and the Camerata Salzburg.

Annual Festivals/Special Events: The Mozarteum is involved in the world-famous Salzburg Festival, which takes place every summer, and hosts the Annual Mozart Week in late January.

SEATING

Capacity: Main Concert Hall – 807 seats; Viennese Hall – 200 seats.

Organization: Most seats are on the ground floor, with a balcony located above.

Best Seats: The best seats are the orchestral stalls downstairs.

Good Seats on a Budget: Seats on the side balconies are inexpensive, although the view is restricted by pillars.

EDUCATION

Guided Tours

Guided tours of the venue take place daily; advance booking is required for groups of ten or more. To arrange a tour, Tel: +43 (0)662 849 097 or Fax: +43 (0)662 847 835. Booking queries can also be addressed to festspielshop@culturmanagement.com

Times: July to August, 9.30 a.m., 2.00 p.m. and 3.30 p.m.; June and September, 2.30 p.m.; January to May and October to December, 2.00 p.m.

Cost: €5.00; for groups of ten or more, €3.70 per person.

Concessions: Children under 12, €2.90; groups of ten or more children under 12, €2.20 per child; schoolgroups, €29.00.

FACILITIES

Services

There are two seats available for wheelchair users in the Grosse Saal.

HOW TO GET THERE

Bus: 20. A concert ticket to the Mozarteum is double of a bus ticket.

Car Parking: Concert-goers can park in an underground car park opposite the Mozarteum.

For those wishing to discover more about the life and works of Mozart, why not pay a visit to one of the several museums and residences dedicated to the composer? The museums of the International Mozarteum Foundation bring together some of the most important historical sites where Mozart's genius compositions originated. For further information and directions, see the website under, 'Museums'.

Salzburger Marionettentheater

Without doubt the most extraordinary theatre in Salzburg, the Salzburger Marionettentheater was founded in 1913 by a sculptor, Anton Aicher. It developed into a family business that is

Schwarzstraße 24
Salzburg
A-5020
Austria
Tel: +43 (0)662 872 4060
Fax: +43 (0)662 882 141
www.marionetten.at

still well established to this day. The auditorium is as decorated as any 'normal' opera house, with a unique twist added in that the company puts on performances of operas, including Mozart and Rossini, with a cast of puppets. As Oscar Wilde famously said: 'There are many advantages in puppets. They never argue. They have no crude views about art. They have no private lives'. So this phrase is replicated at the Salzburger Marionettentheater, adding a unique touch of vivacity and life, helping to seal the theatre's world-wide reputation. The Marionettentheater stays close to its origins as a nomadic theatre, journeying for more than ninety years around the world and to this day touring regularly in France, the USA, Japan, Italy, Switzerland, Germany and South America.

TICKETING

Advance Sales: Tickets go on sale up to one year in advance.

Price Range: Tickets generally range from €18.00 to €35.00.

Concessions: Tickets for under-18s cost €14.00. Tickets for mobility impaired visitors can be purchased for €18.00.

Box Office

The Box Office is open on performance days only, 9.00 a.m.–1.00 p.m., and two hours prior to the start of the performance. The theatre is closed from 21 to 25 December, throughout January and during the Easter period.
Tel: +43 (0)662 872 406
Lines are open Monday to Saturday, 9.00 a.m.–1.00 p.m.
Fax: +43 (0)662 882 141
www.marionetten.at

PERFORMANCES

Performances take place all year round, although the company does tour, so check the performance calendar.

Times: Performances take place at 2.00 p.m., 5.00 p.m. and 7.30 p.m.

Programmes: Free programmes are available in German, English, French, Italian, Spanish and Japanese.

Resident Groups: The Salzburg Marionettes

Annual Festivals/Special Events: The Marionettentheater is involved in the world-famous Salzburg Festival, which takes place every summer, and the Annual Mozart Week in late January.

SEATING

Capacity: 350

Organization: All seats are on the same level.

Best Seats: The best seats are located at the front, closest to the stage.

EDUCATION

Guided Tours

Post performance tours can be arranged in advance. Contact the Box Office to arrange.

Cost: €5.00

FACILITIES

Services

There are two wheelchair places available.

Guide dogs welcome.

All performances are subtitled in German, English, French, Italian and Japanese.

HOW TO GET THERE

Bus: 20. Adult single, €0.80

Car Parking: Concert-goers can park in the underground car park opposite the Marionettentheater.

VIENNA

Der Musikverein

One of the most famous venues in the world, beamed around the world on every New Year's Day with its famous concert of waltzes, the Musikverein is renowned for its near-perfect acoustics. The venue is owned by the Friends of Music Society, whose past directors included Johannes Brahms, after whom the chamber hall is now named. Many of the world famous pieces of classical music, including Brahms' and Bruckner's symphonies and Tchaikovsky's 'Violin Concerto', were first performed in these opulent surroundings, with the hall's gold leaf and chandeliers providing the perfect atmosphere to watch the world's finest musicians.

TICKETING

Advance Sales: Sales of individual tickets begin one month before the performance for members, and three weeks before the performance for non-members.

Price Range: Tickets generally range from €4.00 to €80.00.

Concessions: Concessions are available for disabled visitors and carers at a reduced rate of €12.00. Contact the venue for further information.

Box Office

The Box Office is located at the main entrance and is open Monday to Friday, 9.00 a.m.–8.00 p.m.; Saturday, 9.00 a.m.–1.00 p.m. The Box Office is closed from 1 July to 15 August. Tickets booked online can be collected from the Musikverein Box Office at the entrance on Bösendorferstraße 12. Tel: +43 (0)150 58690

Bösendorferstr 12
Wien
A-1010
Austria
Tel: +43 (0)150 58190
Fax: +43 (0)150 581 9094
www.musikverein.at

Lines are open Monday to Friday, 9.00 a.m.–7.30 p.m.; Saturday, 9.00 a.m.–5.00 p.m.
Fax: +43 (0)150 586 8194
www.musikverein.at

PERFORMANCES

Events take place from September to June.

Times: Times vary, so it is advisable to check with the Box Office for individual performances.

Programmes: Concert programmes can be downloaded from the website, and are also available from the Box Office. Programmes are available in German and in most occasions in English.

Resident Groups: Vienna Philharmonic Orchestra, the Orchestral Association of the Society of Music Lovers, Singverein and the Vienna Radio Symphony Orchestra.

Annual Festivals/Special Events: The New Year's Day concert by the Vienna Philharmonic is world famous. Tickets are allocated in a ballot one year in advance.

SEATING

Capacity: The Large Hall can accommodate 1,744 seated, with room for 300 standing; the Brahms Hall, up to 600; the Glass Hall, 380; and the Metallic Hall, 126.

Organization: The Large Hall is organized into parterre stalls on the ground level, side balconies and a balcony and gallery at the rear. The Brahms Hall is organized into a large parterre, a central balcony and side balconies. The Glass Hall has staggered stalls, and the Metallic Hall stalls on one level only.

Best Seats: The best seats in the Large and Brahms Halls are at the front of the ground floor stalls.

Good Seats on a Budget: There are cheap standing tickets available at the back of the ground floor stalls of the Large Hall.

Seats to Avoid: In the Large Hall, the organ balcony, choir stalls and side balconies all have a restricted view. In the Brahms Hall, the choir stalls and the standing places at the back of the parterre have a restricted view, as well as row 2 and the peripheral seats of rows 1 and 3–5 of the central balcony.

EDUCATION

Guided Tours

Guided Tours take place regularly, although they may be changed due to rehearsals. Check the website, www.musikverein.at for details. Tickets can be booked via Tel: +43 (0)150 58190, and are also available from the doorman at the entrance on Bösendorferstraße 12. Further information can also be obtained by emailing: tickets@musikverein.at

Times: Usually at 1.00 p.m., but check online or by telephone to confirm.

Cost: €5.00

Concessions: Free for under-12s; 12–18 year olds, €3.50.

FACILITIES

Dining

The Imperial Café, next door to the Musikverein, is a popular place for pre-concert dining.

Services

There are 12 seats allocated for wheelchair-users and their carers in the Large Hall. In the Brahms Hall, Metallic Hall and Glass Hall, there are two places each.

Guide dogs welcome.

HOW TO GET THERE

Bus: 3A, 4A and 59A

Overground: Tram lines 1, 2, 62, 65 and 71.

Underground: Lines U1, U2 and U4 to Karlsplatz. Adult single, €1.50 in advance, €2.00 on board; day pass, €5.00.

Car Parking: There are five car parks within a few minutes walk of the Musikverein. Each costs around €4.00 per hour.

Wiener Konzerthaus

The Konzerthaus may not be as gilded or finely decorated as the Musikverein, but it is in no way inferior in the quality of its music making or the comfort of its halls. Run by the Concert Hall Society, the Konzerthaus has enjoyed a colourful and innovative history which has seen it pioneer a wide range of activities since its opening in 1913. In addition to its consistent attention to classical repertoire, the programmes of the 1920s and 30s featured major premieres, jazz and popular concerts, readings by famous writers, lectures on spiritualism, modern dance events, symposia,

Lothringerstraße 20
Wien
1030
Austria
Tel: +43 (0)124 2000
www.konzerthaus.at

conferences, and even world fencing and boxing championships. The troubles of World War II halted many of the creative activities, with the venue being reduced to a propaganda site robbed of its cultural activities. These were revived following the War, with contemporary programmes continuing to feature a wide mix of early music, jazz and new music, contributing to a celebration of classical music in its entirety.

TICKETING

Advance Sales: Tickets are sold in subscription cycles. Check on the website for individual concerts to see if tickets are on general sale. Members of the Concert Hall Society get priority booking.

Price Range: Tickets generally range from €12.00 to €72.00.

Concessions: Children between the ages of five and 16 are eligible for a 50% discount. In addition, all people under 27 can purchase tickets 30 minutes before the start of the concert for €12.00. Disabled visitors can purchase selected tickets at a discounted rate of €8.00.

Box Office

The Konzerthaus Box Office is situated on the left of the entrance foyer on entering from the Lothringerstrasse. The Box Office is open Monday to Friday, 9.00 a.m.–7.45 p.m.; Saturday, 9.00 a.m.–1.00 p.m. In addition, there is an excellent online booking system, where visitors can see the view from their seat before booking. Tickets can be collected from the Box Office on the day of the performance.
Tel: +43 (0)124 2002
Lines are open Monday to Friday, 8.00 a.m.–6.30 p.m.; Saturday, 9.00 a.m.–1.00 p.m. and 4.00 p.m.–6.30 p.m.; Sundays and public holidays, 10.00 a.m.–1.00 p.m. and 4.00 p.m.–6.30 p.m.
Fax: +43 (0)124 200 110
www.konzerthaus.at

PERFORMANCES

Events take place all year round.

Times: Times vary, and it is advisable to check with the Box Office for individual performances.

Resident Groups: The Vienna Symphony Orchestra, Vienna Chamber Orchestra and Wiener Singakademie.

Annual Festivals/Special Events: There are several festivals: The Early Music Festival Resonanzen in January, the Spring Festival in April, the International Music Festival during the summer and a festival of contemporary music, Wien Modern, which takes place in November.

SEATING

Capacity: Large Hall – 1,865; Mozart Hall – 704; Schubert Hall – 336.

Organization: The Large Hall has a large, flat parterre section on the ground floor, boxes at the side, and a balcony and gallery at the back of the hall. The Mozart Hall has a flat parterre and balcony. The Schubert Hall is all one level.

Best Seats: In each hall the best seats are towards the front of the parterre section.

Good Seats on a Budget: In the Large Hall the seats at the back of the gallery are far from the stage, but cheap with a good view. In the Mozart Hall the seats on the balcony are the cheapest.

Seats to Avoid: In each hall, seats at the back of the stalls section have a bad view due to the flat floor, but all seats are comfortable.

FACILITIES

Dining

There are refreshments served at concerts, and a fine in-house restaurant, Weinzirl.

Services

There are several seats available for wheelchair users and accompanying carers, but it is advised to book well in advance.

HOW TO GET THERE

Bus: 4A

Underground: Line U4 to Stadtpark. Transport on the underground and buses is free with a ticket for the Konzerthaus.

Car Parking: There is parking in the wonderfully named Beethoven Garage, opposite the Konerthaus on Lothringerstrasse. Parking costs €6.00 on production of a ticket for the Konzerthaus.

Wiener Staatsoper

The Staatsoper is one of the great opera houses of the world, and its list of musical directors is a veritable who's who of classical music. Mahler, Richard Strauss, Furtwängler, Walter, Böhm and von Karajan have all shaped the musical tradition of this great company. The hall itself was old fashioned even when first built, and was virtually destroyed at the end of World War II. The décor is perhaps excessively opulent, with chandeliers, marble floors and oil paintings, but the acoustics are first rate and with the members of the Vienna Philharmonic in the pit, so is the music.

Opernring 2
Wien
A-1010
Austria
Tel: +43 (0)514 442 250
www.staatsoper.at

TICKETING

Advance Sales: Tickets go on sale one month before each performance.

Price Range: Tickets range from €2.00 to €250.00.

Concessions: A maximum of 100 tickets, but no fewer than 25, are allocated to children below the age of 14 (photo identification necessary) for every performance except premieres and those on New Year's Eve. These tickets can be purchased at a flat rate of €15.00. In addition, any seats unsold on the day of performance can be bought cheaply by holders of a bundestheater.at card, available through the website.

Box Office

> The Box Office is open Monday to Friday, 9.00 a.m. until one hour prior to performances; Saturday, 9.00 a.m.–noon; first Saturday of every month, and during Advent, 9.00 a.m.–5.00 p.m.
> Tel: +43 (0)151 31513
> Lines are open daily from 10.00 a.m.–9.00 p.m.
> Fax: +43 (0)151 444 2969
> www.culturall.com

PERFORMANCES

Performances take place from September to June.

Times: Times vary, and visitors are advised to check with the Box Office for individual performances.

Resident Groups: Orchestra of the Vienna State Opera (from which the members of the Vienna Philharmonic are drawn) and the Vienna Staatsoper.

Annual Festivals/Special Events: The Opera Ball is held annually on the Thursday prior to Ash Wednesday, where the auditorium is transformed into a dancefloor for white tie guests to get in one last waltz before Lent.

SEATING

Capacity: 1,709 seats, with room for 567 standing.

Organization: The Staatsoper is a classic opera house with parterre stalls and four levels of balconies.

Best Seats: The best seats are in the parterre section.

Good Seats on a Budget: For those with stamina, there are plenty of cheap standing places available.

Seats to Avoid: Views of the stage are restricted from the peripheral seating.

EDUCATION

Guided Tours

Guided tours take place most days, although times vary. A tour can be combined with a visit to the Opera Museum. For further information and bookings, see www.staatsoper.at or contact the venue by Tel: +43 (0)151 444 2606 or +43 (0)151 444 2421, Fax: +43 (0)151 444 2626 or email: eva.dintsis@wiener-staatsoper.at

Cost: €5.00

Concessions: Senior citizens, €4.00; Children and students, €2.00.

FACILITIES

Dining

There is a restaurant located at the venue which serves a range of meals and refreshments.

Services

There are four wheelchair spaces at the Wiener Staatsoper, plus four spaces for carers.

HOW TO GET THERE

Bus: 59A

Overground: Trams : 1, 2, D, J, 62, 65.

Underground: Lines U1, U2 and U4, Karlsplatz or Oper. Adult single, €1.50 in advance, €2.00 on board; day pass, €5.00.

Car Parking: Opera-goers can use the Kärntner Ring Garage beneath the Ringstrassengalerien Mall at Mahlerstrasse 8.

> Near the opera house, on Hanuschgasse 3, there is a museum of the history of the Staatsoper. Unfortunately, all the sets and memorabilia were destroyed in the War, so there is nothing older than 1955, when the opera reopened, but it is still worth a visit.

Wiener Volksoper

Up until World War I, the Volksoper was very much seen as Vienna's second opera house. Lagging behind the more luxurious Wiener Staatsoper, the theatre was built in 1898 under the name 'Kaiserjubiläumsstadttheater' (Kaiser's Jubilee Civic Theatre), originally intended for the sole purpose of producing plays.

Währingerstraße 78
Wien
A-1090
Austria
Tel: +43 (0)151 444 3670
www.volksoper.at

Eventually in 1903, operas and operettas became part of the programme, expanding its horizons and gaining status as a popular venue, for operas, operettas, musicals and dance theatre. The first Viennese performances of Tosca and Salome were given at the Volksoper in 1907 and 1910, also playing host to world famous singers such as Maria Jeritza and Richard Tauber. After 1929, the Volksoper decided to focus its repertoire on light opera, and after the devastation caused by World War II, the venue became the alternative to the devastated Wiener Staatsoper, eventually returning to its former role of presenting opera, operetta and musicals. Today, although the venue does remain less opulent than the Staatsoper, it is now by no means second best to this or any other venue.

TICKETING

Advance Sales: Tickets for performances between January and June go on sale on 1 January. Tickets for performances between September and December go on sale on 1 June.

Price Range: Tickets generally range from €18.00 to €70.00.

Concessions: Children of 15 and under are eligible for a 75% reduction, however this only applies when in the company of an adult with a full price ticket. A maximum of three children can accompany one adult, and reduced tickets are only available from the Box Office. Students can purchase any unsold tickets 30 minutes before the performance for a reduced rate of €6.00–€7.50. Patrons of 60 and over are eligible for a 25% reduction upon proof of age. Tickets must be purchased from the Box Office. Disabled persons receive a reduction of 50% at the Box Office with the submission of a disabled pass. For wheelchair users and their carers, the ticket price is €3.50 when tickets are booked at least ten days advance over by telephone or in person. Carers are eligible for reduced ticket prices upon proof of status.

Box Office

The Box Office is located at the main entrance. Tickets can also be purchased from the Staatsoper Box Office. The Box Office is open Monday to Friday, 8.00 a.m.–6.00 p.m.; weekends and public holidays, 9.00 a.m.–noon.
Tel: +43 (0)151 31513
Lines are open daily, 10.00 a.m.–9.00 p.m.
Fax: +43 (0)151 444 3669
www.culturall.com

PERFORMANCES

Events take place from September to July.

Times: Most concerts start at 7.00 p.m., although this can vary.

Resident Groups: The Volksoper Symphony Orchestra, and the Vienna Staatsoper.

SEATING

Capacity: 1,473 seats, with room for 102 standing.

Organization: There are parterre stalls on the ground floor, two balconies and boxes on either side of the stage.

Best Seats: The best seats are at the front of the first balcony.

Good Seats on a Budget: The seats in the second balcony are inexpensive and provide good value for money.

FACILITIES

Dining

The Volksoper does not have a restaurant, but recommends the nearby Weimar Cafe (www.cafeweimar.at). Special catering can be organized for groups of ten or more. To arrange, contact Tel: +43 (0)151 444 3661 or email: tickets@volksoper.at

Services

There are 14 wheelchair places available, plus two for accompanying carers, at a reduced rate of €3.30. Prebooking is essential.

HOW TO GET THERE

Bus: 40A

Overground: Tram lines 40, 41 and 42 stop near the venue.

Underground: Line U6, Währinger Straße. Adult single, €1.50 in advance, €2.00 on board; day pass, €5.00.

Car Parking: Parking is available at the WIFI and AKH parking garages. Parking costs approximately €4.00 per hour.

BELGIUM

ANTWERP

Opera de Flandre – De Vlaamse Opera

The building of the Antwerp Opera House was commissioned in 1899 by Jan Van Rijswijck. At the initiative of the composer Peter Benoit, and under the pressure from a steadily growing group of Flemish nationalists, the venue was built primarily for the growing group of people who wanted a music theatre that would be a match for the French Opera. Erected between 1904 and 1907, it was built in a Neo-Baroque style with sumptuous decoration taken from the period of Louis XVI. The most striking feature of the foyer is its lighting, which consists of four hundred bulbs that create the impression of a star-spangled sky, with the enormous canvas that is attached to the ceiling taking two years for Karel Mertens to paint. The Flanders Opera was started in

Vlaamse Opera Antwerp
Van Ertbornstraat 8
Antwerp
B-2018
Belgium
Tel: +32 (0)3 202 10 11
Fax: +32(0)3 231 07 85
www.vlaamseopera.be

1989 as a merger between theatres in Antwerp and Ghent, quickly surpassing the reputation already gained by the two individual companies with performances of Verdi, Wagner and Puccini. The theatre also features concerts by other ensembles and recitals by the Flanders Opera orchestra and choir as well as ballet. There is also a series of lunchtime recitals.

TICKETING

Price Range: Tickets generally range from €12.00 to €75.00.

Concessions: Spare tickets are sold at €8.00 for under-26s 15 minutes before performances. For the under-8s, tickets cost €7.00 to €14.00. In addition, there is a discount for students which varies according to performances.

Box Office

The Box Office is open from Thursday to Saturday, 11.00 a.m.–5.45 p.m. Visitors can also book tickets online or via telephone. There is €1.00 reservation charge per ticket for remote bookings. Online tickets will be sent if bought at least two weeks before the performance. Otherwise visitors can collect tickets from the Box Office.

Tel: +32 (0) 70 22 02 02
Lines are open Tuesday to Saturday, 11.00 a.m.–5.45 p.m.
www.vlaamseopera.com

PERFORMANCES

Events take place from October to June.

Resident Groups: Flanders Opera

SEATING

Capacity: 1,006

Organization: The hall is organized into stalls, three balconies and two galleries.

Best Seats: The best seats are in the central stalls and in the first balcony.

Good Seats on a Budget: Seats in the side balconies provide good value.

Seats to Avoid: None of the seats has restricted views.

FACILITIES

Dining

There are bars and restaurants.

Services

♿ Disabled access.

HOW TO GET THERE

Bus: Buses and trams stop at Franklin Rooseveltplaats nearby. Trams 2, 3 and 15 stop at the underground station 'Opera', which is located near the venue. A single time-limited ticket costs roughly €1.00. Bus, tram and metro travelcards are available for about €10.00, and are valid for multiple journeys.

Car Parking: The theatre recommends car park Roosevelt, Rooseveltplaats 12. The car parks are open from Monday to Thursday until 1.30 a.m.; and continuously from Friday morning to Sunday night.

> Antwerp is renowned for its festive celebrations, throughout December and January. Events include: Christmas markets in Groenplaats, an open air ice rink in Grote Market, the Antwerp Christmas circus at the Lotto Arena and a Christmas tree burning party to see in the New Year.

BRUGES

Concertgebouw Brugge

The Concertgebouw is situated on the Zand, the largest square in Bruges. The large red building is as striking as it is innovative, and was designed by award-winning architects Paul Robbrecht and Hilde Daem to be a 'haven' for all kinds of music. The theatre presents classic opera, symphonic works, chamber music, recitals, and contemporary classical works. The venue consistently tries to experiment in its performances, staging, amongst other things, shows which combine opera and film, together with a growing contemporary art collection.

TICKETING

Price Range: Tickets generally range from €12.00 to €60.00.

> Concertgebouw Brugge
> vzw 't Zand 34
> Brugge
> B-8000
> Belgium
> Tel: +32 (0) 50 47 6999
> Fax: +32 (0) 50 47 6979
> http://concertgebouw.be

Concessions: People under 26 and 60 and over receive a €5.00 discount.

Box Office

The Concertgebouw Box Office is open Monday to Wednesday and Friday to Sunday from 10.00 a.m.–6.00 p.m; Thursday, 10.00 a.m.–8.00 p.m. The evening Box Office opens one hour before each performance. There is no charge if tickets are collected.
Tel: +32 (0)70 22 33 02
Lines are open Monday to Friday, 9.00 a.m.–7.00 p.m.; Saturday, 9.00 a.m.–12.30 p.m. Closed during various dates each year. Please check the website for more details.
www.concertgebouw.be

PERFORMANCES

Programmes: Programmes are available from the Concertgebouw Box Office.

Annual Festivals/Special Events: Each year, the Festival of Ancient Music, Steinway Anniversary Festival and a special 'Bad Boys' Festival featuring composers such as Steve Reich, take place.

SEATING

Capacity: The large hall seats 1,295, a smaller hall seats 300.

Organization: There are stalls and two balconies in the large hall of the Concertgebouw.

Best Seats: The best seats are in the central stalls and in the front rows of the first balcony.

EDUCATION

Guided Tours

Tours of the venue can be arranged in advance. For further information and booking details contact the venue directly.
Tel: +32 (0) 50 47 6999

Cost: Guided tours cost €100.00 for a maximum of 25 people.

FACILITIES

Dining

There is a restaurant at the Concertgebouw and a bar in the foyer for interval drinks.

Services

There is wheelchair access at the Concertgebouw and special places in the hall are available to book, with 24 spaces specifically designated for wheelchair users.

Guide dogs are not admitted inside the Concertgebouw but staff are available to guide the partially sighted to their seats.

HOW TO GET THERE

Bus: 1, 3, 4, 6, 9, 11, 13, 14, 16 and 23 serve the stop next to the theatre from the train station.

Underground: Brugge Central Station is five minutes walk. Cross the station square and the motorway and take the path to the left through the Albert Park.

Car Parking: Parking is available under the Concertgebouw in the 'Centrum Zand' car park. This car park closes at 1.00 a.m. on Monday to Thursday nights and Sunday nights. On Friday and Saturday it remains open for 24 hours. A special evening rate (maximum €2.50) is available to those attending cultural activities who enter the car park after 7.00 p.m. and leave before 7.00 a.m. or closing time.

BRUSSELS

Palais des Beaux-Arts

Constructing and shaping a venue which brings several elements of the arts together harmoniously under one roof, Belgian architect Victor Horta is credited for this fine building which formed part of his urban development project for the Mont des Arts/Kunstberg (Mount of the Arts). Inside, the lower floor is dedicated to music, with the Chamber Music Room joined by the marvellous Henry Le Bœuf Hall, the oval structure of which gives audiences superb acoustics accompanied by aesthetic delights. In addition, BOZAR music concerts are frequently being held at the Palais des Beaux-Arts and elsewhere in Brussels, with Western classical music from the middle ages to modern times in a great variety of line-ups and genres from chamber ensembles to big bands, and recitals to concert performances of opera.

Rue Ravensteinstraat 23
Brussels
B-1000
Belgium
Tel: +32 (0) 25 07 8200
www.bozar.be

TICKETING

Price Range: Tickets generally range from €15.00 to €77.00.

Concessions: There is a 25% discount for those under 26 years of age and a flat rate of €5.00 for those under 12 years. The 25% discount also applies to senior citizens and the unemployed. In addition, there is a flat fee of €5.00 for disabled patrons.

Box Office

There is a Ticket Office at the Centre for Fine Arts, or visitors are also able to purchase tickets via the telephone, via the NATO Theatre Bureau or the European Parliament's Tourist Office by phone. It is possible to purchase tickets by bank transfer to a/c number, 210–0060441–62. The Box Office is open from September to June: Monday to Saturday, 11.00 a.m.–7.00 p.m. In July and August: Monday to Friday, 11.00 a.m.–5.00 p.m. Outside regular hours the Ticket Office also opens one hour before performances. Transaction charges vary.
Theatre Box Office Tel: +32 (0)25 07 82 00. The European Parliament's Tourist Office Tel: +32 (0)2 284 2080. NATO Theatre Bureau Tel: +32 (0)2 707 4983.

Lines are open Monday to Saturday, 9.00 a.m.–7.00 p.m. In July and August: Monday to Friday, 9.00 a.m.–5.00 p.m. www.bozar.be

SEATING

Capacity: The Henry le Bœuf Hall seats 2,100; the Chamber Music Room seats 476.

Organization: stalls, two balconies, boxes.

Best Seats: The best seats are located in the central stalls and in the front rows of the first balcony.

EDUCATION

Guided Tours

The BOZAR STUDIOS team organizes a special tour, where visitors are invited to explore the whole site, and are provided with information on the historical and artistic context of various works at the venue. Tours are available in French, Dutch and English. For further information and booking details, Tel: +32 (0)25 07 82 00 or email: groups@bozar.be

Cost: €60.00 per group (max. 15) on weekdays and €80.00 per group on weekends.

Concessions: For school-groups under 18 and groups aged over 60, €50.00 per group on weekdays and €80.00 per group on weekends.

FACILITIES

Dining

Bars are open one hour before performances and during the interval.

Services

There is good wheelchair access at the Centre of Fine Arts with spaces in the hall.

HOW TO GET THERE

Bus: 38, 60 and 71 stop at the Beaux Arts. Tram lines 92, 93 and 94 also stop in the vicinity.

Underground: Underground to Gare Centrale or Parc 1 A-B.

Car Parking: There is parking available at the Albertine Congrès rue des Sols (perpendicular to Cantersteen, behind the Gare Centrale) from Monday to Friday, 7.00 a.m.–1.00 p.m.; Saturday, Sunday and holidays from 10.00 a.m.–1.00 p.m. There is a direct entrance to the Palais des Beaux-Arts.

Théâtre Royal de la Monnaie – Opera National

'La Monnaie', the French word for coins, is the title of a venue holding a strong monetary theme which stretches back to the late seventeenth century. Built on the former site of the Herberge van Oistervant mint in 1700, the venue was conceived by Gio Paolo Bombarda, owner of the theatre at the Hooikaai, banker and financial counsellor to Maximilian II Emmanuel of Bavaria and governor of the Spanish Netherlands. Injected with new life across the centuries, including architectural commissions by Napoleon, the venue has undergone several

23, Rue Léopo
Brussels
B-1000
Belgium
Tel: +32 (0) 70 23 39 39
Fax: +32 (0) 22 29 13 84
www.lamonnaie.be

renovations since it was first erected. Today, the theatre hosts a combination of opera, recitals, chamber music, symphonic music, lunchtime concerts and dance events.

TICKETING

Price Range: Tickets generally range from €6.00 to €150.00. Lunchtime concerts cost €7.50.

Concessions: Patrons under 28, those over 65 and the unemployed receive a 25% discount on all seats. In addition, 15 minutes before the start of performances, all spare tickets are sold at €10.00 to these concessionary groups. (The theatre may have selected performances for which concessions are not available.)

Box Office

La Monnaie Box Office is open Tuesday to Saturday, 11.00 a.m.–6.00 p.m. and one hour before each performance (only open for that day's performance). Please note that seats in Category 6 (the cheapest category) cannot be booked online. Online, telephone and fax bookings can be collected in person from the Box Office or sent for a €1.00 charge. For five tickets and over the charge is €2.00.

Tel: +32 (0) 70 23 39 39
Lines are open Tuesday to Saturday, noon–6.00 p.m.
Fax: +32 (0) 22 29 13 84
www.lamonnaie.be

PERFORMANCES

Events take place from September to June.

Programmes: Programmes are available from the La Monnaie bookshop or on special stands in the theatre.

Resident Groups: National Opera

SEATING

Capacity: 1,152

Organization: There are six seating categories. stalls, four balconies and boxes.

Best Seats: The best seats in the stalls and the central balcony.

Seats to Avoid: Some seats have a restricted view of the surtitles.

EDUCATION

Guided Tours

Tours can be arranged individually or in groups in French, Dutch, English, German, Italian or Spanish. Contact: e_vanvolsem@lamonaie.be. Alternatively, join the regular tour every Saturday in two languages. Tel: +32 (0) 22 29 13 72 to book a private tour.

Times: Public tours are conducted every Saturday, starting at noon. Tours last approximately 90 minutes.

Cost: €7.00

Concessions: €4.00

FACILITIES

Services

Disabled access.

HOW TO GET THERE

Bus: 29, 60, 63, 65, 66 and 71 all stop at the De Brouckère bus station. Bus numbers 34, 48, 95 and 96 stop at the Beurs which is also within walking distance of the venue.

Overground: There is an underground tram stop at the De Brouckèreplein which is a stop for lines 23, 52, 55, 56 and 81.

Underground: De Brouckèreplein underground station. Lines 1 A–B. A Metro ticket costs €1.50.

Car Parking: Theatregoers are advised to park their vehicle in one of two car parks situated in the vicinity of La Monnaie, the 'Ecuyer' (open 24 hours) and 'Monnaie' (open till 1.00 a.m.), both situated near the venue.

In 1855, the interior of the theatre was completely destroyed by fire, leaving only Eugène Simonis's 1854 pediment, 'The Harmony of Human Passions', the colonnade and the outside walls intact. The pediment's great resistance in the face of disaster inspired a rapid rebuilding of the theatre, and the revival of its repertoire of opera and dance.

GHENT

Koninklijke Vlaamse Opera

The impetus for building a new Ghent playhouse was given by local rich industrialists in the first half of the nineteenth century. In their desire for a magnificent theatre to advertise their newly acquired wealth, they commissioned municipal architect Louis Roelandt to design an exceptional ensemble of high quality, across the street from the court of justice he had designed only a few years earlier. The opera house has an unusual L shape with elongated halls and rooms; a departure from the traditional squares and circles of classicism. The crowning glory of the theatre is an impressive chandelier on a trompe l'oeil ceiling painted by Philastre and Cambon. Both the Koninklijke Vlaamse Opera and the Antwerp Opera House play host to recitals by the Flanders Opera.

Flemish Opera
Schouwburgstraat 3
Ghent
B-9000
Belgium
Tel: +32 (0) 92 68 10 11
Fax: +32 (0) 92 23 87 26
www.vlaamseopera.be

TICKETING

Price Range: Tickets generally range from €7.00 to €77.00.

Concessions: Spare tickets are sold at €8.00 for under-26s from 15 minutes before performances. For the under-8s, tickets cost €7.00 to €14.00. There is also a discount for students which varies according to performances.

Box Office

The Box Office is open from Tuesday to Saturday, 11.00 a.m.–5.45 p.m. There is €1.00 reservation charge per ticket. Online tickets will be sent if bought at least two weeks before the performance. Otherwise tickets can be collected from the Box Office. Tel: +32 (0) 70 22 02 02 Lines are open during Box Office hours.
www.vlaamseopera.com

PERFORMANCES

Events take place from October to June.

Resident Groups: Flanders Opera

SEATING

Capacity: 965

Organization: The hall is organized into the stalls and five balconies.

Best Seats: The best seats are located in the central stalls and in the first balcony.

Good Seats on a Budget: Seats in the side balconies provide good value.

Seats to Avoid: None of the seats has restricted views.

EDUCATION

Guided Tours

Guided tours are conducted one Saturday every month during performance dates. For further information see the website at www.vlaamseopera. be/buildings_guidedvisits.orb or email: info@vlaamseopera.be for further information. Bookings can also be made by contacting the venue directly. Tel: +32 (0) 70 22 02 02

Cost: €5.00

Concessions: €2.50 for the under-12s.

FACILITIES

Services

Disabled access.

HOW TO GET THERE

Overground: Tram 1, 10, 12 from St Pietersstation stop at Kouter-Korte Meer. Trams 21 and 22 from St Pietersstation stop at Zonnestraat. An unlimited day ticket on the trams costs €3.00.

Car Parking: Car park Kouter is situated next to the opera house. Open every day until 2.00 a.m.; Friday and Saturday until 4.00 a.m.

LIÈGE

Opera Royal de Wallonie

The opera house of Liège was built in 1818, situated on the location of an old Dominican monastery. The site was constructed using the material of two churches which had been broken down during the French Revolution. Inaugurated on the 4 November 1820, the venue served as a music venue until World War I, when the building was requisitioned by the German army, and did not reopen as a music venue until October 1919. The Royal Opera of Wallonie was created in 1967 and to this day continues to delight audiences with its diverse range of performances.

> Rue des Dominicains 1
> Liège
> B-4000
> Belgium
> Tel: + 32 (0) 42 21 47 20
> Fax: +32 (0) 42 21 02 01
> www.operaliege.be

TICKETING

Price Range: Tickets generally range from €5.00 to €60.00.

Concessions: Under-15s accompanied by their parents get approximately 20% discount on the full ticket price.

Box Office

> The Opera Royal Theatre Box Office is open Monday to Saturday, 12.30 p.m.–6.00 p.m. or until the end of the first interval on performance days. On Sundays with a performance from 1.00 p.m. until the end of the first interval, otherwise closed on Sundays. Telephone lines are also open during these hours. There is a €2.00 booking charge for remote bookings.
> Tel: +32 (0) 42 21 47 22
> www.operaliege.be/billeterie

PERFORMANCES

Events take place from September to June.

SEATING

Capacity: 940

Seats to Avoid: Not all seats have a good view of the surtitles, ask at the Box Office for further details.

FACILITIES

Dining

Assorted cold food is available upon reservation at the Box Office no later than 24 hrs before the performance, and costs €8.00. There are dinner tables available upon reservation at the Box Office no later than 48 hours before the performance. The Opéra's Table d'Hôte offers you an aperitif, assorted cold food dessert, coffee, and wine for €40.00 per head.

Services

Surtitles are available in French and Dutch for most performances.

HOW TO GET THERE

Bus: 1, 2, 3 and 4 stop at the exit of the Boulevard de la Sauvenière tunnel. 9, 25, 27, 48, 30, 64, 65, 377 all stop nearby. The St Lambert stop is close to the theatre. Bus tickets in Liège cost €1.20 and are purchased on board.

Car Parking: The Opera Royal de Wallonie, in conjuction with the Neujean car park, offers 400 spaces under permanent guard and video surveillance, for the duration of the performance, at a set price per evening. The car park is open every day.

BULGARIA

SOFIA

Natsionalen Dvorets na Kulturata

Boasting 50 percent more steel within its walls than was used in the Eiffel Tower, and holding a firm place in the heart of Sofian culture, the Natsionalen Dvorets na Kulturata provides its visitors with a synthesis of modern architecture within a multifunctional complex. Opened in 1979, it boasts no less than 14 concert halls which have played host to the finest artists, including Jose Carreras, Andrea Bocelli, Darina Takova, Yuriy Bashmet and Nigel Kennedy. Today, one of the most notable events of the venue is its Annual New Year Music Festival. Founded by celebrated Bulgarian conductor Emil Tchakarov in 1986, the festival showcases some of the finest Bulgarian musicians, ensuring the promotion of local and national music, all set against the beautiful backdrop of the emblematic Vitosha Mountains.

1 Ploshtad Bulgaria
Yuzhen Park
Sofia
Bulgaria
Tel: +359 (0)291 662 300
www.ndk.bg

PERFORMANCES

Times: Evening performances generally start at 6.30 p.m. or 7.00 p.m.

Annual Festivals/Special Events: The Annual New Year Music Festival takes place between 22 December and 10 January.

SEATING

Capacity: There are 14 halls, with capacities ranging from 100 seats to 3,880 seats.

Organization: Hall 1 has stalls and two balconies; others vary.

Best Seats: The best seats in Hall 1 are located in the stalls.

Sofia National Opera

30 Dondoukov blvd.
Sofia
1000
Bulgaria
Tel: +359 (0)2 988 5869
Fax: +359 (0)2 987 7998

The Sofia National Opera was built in 1890. Its location in Bulgaria makes it an ideal point for the cross-fertilization of Russian and Italian opera. It has continued to be a renowned opera house, with many international composers and performers debuting there. As the company evolved under the ensemble system and style, the permanent troupe of soloists, choir, orchestra, ballet, technical and production teams produced up to ten opera and ballet premieres a year. Gradually, the basic repertory of world opera classics was established at the same time as the theatre began to attract Bulgarian composers who created new national works with twentieth century performers such as, Nicolai Ghiaurov, Nicolai Ghiuselev and Ghana Dimitrova all beginning their careers within the structure of the National Opera. Today, the company continues to showcase international artists as well as supporting the artists of the future through various programmes and competitions.

TICKETING

Box Office

Tel: +359 (0)2 987 701 1272
Fax: +359 (0)2 987 1366

PERFORMANCES

Events take place from September to July.

Times: Performances typically start at 7.00 p.m., although times can vary; matinees and morning productions are also available.

Annual Festivals/Special Events: The Easter Festival takes place every April.

CROATIA

SPLIT

Hrvatsko Narodno Kazalište

Established in 1840, the Hrvatsko Narodno Kazalište, or Croatian National Theatre initially grew through an injection of government funding that placed it on a par with many national theatres across Europe. 30 years later in 1870, a National Opera Company was formed, with the Split site joining four other sites in Croatia, including the main site in Zagreb. Throughout its long history, the venue has played host to many famous names, including Ivan Zajc, who was the theatre's first conductor. The theatre's claim to stardom is not limited to local stars either, with international artists such as Sarah Bernhardt, Franz Lehar, Richard Strauss, Vivian Leigh and Laurence

Trg Gaje Bulata 1
Split
HR-21000
Croatia
Tel: +385 (0)21 344 399
Fax: +385 (0)21 344 399
www.hnk-split.hr

Olivier having also graced the National Theatre's grounds.

TICKETING

Box Office

> In addition to the Box Office, tickets for the Habunek Stage can be acquired at the KNAPP-u, from 6.00 p.m.–8.00 p.m. weekdays; 10.00 a.m.–noon on Saturdays; and two hours before the start of performances on Sundays.
> Tel: +385 (0)21 363 014

PERFORMANCES

Events take place from October to June.

Times: Performances typically start at 8.00 p.m. but performance time can vary.

Annual Festivals/Special Events: Split Summer Festival

FACILITIES

Dining

The Amadeus Caffé Bar and Theatre Caffé Bar both serve a range of food and refreshments.

ZAGREB

Hrvatsko Narodno Kazalište

Established in 1840, what today forms one of the main sites of the Croatian National Theatre lies at the heart of Zagreb and takes its place rightly at par with many other European theatres. Joining its partner sites in Split, Rijeka, Osijek and Varazdin, the repertoire is centred around the National Opera Company which was formed in 1870, moving to its current site in 1895. The building itself was constructed by the famous architects Ferdinand Fellner and Herman Helmer and was unveiled by Austro Hungarian Emperor Franz Joseph. Throughout its history many of Croatia's finest artists have worked at the theatre. The famous Croatian director Branko Gavella began his brilliant career here, and many famous international artists have graced the Hrvatsko Narodno Kazaliste's stage,

> Trg Marsala Tita 15
> Zagreb
> HR-10000
> Croatia
> Tel: +385 (0)14 828 511
> Fax: +385 (0)14 828 511
> www.hnk.hr

including Franz Liszt, Franz Lehar, Richard Strauss and Mario del Monoco, forming only some of the names on a long roll call which continues to grow to this day.

TICKETING

Price Range: Tickets generally range from HRK 40.00 to HRK 210.00.

Concessions: For revivals, a discount of 50% is offered to children and students. A 60% discount is offered to senior citizens.

Box Office

The Box Office is open Monday to Friday, 10.00 a.m.–2.00 p.m., and 90 minutes before the curtain rises. During weekends, the Box Office opens 90 minutes before the curtain rises.
Tel: +3851 (0)482 8415
Fax: +3851 (0)488 8417
http://hnkonline.hnk.hr

PERFORMANCES

Events take place from September to June.

Times: Performances typically start at 7.30 p.m. but performance times can vary.

SEATING

Organization: The auditorium is arranged into stalls, a balcony, and boxes.

Koncertna Dvorana Vatroslav Lisinski

Located in the lively Croatian capital, the Koncertna Dvorana Vatroslav Lisinski is the home of the Zagreb Philharmonic Orchestra, and stages a range of classical music performances as well as the occasional jazz concerts. Vatroslav Lisinski, the name of the man after which the concert hall is named was a Croatian composer, and one of the founders of the Illyrian movement, which involved a return to Croatian cultural heritage as a reaction to Magyarisation. This involved a number of ethnic assimilation policies implemented by various Hungarian authorities aimed at imposing or maintaining many Hungarian practices in Hungarian ruled regions during Austro-Hungarian rule. Lisinski composed the first Croatian operas, 'Ljubav i zloba' (Love and Malice) and 'Porin', and numerous works for orchestra, choir and soloists. In an act of patriotism, he changed his name from his christened name Ignaz Fuchs to Vatroslav Lisinski, an idea followed through in the varied yet traditional performances at the Koncertna Dvorana.

TICKETING

Box Office

Trg Stjepana Radića 4
Zagreb
HR-10000
Croatia
Tel: +385 (0)1 612 1173
www.lisinski.hr

The Box Office is open Monday to Friday, 9.00 a.m.–8.00 p.m.; Saturday. 9.00 a.m.–2.00 p.m. The Box Office is also open two hours before the start of a concert or performance. Online booking is also possible, although much of the website for such transactions is only available in Croatia. Tickets purchased online are accompanied by an ID number. Tickets can be collected 60 minutes before the start of the performance, on submission of the ID number issued during the Internet purchase.
Tel: +385 (0)1 612 1167
www.lisinski.hr

PERFORMANCES

Times: Performances typically start at 7.30 p.m., but performance times can vary.

SEATING

Organization: The venue is divided into stalls, arranged into 15 discrete blocks and a balcony. Visitors are able to see the view from each block before purchasing their ticket on the venue's website.

> Perhaps one of its lesser claims to fame, the Koncertna Dvorana Vatroslav Lisinski hosted the 1990 Eurovision Song Contest. In a year which was filled with political statements, forgotten lyrics and technical problems, the troubles began from the start, when, offended about press comments concerning their ages, the two presenters Helga Vlahović and Oliver Mlakar resigned. The chaos continued, with replacement hosts being found. Thankfully the misunderstandings were quickly sorted and Vlahović and Mlakar returned, successfully hosting a contest which saw Italy's Toto Cutugno performing, 'Insieme' becoming the eventual victor.

CZECH REPUBLIC

PRAGUE

Národní Divadlo

The brainchild of Czech patriots, the building which was to become the Národní Divadlo was built on the banks of the River Vlatava and was first inaugurated in 1862, with plans for the Czech theatre properly underway in 1867, and the foundation stone being laid the following year. Twin inspirations for the theatre's décor came from Neo-Rennaisance styles and Slavic mythology. The theatre opened in 1881, to honour the visit of Crown Prince Rudolf. However, a fire destroyed the stage and auditorium in the August of that year. The architect Josef Schulz extended the theatre and unified the styles of its various component parts, before the theatre was reopened in 1883. The theatre was closed again in 1977, when it underwent extensive rebuilding under the supervision of architect Zdeněk Vávra, reopening in 1983 on the centenary anniversary of its opening. It currently serves as the main stage of the National Theatre ensembles of ballet, opera and drama; and stands as an important monument for the maturation of the Czech nation and identity.

TICKETING

Advance Sales: Tickets can be purchased up to five months in advance for all performances of the season.

Price Range: Tickets generally range from CZK 30.00 to CZK 900.00.

Concessions: A 50% discount is offered to students with ISIC, ITIC, EURO 26 study cards (galleries 1 & 2 only). 100% discount for students who attend secondary schools or colleges of the arts from 30 minutes before the performance begins; 20% for all other students 30 minutes before the performance commences. In addition, disabled visitors and carers qualify for a 50% reduction; on presentation of ZTP card.

Ostrovní 1
Prague 1
Prague
CZ-11230
Czech Republic
Tel: +420 (0)224 901 377
Fax: +420 (0)224 931 544
www.narodni-divadlo.cz

Box Office

The Box Office is located in the Administrative Building, Ostrovní 1, 112 30 Prague 1. The office is open Monday to Sunday, 10.00 a.m.–6.00 p.m.; during evenings, the Box Office opens 45 minutes before the performance commences.
Tel: +42 (0)224 901 448
Lines are open daily, 10.00 a.m.–6.00 p.m.
www.narodni-divadlo.cz

PERFORMANCES

Times: Performances typically start at 7.00 p.m. but performances times can vary.

EDUCATION

Guided Tours

Tours of the venue can be arranged by booking in advance. For further information, see the website; or, to book a tour on a weekday, contact M Ševčíková on: +42 (0)224 901 570 or email: m.sevcikova@narodni-divadlo.cz. For tours during weekends, contact the Prague Information Service on Tel: +42 (0)221 714 1512.

HOW TO GET THERE

Overground: Tram lines 6, 9, 17, 18, 21, 22 and 23 stop five minutes from the Národní Divadlo.

Underground: Narodni Trida

Rudolfinum

The home of the Czech Philharmonic Orchestra, the Rudolfinum was commissioned by the Czech Savings Bank and designed by Zítek and Schultz as a building which held both concerts and art exhibitions. Opened in 1885 and attended by the Austrian Crown Prince Rudolf (after whom the building was named), the CPO played its first concert, conducted by Dvořák here in 1896. This was not to be their permanent home however. Between 1920 and 1945, it housed the Czechoslovak Parliament. After

Galerie Rudolfinum
Alšovo nábřeží 12
Prague 1
Prague
CZ-11001
Czech Republic
Tel: +420 (0)227 059 309
Fax: +420 (0)227 059 327
www.rudolfinum.cz

this interlude, the CPO returned to its natural home, restored to its original funtion to allow the public to access great music and art.

TICKETING

Advance Sales: Tickets for performances can be booked at the start of the season.

Box Office

The Box Office is open Monday to Friday, 10.00 a.m.–7.30 p.m.; if the event is a chamber concert, the Box Office is closed between 6.00 p.m.–6.30 p.m.; 10.00 a.m.–3.00 p.m. on Saturdays during O-Series; 2.00 p.m.–5.00 p.m. on Sundays during S-Series. The Box Office is also closed during most of July; Christmas Eve, Christmas Day and Boxing Day. Tel: +42 (0)227 059 352 Fax: +42 (0)227 059 327 www.ceskafilharmonie.cz/en

PERFORMANCES

Events take place from late August to late June.

Times: Performances typically start at 7.00 p.m.; but performances times can vary.

Programmes: Programmes are available for purchase at the Box Office and cost approximately CZK 25.00. English programmes are available for certain performances.

Resident Groups: The Czech Philharmonic Orchestra and the Czech Chamber Music Society.

Annual Festivals/Special Events: Some concerts of the Prague Spring and Prague Autumn festivals are held at the Rudolfinum.

SEATING

Capacity: There are two halls, the Suk and Dvorak Hall. The Suk Hall has a capacity of 220 seats and the Dvorak Hall a capacity of 1,148.

FACILITIES

Dining

A café is located in the building, providing visitors with a range of food and refreshments to enjoy during their visit.

Services

HOW TO GET THERE

Bus: 207 stops at Staroměstská Station.

Overground: Tram lines 17 and 18 to Staroměstská Station.

Underground: Line A to Staroměstská Station.

Car Parking: There is an underground car park located within the building. Parking costs CZK 50.00 per hour.

Státní Opera Praha

The Germanic population of nineteenth century Prague demanded their own theatre, and this wish was realised in 1883 in a building designed by Fellner and Hellmer in a Neo-Rococo style, and named The German Theatre. The theatre was opened in 1888 as 'The German stage', and its first performance was Wagner's 'The Mastersingers of Nürnberg'. Under the leadership of Angelo Neumann and Alexander Zemlinsky became one of Europe's greatest Germanic opera houses, featuring performances by Mahler and Richard Strauss. However, in 1938 it was sold to the Czechoslovak government, who renamed it the Smetana Theatre, and badly neglected it. After the overthrow of the communist government, the opera house was handed over to the May 5th Theatre, which was later to become a part of the National Theatre. Since then, it has celebrated the tradition of the New German Theatre, returning to the fine, traditional performances which brought the former venue so much splendour.

Legerova 75
Prague 1
Prague
CZ-11000
Czech Republic
Tel: +420 (0)296 117 111
Fax: +420 (0)224 229 711
www.opera.cz

TICKETING

Advance Sales: Tickets can be purchased in advance for all performances of the season, although release dates vary throughout the year.

Box Office

The Box Office is open Monday to Friday, 10.00 a.m.–5.30 a.m. There is a transaction charge of CZK 50.00 for remote bookings. Tickets can be collected from one hour before the performance.
Tel: +42 (0)224 227 266
Fax: +42 (0)224 218 167
www.bohemiaticket.cz

PERFORMANCES

Events take place from mid-August to the end of June.

Times: Performances typically start at 7.00 p.m.; but performance times can vary.

Programmes: Programmes are available from the e-shop and from ushers. Programmes generally range from CZK 50.00–CZK 80.00 and are sometimes available in English and German, as well as in Czech.

Resident Groups: The Prague State Opera Orchestra and Prague State Opera Chorus

Annual Festivals/Special Events: The Festival of Italian Opera takes place during the first three weeks of the season.

SEATING

Capacity: 1,058

Organization: The opera hall is organized into a pit and two galleries, with boxes available in all.

Best Seats: The best seats are located in the first row of the first gallery and the pit.

Good Seats on a Budget: Seats in the second gallery provide good value for money.

Seats to Avoid: Some seats are located behind a column, hence have restricted views.

FACILITIES

Dining

Zahrada v Opeře Restaurant is located in the operations centre.

Services

There are two available seats for wheelchair users. However, due to restricted access, wheelchair users are advised to take an escort.

HOW TO GET THERE

Bus: Rimska, line 135.

Underground: Line A to the Muzeum Station.

Stavovské Divadlo

Built by František Antonín Count Nostitz Rieneck as a device to beautify Prague and help educate its citizens, the Stavovske Divadlo was opened in 1783 with Lessing's 'Emilia Galotti'. This choice of play was very much in line with the Enlightenment Principles which saw theatres being erected all over Europe, for the twin purposes of improving the minds of ordinary people, and as monuments of a nation's culture. These principles were further reflected in its classicist style and its location adjacent to the Charles University, which was seen with the theatre as comprising a single body.

Ovocný trh
Prague 1
Prague
CZ-11000
Czech Republic
Tel: +420 (0)224 902 322
Fax: +420 (0)224 224 351
www.estatestheatre.cz

It was instrumental in the formation of the national form of theatre, putting many plays and operas on in Czech language, by playwrights such as J N Štěpánek, Škroup and J J Kolár. Its most notable connection, however, is with Mozart, who premiered 'Don Giovanni' and 'La Clemenza di Tito' in this very theatre. Indeed, the welcome given to Mozart led him to claim 'My Praguers understand me'. Fused with the Národní Divadlo in 1920, it went on to stage the plays of some of the most important Czech writers of the twentieth century, such as Karel Čapek; Milan Kundera was also a producer here. It currently concentrates on ballet and theatre, but still puts an important emphasis on Mozart. It is regarded as one of Europe's most beautiful and historically important theatres.

TICKETING

Price Range: Tickets generally range from CZK 150.00 to CZK 1,200.00.

Box Office

The Box Office is open daily, 10.00 a.m.–6.00 p.m.; during evenings, the Box Office opens 45 minutes before the performance commences.
Tel: +42 (0)902 322
Lines are open daily, 10.00 a.m.–6.00 p.m.
www.narodni-divadlo.cz

PERFORMANCES

Times: Performances typically start at 7.00 p.m. but performance time can vary.

HOW TO GET THERE

Underground: Můstek (line A, B)

DENMARK

AARHUS

Musikhuset Aarhus

The Musikhuset is a beautiful modern concert hall constructed with a glass and steel exterior. Built in 1983, it now hosts a wide range of cultural activities, including the city's symphony orchestra and opera company, as well as musicals, jazz and rock concerts. The venue is home to the Aarhus Symphony Orchestra and the Danish National Opera. Equipped with several stages of varying sizes, this grand theatre has a great stage, small stage, cabaret stage and an amphitheatre for its year-round performances.

Thomas Jensens Allé
Aarhus C
DK-8000
Denmark
Tel: +45 (0)894 09000
Fax: +45 (0)861 33710
www.musikhusetaarhus.dk

TICKETING

Advance Sales: Tickets can be purchased in advance for all confirmed concerts.

Price Range: Tickets generally range from DKK 150.00 to DKK 410.00.

Concessions: There is a DKK 20.00 reduction on all tickets for under-25s. In addition, senior citizens can obtain discounts on Symphony Orchestra concerts.

Box Office

The Box Office is open daily, 10.00 a.m.–9.00 p.m.
Tel: +45 (0)894 04040
Lines are open during Box Office hours.
Fax: +45 (0)861 33710
Tickets for some concerts can be booked via www.billetnet.dk

PERFORMANCES

Events take place all year round.

Times: A typical concert starts at 7.30 p.m., although performance times vary.

Resident Groups: The Aarhus Symphony Orchestra, Den Jyske Opera, FILUREN and DIEM (Danish Centre for Electronic Music).

Annual Festivals/Special Events: The International Jazz Festival in July and the Festuge in September.

SEATING

Capacity: 1,588

Organization: Stalls, with a central balcony and side balconies.

Best Seat: The seats at the front of the balcony have the best view and acoustics.

Good Seats on a Budget: Affordable seats start three rows behind the top price tickets at the front of the balcony.

Seats to Avoid: All seats have a good views and acoustics.

FACILITIES

Dining

There is a café and also a restaurant for fine dining located on-site.

Services

There are places for wheelchair users in all areas of the auditorium, as well as reserved parking.

HOW TO GET THERE

Bus: 16, 17. An adult ticket valid for 10 journeys costs around DKK 78.00.

Car Parking: Parking is available in the adjacent Scandanavian Congress Centre.

> Aarhus has one of the largest student populations in Denmark, and there are many bars and cafés to cater for this audience in the local area. In addition, the city's main art gallery is next door to the concert hall.

COPENHAGEN

Det Kongelige Teater

The Kongelige Teater is one of Europe's classic theatres. Built in 1874 in an opulent style, it was the stage for first performances of Ibsen, Sibelius and Nielsen, and has since undergone several expansion projects. The art deco Stærekassen, now home of the Royal Danish Theatre, was added next door in 1931. The Old Stage still hosts symphony, ballet and opera performances (including a recent Ring Cycle) and traditionalists will love everything about this classic hall, including the lack of space and slightly deficient acoustics. Opera lovers might prefer the brand new opera house, situated on an island in the harbour, which opened in 2005, whose facilities blend modern design with superb innovation, such as a small stage geared to operatic originality, serving to interlace between traditional genres.

> The Royal Danish Theatre
> Postbox 2185
> Copenhagen
> DK-1017
> Denmark
> Tel: +45 (0)336 96933
> Fax: +45 (0)336 96519
> www.kglteater.dk

TICKETING

Price Range: Tickets generally range from DKK 32.00 to DKK 690.00. Unsold tickets on the day of performance are sold with a 50% reduction on the normal price.

Concessions: There is a 65% discount for under-30s and a 50% reduction for over-65s.

Box Office

> The ticket centre for all the buildings is located in August Bournonvilles Passage 1. The Box Office is open Monday to Saturday, 2.00 p.m.–8.00 p.m.
> Tel: +45 (0)336 96969
> www.billetnet.dk

PERFORMANCES

Events take place all year round.

Times: A typical concert starts at 8.00 p.m. from Monday to Saturday; 3.00 p.m. on Sundays, although this is subject to variation.

Resident Groups: The Royal Danish Orchestra and The Royal Danish Opera.

SEATING

Capacity: 1,306.

Organization: The Old Stage is a classic opera house, with a parterre, balcony, two floors and a gallery. The Stærekassen is a smaller house with parterre seating, a balcony and a floor above.

Good Seats on a Budget: The cheapest seats are located in the gallery.

EDUCATION

Guided Tours

Tours of the Old Stage take place at 11.00 a.m. daily; those of the opera house at 9.30 a.m. and 4.30 p.m. on weekends only. For further information see the website or contact the venue directly. Tel: +45 (0)336 96969 or email: dktbooking@kglteater.dk

Cost: Tours of the Old Stage cost DKK 75.00; tours of the opera house, DKK 100.00.

Concessions: Tours for schoolchildren cost DKK 75.00.

FACILITIES

Dining

Operaens Restaurant & Café at the opera provides visitors with a range of food and refreshments. Tables are available for guests on all performance days from 5.00 p.m onwards. Tables can be reserved for the entire evening, including refreshments during intermissions, with lunch and dinner menus reflecting the changing seasons. Tel: +45 (0)336 96619 for reservations.

Services

Wheelchair access to the Old Stage is available from the ramps to the left of the main entrance. Space has been allocated to wheelchairs on the left-hand side of the stalls/parterre, i.e. rows 16 and 27. Disabled theatregoers in need of assistance are requested to contact the staff.

An induction loop hearing system is installed.

HOW TO GET THERE

Bus: 26

Underground: Lines M1 and M2 to Kongens Nytorv. An all day ticket costs DKK 105.00 (adult), DKK 53.00 (child).

Tivoli Concert Hall

The world famous Tivoli Gardens, which have proven an inspiration even for Disney World, are perhaps the most popular tourist attraction in Copenhagen. Full of rides and attractions, the centrepiece for music lovers is undoubtedly the Concert Hall. Built in 1956 to replace the one which was burnt down in 1944, the site is in keeping with the funfair atmosphere, playing host to a fine tradition of light music,

Tivoli A/S Vesterbrogade 3
Postboks 233
Copenhagen
DK-1630
Denmark
Tel: +45 (0)331 51001
Fax: +45 (0)337 50347
www.tivoli.dk

starting with its first musical director Hans Christian Lumbye, composer of Strauss-style waltzes and polkas. The glass hall was extensively renovated in 2005, with a dramatic new entrance in a Garden Foyer, as well as the new Balanchine Lounge, which provides a breathtaking view of the gardens and the city of Copenhagen.

TICKETING

Price Range: Tickets generally range from DKK 177.00 to DKK 990.00. In addition, there are often events in the surrounding park, the admission price of which is DKK 75.00.

Concessions: For some concerts, children under the age of 12 are eligible for tickets costing only DKK 35.00 when accompanied by a paying adult. All students are entitled to a 50% discount upon proof of status. Tickets must be booked seven days in advance.

Box Office

The Box Office is open daily, 11.00 a.m.–8.00 p.m. from April to September and November to December. From January to March the Box Office opens Monday to Friday, 9.00 a.m.–5.00 p.m. All prices are inclusive of booking fees.

> Free access to the Gardens is included with tickets for the Concert Hall on the day of the concert.
> Tel: +45 (0)331 51012
> www.billetnet.dk

PERFORMANCES

Events take place all year round.

Times: Performance times vary. Please check with the Box Office for individual performances.

Resident Groups: Copenhagen Philharmonic, also known as the Tivoli Symphony Orchestra, the Tivoli Big Band and The Pantomime Theatre.

SEATING

Capacity: 1,800

FACILITIES

Dining

The park has no less than 38 restaurants and cafés, ranging from gourmet dining to fast food outlets. The Concert Hall Café, located in the Hall itself, provides a range of refreshments including tapas, coffees and a special children's menu. In addition, the Balanchine Lounge seats up to 45 persons and can be used for special dining arrangements. For further information, Tel: +45 (0)33 75 02 47.

Services

The Concert Hall features several toilets and lifts for disabled persons, as well as level-free access to almost the entire building.

Guide dog access is available, although visitors wishing to do so are advised to contact the Tivoli's service centre.

HOW TO GET THERE

Bus: 250S

Overground: København H

Car Parking: Parking is available by the main entrance at the cost of DKK 35.00 per day.

> The Tivoli's lounge plays host to Europe's longest salt water aquarium, home to more than 1,600 tropical fishes. The aquarium, containing sharks, rays and other marine life adds an extra dimension to an already colourful venue, and is open all day long for visitors wishing to see this amazing spectacle.

ODENSE

Odense Concert Hall [Nielsen Hall]

Designed by Hougaard Nielsen, C J Nørgaard Pedersen, Lars Møller and Birte Rørbæk, the Odense Concert Hall is, by some distance, the most impressive building in its vicinity. The building plays house to the resident Odense Symphony Orchestra, established in 1946, though with roots stretching back much further to the beginning of the nineteenth century. Today, many of the concerts are conducted in the Carl Nielsen Hall, which provides audiences with excellent acoustics, and among other facilities a large 46-stops organ built by Marcussen & Son, one of the world's leading organ builders. In addition, because of its large size and impressive stature, part of the building is below ground, with its angles

Claus Bergs Gade 9
Odense C
DK-5100
Denmark
Tel: +45 (0)66 12 00 57
Fax: +45 (0)65 91 00 47
www.odensesymfoni.dk

correlated with the surrounding buildings.

TICKETING

Price Range: Tickets generally range from DKK 70.00 to DKK 185.00.

Concessions: Students can buy tickets for DKK 20.00 on the day of the concert. Carers may accompany disabled visitors free of charge.

Box Office

> The Box Office is open Monday and Tuesday, 2.00 p.m.–5.00 p.m. and on the day of the concert, 4.00 p.m.–8.00 p.m.
> Tel: +45 (0)66 12 00 57
> Fax: +45 (0)65 91 00 47
> www.odensesymfoni.dk

PERFORMANCES

Events take place from August to June.

Resident Groups: Odense Symphony Orchestra

Annual Festivals/Special Events: The Carl Nielsen International Music Competition takes place annually, although it does not take place once every four years (last time being 2007), typically 31 May–9 June.

SEATING

Capacity: 1,212

Organization: The auditorium is arranged into stalls and a balcony, together with some seats behind the orchestra.

Best Seats: The best seats are located in the stalls and the balcony.

Good Seats on a Budget: The seats in C section provide good value for money.

Seats to Avoid: The seats behind the orchestra have restricted views.

FACILITIES

Services

HOW TO GET THERE

Bus: 41, 42, 82, 92, 21, 22, 23, 24, 51, 61, 62 and S5 all stop less than 100 m from the Odense Concert Hall.

Overground: Odense Train Station is approximately a ten minute walk from the venue.

Car Parking: Parking is available in the building and costs around DKK 4.00 per hour.

> Odense City Hall bears a small scar from a 1945 battle between the Germans and members of the Danish Resistance. The city's coat of arms, located above the main entrance to City Hall, still shows the damage caused by the conflict and on close inspection, visitors can see where the kneecap of Saint Canute was penetrated by a bullet.

ESTONIA

TALLINN

Estonian National Opera

Situated in the beautiful old town of Tallinn, the National Opera dates back to the beginning of the twentieth century, when it was established as the largest building in Estonia. War and Soviet rule destroyed the original building, and the current theatre dates from 1947, albeit in a more sombre form than the original. Recent renovation has made this beautiful little theatre a comfortable and intimate venue, home to a serious opera company that mounts performances of new operas, neglected operas and classics from the core repertoire.

TICKETING

Price Range: Tickets generally range from EEK 50.00 to EEK 380.00.

Box Office

Estonian National Opera
Estonia Avenue 4
Tallinn
EST-10148
Estonia
Tel: +372 (0)683 1260
Fax: +372 (0)683 1246
www.Opera.ee

The Box Office is located in the main building. Tickets are also available at Piletimaailm and Piletilevi ticket centres all over Estonia.

The Box Office is open daily,
11.00 a.m.–7.00 p.m.
Tel: +372 (0)683 1215 or
+372 (0)683 1214
Lines are open Monday to
Friday, 10.00 a.m.–4.00 p.m.
Fax: +372 (0)683 1246
No online booking. Help for
booking from the UK can be
found at
www.Operasabroad.com

PERFORMANCES

Events take place from September to July.

Times: Performances take place at midday and 7.00 p.m.

Resident Groups: Estonian National Opera

Annual Festivals/Special Events: Estonian Opera Festival

SEATING

Capacity: 700

Organization: Main level – 416; first balcony – 118; second balcony – 166.

Best Seats: The best seats are in a box in the centre of the first balcony.

Good Seats on a Budget: For concert-goers used to UK prices, even the top priced tickets will seem cheap. However, for those on a shoestring budget, the seats at the front of the second balcony offer a great view, all for less than the price of a programme in the UK.

Seats to Avoid: All the seats in this intimate theatre are comfortable. The seats at the back of each level are underneath a balcony, so may have slightly less favourable acoustics. In addition, although all operas are performed in the original language, visitors can check whether performances have subtitles (also in foreign languages) by clicking on the name of the performance at the 'homepage Repertoire' section on the website. Subtitles cannot be seen in the last rows of the parterre (the red price area on the hall plan).

FACILITIES

Dining

The Estonian National Opera catering service offers snacks and drinks during the intermissions in the White and Blue Halls, and in the Colombina Café and Harlequin Bar.

Services

♿ Wheelchair users will be provided the best possible seats available in the hall, but visitors are advised to inform the Box Office when purchasing a ticket. There is a lift and a toilet for disabled persons in the theatre.

HOW TO GET THERE

Bus: 9, 11, 14, 18, 20, 20A, 40, 46 and 48. Adult single, EKK 10.00 in advance; EKK 15.00 on board; ten ticket carnet, EKK 85.00.

Overground: Balti Jaam

Car Parking: Street parking is available near the theatre. Parking costs EKK 12.00 per 15 minutes.

The opera house also incorporates a new chamber hall which benefits from a flexible seating configuration, and the multi-purpose Winter Gardens conservatory that is occasionally used for concerts amongst the plants. There are many other theatres and museums nearby, including the Estonian Art Museum, which comprises several different complexes showcasing the best in Estonian art in this most cultured of small cities.

Linnahall

A relic from the 1980 Moscow Olympics, Taillin's Linnahall was constructed following the city's failure to provide a suitable venue to host the sailing regatta. The event centre, which possesses a distinctly Soviet feel was constructed on the harbour, just beyond the walls of the old town, where it stands to this day as a large imposing structure. For this reason, the building has gained criticism from many sides, and has been in disrepair for a number of years. Fears are that this is how the building will remain for the foreseeable future, as the outside is protected as a historic site and hence cannot be removed. However, these factors should not distract from the events within, as the Linnahall

---

Mere pst. 20
Tallinn
EST-10111
Estonia
Tel: +372 (0)641 2250
Fax: +372 (0)644 9847
www.linnahall.ee

plays host to a wide variety of musical performances which surely overshadow the building's aesthetic problems.

TICKETING

Price Range: Tickets generally range from EEK 10.00 to EEK 240.00.

PERFORMANCES

Performances take place all year round.

Times: A typical concert starts at 7.00 p.m., although performance times vary.

SEATING

Capacity: 4,200

Organization: The seating is all on one level, with seats arranged in a large semicircle.

Good Seats on a Budget: Most of the seats have similar views and levels of comfort.

Seats to Avoid: The seats at the back are a long, long way from the performance area and should be avoided where possible.

HOW TO GET THERE

Bus: 3. Adult single, EKK 10.00 in advance; EKK 15.00 on board; ten ticket carnet, EKK 85.00.

Overground: Balti Jaam Station is approximately ten minutes walk from the venue.

Car Parking: The Linnahall has a car park located on-site.

FINLAND

HELSINKI

Finlandia Concert Hall

Designed by the great Finnish architect Alvar Aalto and completed in 1971, the Finlandia Hall is set overlooking Töölönlahti Bay. The extensive use of marble both on the façade and in the interior makes this cool, white building one of the most elegant halls in Europe. Standards of classical music in Finland are exceptional, and there is always a full programme of symphonic concerts and organ recitals. Apart from the main auditorium, the main feature of the interior is the shallow and broad 'Venetian' staircase leading from the ground floor foyer to both the main auditorium and the chamber music hall, adding yet another touch of innovation to a popular and delightful music venue.

Mannerheimintie 13e
Helsinki
FIN-00100
Finland
Tel: +358 (0)940 241
Fax: +358 (0)944 6259
www.finlandiatalo.fi

TICKETING

Price Range: Tickets generally range from €6.00 to €17.50.

Concessions: Reductions are available on all concerts. The

Helsinki Philharmonic provides large reductions for children, students and unemployed.

Box Office

The Box Office is located at the main entrance and is open Monday to Friday, 9.00 a.m.–3.45 p.m. There is a €0.50 per ticket additional booking charge for reservations by telephone or fax. For online bookings there is a transaction charge of €4.50 for a paper ticket, and €1.00 for an e-ticket (available only within Finland).
Tel: +358 (0)940241 or +358 9 409 611 on concert evenings. Lines are open Monday to Friday, 9.00 a.m.–4.00 p.m.
Fax: +358 (0)9 4024249
www.lippu.fi

PERFORMANCES

Times: A typical concert starts at 7.00 p.m., although performance times vary.

Resident Groups: The Helsinki Philharmonic Orchestra and the Finnish Radio Symphony Orchestra.

SEATING

Capacity: There are two concert spaces – the main Finlandia Hall seats 1,700 and the smaller Helsinki Hall seats 340.

Organization: The Finlandia Hall has 1,200 seats in the ground stalls and 500 in the balcony. The Helsinki Hall is on one level, with seats arranged in a 'V' shape about the stage.

Best Seats: The best seats are located in the centre of the stalls downstairs.

Good Seats on a Budget: Concerts in Helsinki are inexpensive. The balcony seats are cheaper than the stalls.

Seats to Avoid: Architect Alvar Aalto designed the Hall based on a classical Greek theatre. However, while such a form was suited for theatre and classical oratorios, it is not suitable for a concert hall. As a result, the upper floor balconies overhang the last few rows of seats in the ground floor stalls, thus muffling the sound in those seats.

EDUCATION

Guided Tours

For information on guided tours of the venue, as well as specific dates, see the events calendar on the website. The tour begins at the Finlandia Hall InfoShop by the concert hall entrance on Mannerheimintie. Tours for groups should be agreed in advance. Tel: +358 (0)9 40241 or email: infoshop@finlandiatalo.fi

Times: Tours usually begin at 1.00 p.m.

Cost: €6.00

Concessions: €4.00

FACILITIES

Dining

There is a fine restaurant located on-site, reservations for which can be made by Tel: +358 (0)9 4024 500.

HOW TO GET THERE

Bus: 43

Underground: The main central station is situated approximately ten minutes from the venue. A single journey costs €2.20 (adult) and €1.10 (child).

A Tourist one day ticket costs €6.00 and €3.00 respectively.

Car Parking: 400 parking spaces are available in the Hall car park.

> The Finlandia Hall is situated on Mannerheimintie, one of the grand boulevards in Helsinki. Concert-goers can also take in the nearby Stockmann department store and the Kiasma Museum of Modern Art, a daring contemporary building.

LAHTI

Sibeliustalo (Sibelius Hall)

It is a happy coincidence for concert lovers that Finland's finest artistic achievements in modern times have been classical music and architecture. Inspired by Sibelius and Alvar Aalto, the small town of Lahti (population

> Ankkurikatu 7
> Lahti
> FIN-15140
> Finland
> Tel: +358 (0)381 42801
> Fax: +358 (0)381 42820
> www.sibeliustalo.fi

100,000) has built up a world-class orchestra under the direction of Osmo Vänskä and a stunning modern concert hall by young architects Hannu Tikka and Kimmo Lintula. Set beside Lake Vesijärvi, the hall was originally a dilapidated carpentry factory used by the Finnish army for manoeuvres. The architects conceived a brilliant structure of glass and wood that provides a light, warm, and natural ambience and an auditorium with magnificent acoustics, helped by modern echo chambers and a movable canopy above the stage. Whereas some local residents initially begrudged the expense when the hall opened in 2000, the town now boasts a unique concert hall and, as those familiar with the local orchestra's recording of Sibelius will know, a first rate ensemble to compliment it.

TICKETING

Price Range: Tickets generally range from €10.00 to €40.00.

Concessions: Selected seats are available for children, students, and the unemployed at a special rate of €6.00. In addition, these groups also receive a 50% discount on tickets for the Sibelius Festival. For senior citizens, there is a small discount available on top priced tickets.

Box Office

The Box Office is open Monday to Friday, 11.00 a.m.–5.00 p.m. On weekends the Box Office opens one hour before the performance. Transaction charges vary.
Tel: +358 (0)3 814 2801
www.lippupalvelu.fi

PERFORMANCES

Events occur all year round, except for July.

Times: Evening performances typically start at 7.00 p.m., although start times vary. Occasional lunchtime concerts are conducted at 1.00 p.m., together with selected afternoon concerts.

Resident Groups: Sinfonia Lahti

Annual Festivals/Special Events: The Sibelius Festival takes place each September in celebration of the music of Finland's national composer.

SEATING

Capacity: 1,100 seats in the main hall plus 129 in the choir balcony.

Organization: 650 stall seats on the ground floor, plus two balconies and choir stalls.

Best Seats: www.sibeliustalo.fi provides panoramic views of the auditorium with views from the stage and from the balcony. The Box Office recommends the front of the first balcony for the best views.

Good Seats on a Budget: The choir stalls are the cheapest seats. If these are not available, the side balconies represent the best value.

Seats to Avoid: All seats have a reasonable view, without any major obstructions. The acoustics are excellent in all areas of the auditorium.

EDUCATION

Guided Tour

Tours of the venue can be arranged in advance. For further details contact the Sibeliustalo directly. Tel: +358 (0)3 814 2811

Cost: Groups of up to 12 persons cost €48.00 (Monday to Saturday), €96.00 (Sundays and public holidays), extra people are charged at a rate of €4.00 per person.

FACILITIES

Dining

The Restaurant Lastu provides café and bar services, and the terrace is open in the summer. The restaurant is known for its good value, fine cuisine and spacious, contemporary décor. For more information, or to book in advance, please visit the venue website.

Services

12 specially designated places are available for wheelchair users.

An area exists at the back of the auditorium for sign-interpretation. Contact for availablility.

HOW TO GET THERE

Bus: 17. Adult single, €3.00; Child single, €1.50.

Car Parking: All-day parking is available beside the hall. Parking is free of charge for patrons.

Together with the main auditorium, the Sibelius Hall hosts a Congress Centre comprising the Forest Hall for banqueting and exhibitions, a Congress Wing, a Carpentry Factory that provides meeting rooms, and – in a very Finnish touch – a sauna. Concert-goers can take a boat trip on the adjacent Lake Vesijärvi, and watch the 'musical fountain' that performs daily. In addition to the Sibelius Hall, the Church of the Cross, designed by Alvar Aalto hosts regular organ concerts. For those less culturally inclined, Lahti is also famous for its ski jumping and ice hockey.

FRANCE

BORDEAUX

Grand Théâtre de Bordeaux

The Grand Théâtre de Bordeaux dates back to 1780, and is a grand, stone building, with a Neo-Classical façade of pillars and statues. Built using a wooden frame, the Grand Théâtre remains the oldest opera house in Europe still standing without ever been damaged by fire. The façade is endowed with a portico of 12 Corinthian style columns supporting 12 statues including the Roman goddesses Venus, Juno, and Minerva. The venue has been showcasing opera since its inauguration, except in 1871 when it served as the French parliament building. It now presents a varied programme of opera and ballet to a high standard. The auditorium was renovated in the early 1990s, and is now opulent and gilded in its original colours of blue and gold.

Opéra National de Bordeaux
Grand-Théâtre, Place de la Comédie
B P 95
Bordeaux
F-33025
France
Tel: +33 (0)556 008 595
www.opera-bordeaux.com

TICKETING

Advance Sales: Tickets for the season can be booked from the beginning of September.

Price Range: Tickets generally range from €13.00 to €80.00.

Concessions: A 50% reduction is available on all tickets for young people, students and the unemployed.

Box Office

There are Box Offices in the theatre building, FNAC and Virgin stores and Kiosque Bordeaux Culture, Allées de Tourny. The theatre Box Office is open Monday to Saturday, 11.00 a.m.–6.00 p.m.
Tel: +33 (0)556 008 595
www.opera-bordeaux.com

PERFORMANCES

Events take place from September to July.

Resident Groups: Opéra National de Bordeaux

SEATING

Capacity: 1,205

HOW TO GET THERE

Bus: 4, 15, 50. An adult ticket valid for ten journeys costs €8.60.

Théâtre Femina

Established in 1921, the Théâtre Femina in its heyday was the centre of both theatrical and cinematic performances; and even today remains one of the largest cinema complexes in Bordeaux. However, the venue also boasts of an array of contemporary comedy, dance and musical acts. The décor of the lobby and film room is that of a twenties picture house, featuring a retro chic true to its origins, and incorporating an intriguing mix of design alluding to the grandeur of the Louis XVI period. This careful renovation has successfully created an inviting and warm environment for its patrons. Recent spatial innovations made in the auditorium allow a more interactive experience, resulting in a fusion of spectacle and real life.

20 rue Grassi
Bordeaux
F-33000
France
Tel: +33 (0)556 524 519
Fax: +33 (0)556 482 140
www.theatrefemina.fr

TICKETING

Price Range: Price ranges vary according to performances.

Box Office

The Box Office is open Monday to Friday, 10.00 a.m.–7.00 p.m.; Saturday, 10.00 a.m.–6.00 p.m.
Tel: +33 (0)556 482 626
www.boxoffice.fr

SEATING

Capacity: 1,175

Organization: The auditorium is arranged into stalls and a balcony.

FACILITIES

Services

Disabled access.

LILLE

Opéra de Lille

The Opéra de Lille dates back to 1907 when the city council of Lille, the fourth largest city in France, built a new Italianate theatre to replace the former building that had been destroyed by fire. On the verge of its completion a setback occurred in 1914, when the building was requisitioned by the German army. However, this did not prevent performances from taking place, over one hundred performances were staged in the subsequent years despite the occupation. The theatre was modernized in the late 1990s, and the latest technologies have been added to ensure the venue can accommodate a diverse range of productions, with the company now presenting a full programme of opera and ballet.

TICKETING

Advance Sales: Tickets go on sale at various intervals throughout the year. Check with the website for details.

2 Rue des bons-Enfants
Lille
F-59001
France
Tel: +33 (0)328 384 050
Fax: +33 (0)328 384 054
www.opera-lille.fr

Price Range: Tickets generally range from €5.00 to €60.00.

Concessions: A 10% reduction on the ticket price is available for children under 12. Those under 26 can get tickets for €5.00 if they purchase a Place Aux Jeunes card for €10.00.

Box Office

The Box Office is located at the main entrance. Tickets can also be purchased from FNAC stores. The Box Office is open from Tuesday to Saturday, noon–7.00 p.m. For remote bookings there is a transaction charge of €3.00 per ticket.
Tel: +33 (0)820 48 9000
www.opera-lille.fr

PERFORMANCES

Events take place from September to July.

Resident Groups: Opéra de Lille

SEATING

Organization: The Opéra is a classic theatre with a parterre section and four balconies.

Best Seats: The best seats are located within the first balcony.

Good Seats on a Budget: The fourth category tickets are inexpensive with good views of the stage.

Seats to Avoid: The seats on the top balcony have very restricted views.

FACILITIES

Services

There are wheelchair places in all price categories. Check with the Box Office for access details.

HOW TO GET THERE

Bus: 3, 4, 6, 9, 12A and 13

Underground: Lines 1 and 2 to Gare Lille Flandres. A single journey costs €1.20.

Car Parking: There is a car park in Place de Gaulle, near the opera.

Lille was elected European Capital of Culture in 2004 and possesses many theatres and cultural highlights.

LYON

L'Auditorium Maurice Ravel

Adjoining the National Orchestra of Lyon, where Emmanual Krivine was conductor for a decade, L'Auditorium Maurice Ravel provides its audiences with a programme which is essentially classical, with added touches of music from far-flung countries like Burundi and Brazil. The venue is named after the French composer and pianist Joeeph Maurice Ravel, who was well-known for the unique subtlety, richness and poignancy of his music. Often compared to Claude Debussy, Ravel preferred the comparison to Mozart and Couperin, whose compositions were more structured and classical in form. However, Ravel took inspirations from around the world, with hints from America, Asia and traditional folk songs from Europe. Today, Ravel's classical affiliation is fulfilled through traditional performances, improved acoustics,

149 Rue Garibaldi
Lyon
F-69003
France
Tel: +33 (0)478 959 595
www.auditorium-lyon.com

and a range of shows which also demonstrate the venue's versatility.

TICKETING

Price Range: Tickets generally range from €5.00 to €50.00.

Concessions: Children, students, disabled visitors, carers and the unemployed qualify for a 50% discount on full price tickets.

Box Office

The Box Office is located at the main entrance. Tickets can also be purchased from FNAC stores.
The Box Office is open Monday to Saturday, 11.00 a.m.–6.00 p.m.
Tel: + 33 (0)478 959 595
Lines are open Monday to Saturday, 11.30 a.m.–6.00 p.m.

PERFORMANCES

Events take place from September to July.

Times: A typical symphony concert starts at 8.30 p.m., though performance times vary.

Resident Groups: Orchestre National de Lyon

SEATING

Capacity: 2,150

Organization: The auditorium is arranged in three semi-circular levels.

Best Seats: The best seats are in the centre of the auditorium in the stalls and first balcony.

Good Seats on a Budget: The cheaper seats are at either side of the auditorium.

Seats to Avoid: All seats are comfortable with decent views.

EDUCATION

Guided Tours

There are free guided tours of the venue conducted on a handful of dates throughout the year. Check the website for further information. Other than these dates, tours can be specially arranged for €6.00 per person (min. ten people).
Tel: +33 (0)478 959 548 to book a private tour.

FACILITIES

Dining

Café-comptoir provides visitors with the perfect place to purchase refreshments during the interval, when visitors can also enjoy a sitdown meal.
Tel: +33 (0)478 959 565 for reservations.

Services

There are wheelchair places in all areas of the auditorium.

Guide dogs welcome.

HOW TO GET THERE

Bus: 1, 25, 28, 36, 37, 41, 47, 59, 70 and 99

Underground: Line B to Part-Dieu Servient. A single journey costs €1.50.

Among his other famous works, Maurice Ravel was the man responsible for the composition called Bolero, which made Torvil and Dean, an ice skating couple, household names. Ravel originally wrote the piece as a ballet score which was premiered in 1928.

The ice-skating couple gained international fame after using the composition during the 1984 Winter Olympics when they became the only couple in the competition with a perfect score from every judge, a record which still stands today.

Opéra National de Lyon

With an auditorium lined in sleek black in a scene vaguely reminiscent of a Star Wars movie, the Opéra National de Lyon stands proudly as one of the most important music venues in France. Founded in 1831, the inaugural performance of François-Adrien Boïeldieu's "La Dame blanche" was given on 1 July of that year. It became the venue for first performances in France of important operas by Wagner and Moussorgsky, including

Opéra de Lyon
Place de la Comédie
Lyon
F-69203
France
Tel: +33 (0)826 305 325
www.opera-lyon.com

Wagner's 'Die Meistersinger'. The grand old building was expanded and modernized in 1993 and is now a magnificent modern theatre.

TICKETING

Price Range: Tickets generally range from €5.00 to €90.00.

Concessions: There is a discount of between 10% and 50% available for children under 16, depending on the production. In addition, any remaining unsold tickets are available to students, seniors over-65 and the unemployed for a discounted price of €8.00 from 30 minutes before the performance. Wheelchair places are available for €10.00. Registered blind customers get 50% discount. These same discounts are available for carers accompanying disabled customers.

Box Office

The Box Office is located at the main entrance. Tickets can also be purchased from FNAC stores.
The Box Office is open Tuesday to Saturday, noon–7.00 p.m. The Opéra is closed completely in August. For remote bookings, a transaction charge of €2.00 per ticket applies.
Tel: +33 (0)826 305 325
www.opera-lyon.com

PERFORMANCES

Events take place from September to July.

Resident Groups: Opéra National de Lyon

SEATING

Capacity: 1,350

Organization: The Opera stage is placed within a very high auditorium with parterre stalls and six balconies of seating.

Best Seats: The best seats are located in the front of the first balcony.

Good Seats on a Budget: The seats in the side balcony on the fourth gallery are the cheapest seats located near the stage.

Seats to Avoid: All seats are comfortable with decent views.

EDUCATION

Guided Tours

Guided tours take place every Saturday in French or on special request in English. For all foreign language tours, advance booking is essential. Tel: +33 (0)472 776 969 to arrange a private tour.

Times: Regular tours in French are conducted every Saturday at 1.00 p.m.

Cost: €9.00

Concessions: €5.00

FACILITIES

Dining

There are several bars and a fine restaurant, Les Muses de l'Opéra located on-site. Reservations can be made at the Box Office.

Services

There are wheelchair places in all areas of the auditorium.

HOW TO GET THERE

Bus: 13

Overground: Lyon-Part-Dieu

Underground: Lines A and C to Hôtel de Ville. A single journey costs €1.50.

Car Parking: There is parking available at Parc Opéra. Tickets can be booked at the Box Office.

Capital of the Rhône-Alpes région, Lyon is also considered by some the gastronomic capital of France, and the old town, across the river from the Opéra is full of quaint narrow streets filled with an array of interesting shops, traditional restaurants and historic sites.

For those less culturally inclined, there is the city's football team, Olympique Lyonnaise, the most successful French team of recent years and are renowned for the jubilant atmosphere of their stadium and flamboyant playing style.

Lyon is a child-friendly city and many of the major museums and tourist sites offer a wide range of itineraries for children. In particular, Tête d'Or Park is highly recommended for a family excursion.

MARSEILLE

Opéra Municipal

Constructed on the site of a former tennis court, the Opéra Municipal in Marseille was the second opera house to be built in France after Bordeaux. The theatre flourished in the years following the French Revolution, hosting many major opera presentations including Verdi's 'Rigoletto' and 'Il Trovatore'. Unfortunately for the Opéra Municipal, technological advancements were to prove ill-fated, as some years after the installation of electricity, the site caught fire, completely destroying the building, and leaving only its shell. The present day site opened its doors in 1924. Keen on preserving as much of the original exterior as possible, the new design preserved the stone colonnade and placed the surviving original Box Office in the centre of the entrance hall.

Opéra Municipal de Marseille
2 Rue Molière
Marseille
F-13001
France
Tel: +33 (0)491 551 499
Fax: +33 (0)491 552 165
www.marseille.fr

Contemporary times have seen many singers make their French debuts at this opera house, with artists such as Alfredo Kraus, Plácido Domingo and Renata Scotto all choosing the Opera Municipal as a venue for their first outing on stage.

TICKETING

Advance Sales: Tickets go on sale at various times throughout the year. Check with the website for details.

Price Range: Tickets generally range from €8.00 to €75.00.

Concessions: Children qualify for a 50% discount on ticket prices. Students, disabled visitors and their carers qualify for a 25% discount, with senior citizens eligible for a 15% discount on the ticket price.

Box Office

> The Box Office is open Tuesday to Saturday, 10.00 a.m.–5.30 p.m.
> Tel: +33 (0)491 551 110

PERFORMANCES

Events take place from September to July.

Times: A typical performance starts at 8.00 p.m., but performance times vary.

SEATING

Capacity: 1,837

Organization: The auditorium is a classic urn-shaped auditorium, with three rings of boxes, two balconies and a gallery.

FACILITIES

Services

There are wheelchair places. People with reduced mobility should call +33 4 91 55 11 10 before the concert.

HOW TO GET THERE

Underground: Metro line 1 to Vieux-Port. Single ticket €1.70. Day ticket €4.50.

METZ

L'Arsenal

L'Arsenal opened in 1989 as a cultural centre for Metz. The main hall is a large, wooden-panelled auditorium with a reverberant acoustic. The season consists of visiting artists and orchestras of international quality for a varied programme of baroque, symphonic, jazz and world music. Since its opening, the Arsenal has developed an ambitious artistic policy, based on music and contemporary dance, regularly inviting composers and choreographers for periods in residence. Each year, the seasons operate within set themes, allowing companies to explore varying ideas within concentrated parameters, as well as performing rediscovered works within these genres.

Arsenal de Metz
Avenue Ney
Metz
F-57000
France
Tel: +33 (0)387 399 200
Fax: +33 (0)387 752 152
www.mairie-metz.fr/arsenal

TICKETING

Advance Sales: Tickets go on general sale 30 days before each concert.

Price Range: Tickets generally range from €17.00 to €40.00.

Concessions: All tickets are €8.00 for those under 26. Students from universities of Metz or Nancy can buy tickets for €6.60. There are also reductions available for the over-60s and the unemployed.

Box Office

The Box Office is open Monday to Saturday, 1.00 p.m.–6.00 p.m. The Box Office is closed from Bastille Day (14 July) to the end of August.
Tel: +33 (0)387 741 616
Lines are open Tuesday to Saturday (must be purchased at least 3 days in advance), 9.00 a.m.–noon; Tuesday to Friday, 1.00 p.m.–6.00 p.m.; Saturday 1.00 p.m.–6.00 p.m.

PERFORMANCES

Events take place from September to July.

Times: A typical concert starts at 8.30 p.m., although performance times vary.

Resident Groups: Orchestre National de Lorraine

SEATING

Capacity: Grande Salle – 1,354; Salle de l'Esplanade – 352.

Organization: The seating is arranged in one large bank of stalls.

Best Seats: The best seats are in the middle of the stalls section.

Good Seats on a Budget: The seats at the back of the hall have a great view.

Seats to Avoid: All seats are comfortable with decent views.

HOW TO GET THERE

Bus: 6, 8, 16, 17, 27. Adult single costs €1.00.

Car Parking: There is a car park located in Place de la Republique, near the opera.

Opéra - Théâtre

The Opéra - Théâtre is a small eighteenth century theatre set on a small island on the River Moselle. It prides itself on opera productions in the traditional style in intimate surroundings. The building, classed as a 'monument historique', is one of the oldest theatres in France and is a venue where operas, comedies, ballets, dramatic performances, and opérettas shape a varied programme. Approximately 115 performances are staged each year. It is also one of the last theatres to have its own workshops where costumes and decorations for its latest performances are created.

TICKETING

Advance Sales: Tickets for the coming season go on general sale in September.

4-5 place de la Comédie
Metz
F-57000
France
Tel: +33 (0)387 754 050
Fax: +33 (0)387 313 237
www.mairie-metz.fr/opéra

Price Range: Tickets generally range from €5.00 to €40.00.

Concessions: There are reductions available for young people under 26. Students from universities of Metz or Nancy can buy tickets for €6.60. In addition, special rates are also available for the over-60s and the unemployed.

Box Office

The Box Office is open Monday to Friday, 9.00 a.m.–12.30 p.m. and 3.00 p.m.–5.00 p.m. Tel: +33 (0)387 754 050 (payment by cheque only, payable to Trésorerie Principale de Metz Municipale) www.mairie-metz.fr/opéra

PERFORMANCES

Events take place from September to July.

Times: A typical concert starts at 8.30 p.m., although performance times vary.

SEATING

Capacity: 700

Organization: The auditorium is small, and consists of a parterre section and three balconies.

Best Seats: The best seats are located in the parterre section.

Good Seats on a Budget: The third category seats on the third balcony have a reasonable view.

FACILITIES

Dining

There is a café-bar that serves light meals before performances.

HOW TO GET THERE

Bus: 5, 9, 25, 29. Adult single costs €1.00.

Car Parking: There is parking in the Place de la Comedie next to the Théâtre.

MONTPELLIER

Opéra Berlioz et Salle Pasteur

Home to both the Opéra Berlioz and Salle Pasteur, a prime venue for conferences and major events, Le Corum in Montpellier serves as a multi-purpose venue for a variety of professional events. Designed by architect Claude Vasconi, and situated in the centre of Montpellier, Le Corum forms an extension to Montpellier's historic centre and its pedestrian and commercial areas. Building Le Corum's pink marble walls proved a real challenge for both architects and executers, involving the creation of a structure that had never been built before, incorporating a number of outstanding areas, each with its own particular function. Today opéra Berlioz's main musical output is centred around the festival in July which includes over 100 performances of opera, chamber music, and jazz.

Le Corum
Esplanade Charles de Gaulle
Montpellier
F-34000
France
Tel: +33 (0)467 616 761
Fax: +33 (0)467 616 700

TICKETING

Price Range: Tickets generally range from €17.00 to €48.00.

Concessions: Reductions are available for the under-27s, over-60s and the unemployed.

Box Office

Tel: +33 (0)467 020 201
Lines are open Monday to Friday, 8.00 a.m.–7.00 p.m.
Festival concerts can be booked at www.festival-rfmontpellier.com

PERFORMANCES

Times: Performance times vary. Check with the Box Office for individual performances.

Annual Festivals/Special Events: There is a festival of opera and concerts, the Festival de Radio France et Montpellier Languedoc-Roussillon which takes place every July.

SEATING

Capacity: 2,010

Organization: There is a large parterre section on the ground floor and a balcony, and boxes along the sides of the auditorium.

Best Seats: The best seats are located in the stalls.

Good Seats on a Budget: The boxes above the balcony are cheapest.

Seats to Avoid: All seats are comfortable with decent views.

HOW TO GET THERE

Bus: 4

Overground: Tram line 1 to Corum. A single journey costs €1.30.

Car Parking: There is underground parking situated underneath the hall.

Opéra-Comédie

Located in the heart of Montpellier, the Opéra-Comédie is surrounded by many of the city's top attractions, including the Esplanade Charles de Gaulle, a unique tree-lined space where visitors come to stroll and relax. Until the eighteenth century Montpellier had no theatre at all, and often held events in the residences of the noblemen of the city. In 1721, the 'Académie de Musique' was created, with Louis Armand de Vignerot of Plessis, Duc of Richelieu, appointed 'Premier gentilhomme de la chambre chargé des spectacles' ('First gentleman of the room charged with the spectacles'), whose job was to begin the construction of a new venue for the city. The building was inaugurated in 1755, and was crowned with a performance of François Rebel and François Francœur's 'Pyrame and Thisbé'. During the next 100 years, the theatre was damaged twice by fire, with the blaze of 1881 being particularly fierce, destroying the building completely. The construction of today's Opéra-Comédie was much influenced by the Palais Garnier in Paris, and continues to this day to steer its repertoire towards classical yet modern themes.

TICKETING

Advance Sales: Tickets for the concerts go on general sale in September. Tickets for opera go on sale at various points

---

Opéra National de Montpellier
11 Boulevard Victor Hugo
Montpellier
F-34967
France
Tel: +33 (0)467 601 980
Fax: +33 (0)467 601 990
www.opéra-montpellier.com

throughout the year – check the website for details.

Price Range: Tickets generally range from €17.00 to €48.00.

Concessions: Reductions are available for the under-27s, over-60s and the unemployed.

Box Office

> The Box Office is open Monday, 2.00 p.m.–6.00 p.m.; Tuesday to Saturday, noon–6.00 p.m.
> Tel: +33 (0)467 601 999

PERFORMANCES

Events take place from November to July.

Times: Performance times vary – check with the Box Office for individual performances.

Resident Groups: The Opéra National de Montpellier and the Orchestra National de Montpellier.

SEATING

Capacity: 1,200

Organization: The Opera is a classic theatre with a parterre section and four balconies.

Best Seats: The best seats are at the front of the first balcony.

Good Seats on a Budget: The cheapest seats are located in the fourth balcony.

HOW TO GET THERE

Overground Tram line 1 to Comedie. A single journey costs €1.30.

Car Parking: There is underground parking in the Place de la Comedie next to the Theatre. Parking costs €1.90 per hour.

Ladies please note that, in accordance with a somewhat antiquated rule from 1891 still in force, you must check your hats at the cloakroom.

While in Montpellier, why not visit the celebrated fourteenth century cathedral of Saint-Pierre? In the nineteenth century, Pierre-Henri Revoil and August Baussan worked on its renovation, with new stained glass from Edouard Didron and Paul Nicod.

Also of note are the famous Botanical Gardens at the Boulevard Henri IV, built in 1635, which are a model of exquisite design.

NANTES

Théâtre Graslin

The Théâtre Graslin was inaugurated on 23 March 1788 after plans by the architect Mathurin Crucy were brought to life. The building was devastated by a fire during the late eighteenth century which forced the site to close for a while. The venue was quickly rebuilt, reopening in 1811 to the delight of its audiences. The façade of the building is as grand as the repertoire within, with eight muses overhanging each of the eight columns which stand proudly at the face of the venue, joining two statues of the French dramatists Molière and Jean Racine which appear on the main staircase. Today, the venue, together with its resident organization the Opéra de Nantes, offers a great selection of classical repertoire in an equally apt and grand venue.

1, Rue Molière
10929
Nantes
F-44009
France
Tel: +33 (0)24 089 8400
www.angers-nantes-opera.com

TICKETING

Advance Sales: Tickets can be booked from the start of the season in May.

Price Range: Tickets generally range from €5.00 to €50.00.

Concessions: Discounts vary, depending on nature of performance; some performances can be seen for as little as €5.00.

Box Office

The Box Office is open Tuesday to Saturday, noon–4.00 p.m.
Tel: +33 (0)24 069 7718
Fax: +33 (0)24 089 8422
www.angers-nantes-opera.com

PERFORMANCES

Performances are held all year round.

Times: Performances usually begin at 8.00 p.m.

Resident Groups: Opéra de Nantes

SEATING

Capacity: 784

Organization: The auditorium is arranged into stalls and four balconies.

Best Seats: The best seats are located in the stalls, and first balcony.

Good Seats on a Budget: Seats in the third balcony provide good value for money.

Seats to Avoid: The fourth balcony has restricted views.

FACILITIES

Dining

There is a bar serving a range of light snacks and refreshments.

Services

Guide dogs welcome.

NICE

Acropolis – Grand Auditorium Apollon

Grand by name, grand by design, the Acropolis in Nice is a convention and exhibition centre which has delighted audiences for more than twenty years. Opening in 1984, the joint management of the site, the Acropolis Congrès and Acropolis-Expositions, has ensured that the venue boasts no less than four auditoriums, all fully equipped for a diverse range of events. The biggest of these halls is the prestigious and unique Apollon Auditorium, with a capacity of 2,500. The auditorium was opened in 1985 and still continues to lead the way with fresh approaches to music and arts, providing visitors with one of the world's most efficient convention centres with its technically sophisticated equipment, its design and above all its dynamism.

1, Esplanade Kennedy
Nice
F-06302
France
Tel: +33 (0)4 93 92 83 00
Fax: +33 (0)4 93 92 82 55
www.nice-acropolis.com

Opéra de Nice

PERFORMANCES

Performances take place on selected dates throughout the year. Specific dates and events are listed on the website under 'Discovering Acropolis/Programme'.

SEATING

Capacity: The main Apollon Hall has a capacity of 2,500.

HOW TO GET THERE

Car Parking: A nearby car park has 2,000 places. See the website for a full map of the area.

An elegant building hidden away in Nice's back streets, the Opéra de Nice has a history which stretches back to the eighteenth century with an original site constructed in timber. This structure was replaced by a glorious Italian style building in 1826 which was badly destroyed when the great curtain in the auditorium caught fire. The building as

4&6 Rue Saint-Francois-de-Paule
Nice
F-06300
France
Tel: +33 (0)49 217 4000
Fax: +33 (0)49 380 3483
www.opéra-nice.org

visitors know it today was erected in 1882 and subsequently declared a historic monument in 1993. Possessing a unique pink façade, the Opéra de Nice may be tucked away among souvenir shops and away from the limelight it deserves, '...but this takes nothing away from the majestic splendour of the building, still flourishing through a busy repertoire.'

TICKETING

Price Range: Tickets generally range from €7.00 to €85.00.

Concessions: Some concerts have specific discounts. See the website or contact the venue directly for further information. Disabled patrons qualify for a 10% discount.

Well worth a visit is the *Observatoire de Nice* (Nice Observatory), which is located on the summit of Mont Gros. The observatory was erected in 1879 by the banker Raphaël Bischoffsheim. The architect was Charles Garnier, and Gustave Eiffel designed the main dome.

PARIS

Cité de la musique

Located away from the limelight of central Paris, the Cité de la musique is a self-contained musical world, incorporating a concert hall, museum and the Paris Conservatoire that opened in 1995 in the run-down nineteenth arrondissement, or district of Paris. A shining set of glass and concrete buildings, the site's museum is also worth a visit, containing an important collection of classical music instruments dating mainly from the fifteenth to the twentieth century, together with exhibition halls, workshops and archives. A larger auditorium is currently in development, which will see the main concert hall more than double in capacity, and is due to open to the public in 2012.

221 Avenue Jean Jaurès
Paris
F-75019
France
Tel: +33 (0)1 44 84 45 00
www.cite-musique.fr

TICKETING

Price Range: Tickets generally range from €15.00 to €25.00.

PERFORMANCES

Times: A typical concert starts at 8.00 p.m., although performance times vary.

Programmes: Programmes can be downloaded for free from the website 48 hours before the concert.

Resident Groups: The Ensemble intercontemporain and Conservatoire national supérieur de musique et de danse de Paris

SEATING

Capacity: 800–1,000

EDUCATION

Guided Tours

Tours of the venue include the adjacent museum and are conducted from Tuesday to Saturday. There are different tour options for adults and children of different ages. Tel: +33 (0)1 44 84 44 84 or see the website for further information and bookings.

Times: Visitors can take an unguided tour at any time between noon–6.00 p.m. Those wishing to participate in a guided tour can join one at various intervals between 9.00 a.m.–4.00 p.m.

Cost: €10.00

Concessions: €5.00 (children)

FACILITIES

Dining

Café de la musique is situated next to the concert hall.

Services

Although there are no specific braille prgrammes for the visually impaired, visitors are invited to join a special tour of the site's museum, allowing them a special sensory tour, exploring materials used in instrument-making by touch, as well as participating in a specially designed workshop. Tours cost €50.00, and last from between one and two hours. Tel: +33 (0)1 44 84 46 13 for further information.

HOW TO GET THERE

Bus: 75, 151. For ticket holders there is a free bus service after concerts to the centre of Paris.

Underground: Métro line 5 to Porte de Pantin. A single journey costs €1.40. Check www.ratp.info for various types of tickets.

Car Parking: There is an underground car park located at the Cité de la musique. For information on 24-hour parking facilities, Tel: +33 (0)1 44 84 44 84.

IRCAM

IRCAM is the baby of composer/conductor Pierre Boulez, which opened in 1977 as a shrine to modernism. An addition to the Pompidou Centre, and designed by Richard Rogers and Renzo Piano, it strives to promote modernist electronic music by public performances and education of composers. Many of today's leading composers, including Kaija Saariaho and Harrison Birtwistle, have worked there. Depending on individual tastes, the venue has been seen both as pushing the boundaries and disappearing into its own ego. Either way, nobody can deny the pioneering role the IRCAM has played in the advancement of contemporary classical music, serving more as a producer of dialogue between composer and audience than a passive venue for audiences to consume harmonies. The centre continues to support the young performers and composers of the future, all within the unique environment of the inside-out architecture at the Pompidou, and the modern ingenuity of the facilities within.

TICKETING

Advance Sales: Tickets for the season can be booked from July onwards.

Price Range: Tickets generally range from €5.00 to €24.00.

Concessions: Reduced rates are available for under-25s, including a 50% reduction for students. The unemployed are also eligible for a 50% discount on ticket prices.

Box Office

The Box Office is open Monday to Friday, 2.00 p.m.–5.30 p.m.
Tel: +33 (0) 1 44 78 12 40
Fax: +33 (0) 1 44 78 43 55
www.ircam.fr

1 Place Igor-Stravinsky
Paris
F-75004
France
Tel: +33 (0)1 44 78 48 43
Fax: +33 (0)1 44 78 15 40
www.ircam.fr

PERFORMANCES

Events take place from September to July.

Times: A typical concert starts at 8.00 p.m., although performance times vary.

Resident Groups: IRCAM has a series of resident and visiting composers who create their music electronically with invited instrumentalists.

Annual Festivals/Special Events: Festival Agora, a multi-disciplinary festival of modernism, takes place every June.

SEATING

Capacity: There are two concert spaces, the Main Hall and the Salle Stravinsky, both of variable configuration.

Good Seats on a Budget: Tickets are all the same price.

EDUCATION

Guided Tours

Visits are arranged on request. Visitors can tour the spaces of the building, or take an architectural tour, or a tour of the technical equipment aimed at composers and musicians.
Tel: +33 (0)1 44 78 48 16 or

email: visites@ircam.fr for further information or to arrange a tour.

Cost: €70.00 per group (max. 20 people), €50.00 for a group of students, or €5.00 per individual.

FACILITIES

Dining

Restaurant Georges provides visitors with great views in the Pompidou Centre. There are also cafés in the Centre. Tel: +33 (0)144 78 47 99 for restaurant reservations.

HOW TO GET THERE

Bus: 75, 76

Underground: Métro lines 1, 4, 7, 11 and 14 to Châtelet. A single journey costs €1.40. Check www.ratp.info for various types of tickets.

Car Parking: IRCAM is located within a pedestrianized area, therefore visitors are advised to use public transport.

IRCAM is located next door to the Pompidou Centre, an important gallery of modern art. It is also in a pedestrianized area full of bars and restaurants to enjoy before or after a show. Its multimedia library was established in 1996. It is one of the very first music hybrid libraries to have been created with around 1,000 hours of recorded music and over 2,000 scientific articles available online, in addition to its physical collections of sheet music, books on music and related domains.

Opéra Bastille

With his opinion that 'the most elegant solution for the problem of opera is to blow up the opera houses', the controversial composer Pierre Boulez may have been expected to be responsible for a reduction in the number of opera houses. Instead, his

Opéra Bastille
Place de la Bastille
Paris
F-75012
France
Tel: +33 (0)1 43 43 96 96
Fax: +33 (0)1 43 73 13 74
www.opéradeparis.fr

suggestion of a new type of house inspired President Mitterand to create one of his grand projects, and the shining new Opéra Bastille opened in 1989, on the bicentennial anniversary of the storming of the Bastille prison, after five years of construction on the site of the former Bastille train station. Bringing modernity where the Garnier brings tradition, the Opéra Bastille was built to entice opera away from its predecessor, though over the years some critics have viewed the venue as inferior to its older sibling. Highly modern, it has also been described as impersonal by some, although modern facilities allow the Bastille the sheer stage volume to put on shows which are highly polished. The venue opened with a dazzling gala concert conducted by Georges Prêtre, featuring singers such as Teresa Berganza and Plácido Domingo. However, it did not see its first opera performance until 1990, with Berlioz's 'Les Troyens'.

TICKETING

Advance Sales: The first tickets for the season go on sale at the beginning of July. Other tickets go on sale throughout the year, check with the website for details.

Price Range: Tickets generally range from €5.00 to €150.00.

Concessions: Reductions for under-28s are available when buying tickets for subscription series. Over-60s can purchase a card Pass Opéra Seniors for €45.00 which entitles them to discounts. In addition, there are seats reserved for disabled and visually impaired customers. Tel: +33 (0)1 40 01 18 50 to reserve tickets, Monday to Friday, 10.00 a.m.–1.00 p.m.

Box Office

The Box Office is located at the main entrance. Tickets may also be purchased at the Palais Garnier Box Office. Opening hours are Monday to Saturday, 10.30 a.m.–6.30 p.m. The Box Office opens 45 minutes before the performance for ticket collection. Tickets purchased within two weeks of the performance must be collected from the Box Office.
Tel: +33 (0)1 72 29 35 35
Lines are open: Monday to Friday, 9.00 a.m.–6.00 p.m.; Saturday, 9.00 a.m.–1.00 p.m.
www.opéradeparis.fr

PERFORMANCES

Events take place from September to July.

Times: Performance times vary – check with the Box Office for individual performances.

Resident Groups: The Opera National de Paris

SEATING

Capacity: 2,723

Organization: The Bastille has a large ground floor section, two balconies and galleries at the side of the auditorium.

Best Seats: The best seats are located in the orchestra stalls on the ground floor.

Good Seats on a Budget: The galleries on the side are inexpensive with a good view, although the subtitles (in French) are not visible from these seats.

Seats to Avoid: Every seat has an unrestricted view of the stage.

EDUCATION

Guided Tours

Tours of the venue are available at various times. Tel: +33 140 01 1970 for further information or see www.visites.opéradeparis.fr.

Cost: €11.00

Concessions: €9.00/€6.00 (children)

FACILITIES

Dining

There are several bars located within the venue where a variety of food is served.

Services

Disabled access.

HOW TO GET THERE

Bus: 20, 29, 65, 69, 76, 86, 87 and 91

Underground: Métro lines 1, 5, 8 to Bastille. A single journey costs €1.40. Check www.ratp.info for various types of tickets.

Palais Garnier

Lavish and opulent, Palais Garnier is one of the most extravagant and best known opera houses in the world. Built during the reign of Napoleon III, its motto could be 'more is more'. Marble, paintings and chandeliers fill the venue, which includes an enormous hall, and foyers which are unsurpassed in their magnificence. An ornate building, the style is monumental, with giant columns of the theatre's façade accompanied by bronze busts of many of the great composers, including Mozart and Beethoven. The interior is rich, with velvet, gold leaf, cherubs and nymphs, together with a central chandelier weighing over six tons. The ceiling area, which surrounds the chandelier, was given a new painting in 1964 by Marc Chagall. This painting proved controversial with many people who felt Chagall's work clashed with the style of the rest of the theatre. Nevertheless, the results today are as magnificent as they were during its inauguration in the

Place de l'Opera
Paris
F-75009
France
Tel: +33 (0)1 43 43 96 96
Fax: +33 (0)1 43 73 13 74
www.operadeparis.fr

nineteenth century, with the site hosting an extensive programme of opera, recitals and a large ballet programme.

TICKETING

Advance Sales: The first tickets for the season go on sale at the beginning of July. Other tickets go on sale throughout the year, check with the website for details.

Price Range: Tickets generally range from €5.00 to €160.00.

Concessions: Reductions for under-28s are available when buying tickets for subscription series. Over-60s can purchase a card Pass Opéra Seniors for €45.00 which entitles them to discounts. In addition, there are seats reserved for disabled and visually impaired customers. Tel: +33 (0)1 40 01 18 50 to reserve tickets (Monday to Friday, 10.00 a.m.–1.00 p.m.).

Box Office

The Box Office is located in Place de Opera. Tickets may also be purchased at the Bastille Opera Box Office. The Box Office is open Monday to Saturday, 10.30 a.m.–6.30 p.m. The Box Office opens 45 minutes before the performance for ticket collection. Tickets purchased within two weeks of the performance must be collected from the Box Office. Tel: +33 (0)1 72 29 3535 Lines are open Monday to Friday, 9.00 a.m.–6.00 p.m.; Saturday, 9.00 a.m.–1.00 p.m. www.opéradeparis.fr

PERFORMANCES

Events take place from September to July.

Times: Performance times vary – check with the Box Office for individual performances.

Resident Groups: The Opera National de Paris

SEATING

Capacity: 1,979

Organization: The Palais Garnier is a classic opera theatre with a parterre section and five levels of boxes.

Best Seats: The best seats are located in the orchestra stalls on the ground floor.

Good Seats on a Budget:
The cheapest seats are situated in the upper balconies, but can only be purchased from the Box Office in person.

EDUCATION

Guided Tours: Regular guided tours take place on Wednesdays, Saturdays and Sundays. In addition, the building is open for exploring between 10.00 a.m.–5.00 p.m. every day. Tel: +33 (0)1 41 10 08 10 or email: contact@purplebeam.com for further information or to book a tour ticket. Visitors can also browse vivites.operradeparis.fr

Times: 11.30 a.m. and 3.30 p.m. in French and 11.30 a.m. and 2.30 p.m. in English.

Cost: Tours cost €6.00 without a guide and €11.00 with a guide.

Concessions: Tours for concessionary groups cost €4.00 without a guide, €9.00 with. Special guided tours for children are conducted at a rate of €6.00.

FACILITIES

Dining

There are several bars in which food is served.

Services

Disabled access.

HOW TO GET THERE

Underground: Métro lines 3, 7, 8 to Opera. A single journey costs €1.40. Check www.ratp.info for various types of tickets.

Bus: 21, 22, 27, 29, 42, 53, 66, 68, 81 and 95

Car Parking: There is parking available at Place Vendôme.

The ideal model for several subsequent opera houses across Europe, the Palais Garnier did not always run as smoothly as it does today, and initially, the construction of the opera house was plagued by numerous setbacks. One major problem which postponed the laying of the concrete foundation was the extremely swampy ground under which flowed a subterranean lake, requiring the water to be removed by continual pumping which took eight months. On a more positive note, the subterranean lake also provided inspiration for the 'Phantom Of The Opera', which provides the backdrop for Gaston Leroux's famous Gothic novel, and all its incarnations.

Salle Gaveau

With a beautiful auditorium which has survived both bankruptcy and war, the Salle Gaveau has proven resilient in even the most testing of times. Completed in 1907, the building is constructed in white painted wood, and makes the most of a beautiful organ located above the stage. During World War I, the venue continued to provide entertainment to soldiers and citizens alike, continuing with the same stance during World War II when the venue was used as a site for official receptions as well as accommodating the famous classical musicians of that time. In 1963, the Gaveau went into receivership, and was sold to an insurance company, whose intention was to turn the site into a car park intended for profit. Fortunately, two musicians, Chantal and JeanMarie Fournier bought back the venue, which has since undergone several renovations, significantly improving the site whilst trying to maintain many of the original designs of 1907.

45 Rue la Boetie
Paris
F-75008
France
Tel: +33 (0)1 49 53 05 07
Fax: +33 (0)1 49 53 05 08
www.sallegaveau.com

TICKETING

Price Range: Tickets generally range from €10.00 to €55.00.

Box Office

The Box Office is open Monday to Friday, 10.00 a.m.–6.00 p.m.
Tel: +33 (0)1 49 53 05 07
www.sallegaveau.com

PERFORMANCES

Events take place from September to June.

Times: A typical concert starts at 8.30 p.m., although performance times vary.

SEATING

Capacity: 1,020

Organization: The Salle Gaveau has orchestra stalls on a flat floor and two levels of balcony and side balcony.

Best Seats: The best seats are located in the 'Loge d'honneur' on the first balcony.

Good Seats on a Budget:
The seats on the second balcony have good views. Some concerts have the same price for all seats.

Seats to Avoid: All seats are comfortable with decent views. A preview of the view of each seat can be seen on the website.

HOW TO GET THERE

Bus: 43, 52, 83 and 93

Underground: Métro lines 9 and 13 to Miromesnil. A single journey costs €1.40. Check www.ratp.info for various types of tickets.

Car Parking: Parking is available at 164 Bd Haussmann.

Salle Pleyel

The Salle Pleyel was originally opened in 1927 by the piano manufacturer Pleyel. Its initial inauguration proved to be shortlived, as a fire ravaged the auditorium less than nine months after its opening. The impact of the fire was so immense that both the acoustics and the building suffered from the event. The venue eventually became the property of the Crédit Lyonnais bank, an unusual enterprise which, surprisingly perhaps, was to prove highly successful. The Salle Pleyel became known as the most celebrated concert location in Paris, and was the location where Stravinsky returned to direct 'Agon' in 1957, then 'Threni' in 1958, and where Otto Klemperer gave his highly intense spiritual interpretations of Mahler's Ninth Symphony and Beethoven's 'Heroica'. In addition, artists as diverse as Louis Armstrong, Ravi Shankar and Jorge Bolet have all played in this pioneering concert hall which

252, Rue du faubourg Saint-Honoré
Paris
F-75008
France
Tel: +33 (0)1 42 56 13 13
www.sallepleyel.fr

literally rose like a phoenix from the flames. The Pleyel reopened in 2006 after an extensive and successful renovation. An art deco building, the auditorium is now a very smart hall with white walls, plum coloured seats and wooden fixtures. More importantly, the foyer that was lost in the 1960s has been converted back from dance studios into a spacious and bright area. It is now the principal hall in Paris for symphonic concerts.

TICKETING

Advance Sales: Bookings for individual performances in the coming season can be made from 1 June by telephone or via the website, and from 1 September at the Ticket Office.

Price Range: Tickets generally range from €10.00 to €130.00.

Concessions: Any remaining tickets are available to under-28s, seniors and the unemployed at a special rate of €10.00, from one hour before the performance. Disabled customers are entitled to a 15% discount on seats, except for category 5 (subject to availability and on presentation of proof of status). For each concert a quota of seats is allocated for people with reduced mobility.

Box Office

The Box Office is open Monday to Saturday, 10.00 a.m.–7.00 p.m. Visitors should be aware that any tickets that have not been paid for and collected half an hour before the start of the concert will be automatically cancelled.
Tel: +33 (0)1 42 56 1313
Lines are open Monday to Saturday, 11.00 a.m.–7.00 p.m.; Sunday, 11.00 a.m.–5.00 p.m.
www.sallepleyel.fr (full price tickets only)

PERFORMANCES

Events take place from September to July.

Times: A typical concert starts at 8.00 p.m., although performance times vary.

Resident Groups: The Orchestre de Paris and the Radio France Philharmonic Orchestra.

SEATING

Capacity: 1,913

Organization: There are stalls on the sloped ground floor and two balcony levels, side balconies and a choir balcony.

Best Seats: The best seats are located in the ground floor stalls.

Good Seats on a Budget: The cheapest seats are at the very back of the second balcony. They are far away but have a good view.

Seats to Avoid: All seats are comfortable with decent views.

HOW TO GET THERE

Bus: 43 and 93

Underground: Métro line 2 to Ternes; or Métro lines 1, 6 to Charles de Gaule-Etoile. A single journey costs €1.40. Check www.ratp.info for various types of tickets.

Although slightly nondescript, the Rue du Faubourg Saint-Honoré is perhaps one of the most fashionable streets in the world, in that every fashion house worth visiting has a shop here.

Théâtre de l'Opéra Comique – Salle Favart

Housed in the oldest theatre in Paris, the Théâtre de l'Opéra Comique was devised as an antidote to the Italian opera that dominated the continent during the eighteenth century. Some of the operas that received their premiere here, including Bizet's 'Carmen', Berlioz's 'La damnation de Faust' and Debussy's 'Pelleas et Melisande', have lasted longer than their competitors. Virtually every opera house in France has suffered damages and destruction by fire at one stage or another, and this incarnation of the Salle Favart dates from 1898, replacing two previous buildings that had been reduced to cinders. Today, the Théâtre de l'Opéra Comique stages a range of performances, including many new shows that push the boundaries of comedy and opera, as well as classic operetta.

Opéra-Comique
5 Rue Favart
Paris
F-75002
France
Tel: +33 (0)1 42 44 45 40
Fax: +33 (0)1 42 86 85 78
www.opéra-comique.com

TICKETING

Price Range: Tickets generally range from €7.00 to €100.00.

Concessions: Large reductions are available for individuals under 26, over 60 and the unemployed in the third category seats.

Box Office

The Box Office is open Monday to Saturday, 9.00 a.m.–9.00 p.m.; Sunday, 11.00 a.m.–7.00 p.m. There is a €2.50 transaction charge for remote bookings. Tickets can be collected from the Box Office on the day of the performance. Visitors are advised that any tickets not picked up 30 minutes before the start of the performance will be re-sold.
Tel: +33 (0)1 42 44 4546
Fax: +33 (0)1 49 26 05 93
www.opéra-comique.com/reservation

PERFORMANCES

Events take place from September to July.

Times: A typical concert starts at 8.00 p.m., although performance times vary.

SEATING

Capacity: 1,331

Organization: The Salle Favart has a parterre section, together with four levels of balconies.

Best Seats: The 'gold square' tickets – armchairs beside the orchestra pit are said to possess the best views and most prestigious locations in the auditorium.

Good Seats on a Budget: The cheapest seats are located in the top balcony.

HOW TO GET THERE

Bus: 20, 27, 39, 48, 52, 67, 74, 85, 95

Underground: Métro lines 8, 9 to Richelieu-Drouot, Métro line 3 to Quatre-Septembre. A single journey costs €1.40. Check www.ratp.info for various types of tickets.

Car Parking: There is public parking nearby at Chaussee d'-Antin.

Théâtre des Champs-Elysees

Representing one of the few examples of Art Nouveau in Paris, the Théâtre des Champs Elysees was founded by journalist and showman Gabriel Astruc to provide a lighter edge to contemporary music and dance, as opposed to other institutions such as the Opéra National de Paris which were deemed much more conservative. On its opening night, the venue played host to the world premiere of Igor Stravinsky's highly influential 'Le Sacre du printemps' or, 'The Rite of Spring'. Today, the venue is most famous for its more modest showcases, staging approximately three operas every year and concentrating on a classical repertoire which plays host to two fine resident orchestras, as well as being the French base for the Vienna Philharmonic Orchestra.

15 Avenue Montaigne
Paris
F-75008
France
Tel: +33 (0)1 49 52 50 50
Fax: +33 (0)1 49 52 07 41
www.theatrechampselysees.fr

TICKETING

Price Range: Tickets generally range from €5.00 to €150.00.

Box Office

Online reservation is recommended. All online transactions incur at a €2.00 per ticket booking fee.
www.theatrechampselysees.fr

PERFORMANCES

Times: Many performances start at 7.30 p.m. or 8.00 p.m.

Resident Groups: The Orchestre National de France and Orchestre Lamoureux.

SEATING

Capacity: 2,000

Organization: The theatre has a parterre section and five balcony levels.

Best Seats: The best seats are located in the centre of the parterre section.

Good Seats on a Budget: The fourth balcony offers the best balance of view and expense.

Seats to avoid: The seats on the top balcony (categories 6 and 7) have very restricted viewing – rather like watching an opera from inside a postbox and should be avoided where possible.

FACILITIES

Dining

Bars and designated snack areas provide a variety of refreshments for guests to enjoy before the performance and during the interval.

HOW TO GET THERE

Bus: 42, 63, 72, 80 and 92

Underground: Métro line 9 to Alma-Marceau or Franklin-Roosevelt. A single journey costs €1.40. Check www.ratp.info for various types of tickets.

Car Parking: There is parking available nearby at Alma-Geaorge V.

Théâtre Mogador

Designed by Bertie Crewe and built in 1913, the Théâtre Mogador was used mainly as a vehicle for staging operettas, following from its original purpose – as a venue for hosting music-hall shows. From 1920 the venue gained fame with such performances as Sergei Diaghilev's 'Ballets Russes' and through the 'Thés Mogador', or performances of operettas and plays in the afternoon. Glitz and glamour were even brought to the venue when in 2005 it hosted the nineteenth Molière (French theatre awards). Today, the venue still plays host to operettas, although the stage has also made way for popular musicals such as 'Les Miserables', and most recently 'The Lion King'.

TICKETING

Price Range: Tickets generally range from €13.00 to €92.00.

Concessions: Concessions vary according to the promoter.

SEATING

Capacity: 1,800

Organization: The auditorium is arranged into stalls and three balconies with boxes.

Best Seats: The stalls and first balcony provide the best seats for visitors.

25 Rue de Mogador
Paris
F-75009
France
Tel: +33 (0)1 53 32 32 32
Fax: +33 (0)1 48 78 90 99
www.mogador.net

Good Seats on a Budget:
Second and third balconies

FACILITIES

Services

♿ Disabled access throughout the building. Contact in advance for further information.

🐕 Guide dogs welcome.

HOW TO GET THERE

Bus: 20, 21, 22, 24, 26, 27, 29, 32, 42, 43, 53, 66, 68, 81 and 95 can be taken to the venue.

Underground: Métro line 12 to Trinité, Métro lines 7 and 9 to Chaussée d'Antin or Métro lines 3, 12 and 13 to Saint Lazare. A single journey costs €1.40. Check www.ratp.info for various types of tickets.

Car Parking: Haussmann-Lafayette has parking spaces located three minutes from the theatre.

Théâtre Musical du Châtelet

Once a venue for the silver screen, the Théâtre Musical du Châtelet has evolved since its opening in 1862 to become a venue showcasing a variety of top quality performances and concerts. The Théâtre is encompassed by its very own fortress, with the centre drawing focus to a commemorative sphinx endowed fountain, erected in 1808 to celebrate Napolean's victory in Egypt. Originally used for drama performances, the twentieth century has seen the venue play host to companies as varied as Diaghilev's 'Ballets Russes' and the contemporary Kirov Opera. In addition, musical heavyweights including Tchaikovsky, Gustav Mahler and Richard Strauss have all made appearances at the theatre, which has recently been renovated, improving acoustics, and bringing superiority to an already prominent venue.

Théâtre du Châtelet
2, Rue Edouard Colonne
Paris
F-75001
France
Tel: +33 (0)1 40 28 28 28
Fax: +33 (0)1 42 36 89 75
www.chatelet-theatre.com

TICKETING

Advance Sales: Tickets for the coming season go on sale in May (June for online booking).

Price Range: Tickets generally range from €10.00 to €80.00.

Concessions: There are reductions available for individuals under 26, senior citizens and the unemployed, subject to availability.

Box Office

The Box Office is open daily, 11.00 a.m.–7.00 p.m. Transaction charges range from €2.00–€2.50, depending on how far in advance tickets are booked.
Tel: +33 (0)1 40 28 2840
Lines are open Monday to Saturday, 10.00 a.m.–7.00 p.m.
www.chatelet-theatre.com

PERFORMANCES

Events take place from September to July.

Resident Groups: The Orchestre Philharmonique de Radio France

SEATING

Capacity: 2,300

Organization: The theatre has a parterre section and five balcony levels.

Best Seats: The best seats are located in the centre of the parterre section.

Good Seats on a Budget: The fourth category tickets are inexpensive with good views of the stage.

HOW TO GET THERE

Bus: 58 and 81

Underground: Métro lines 1, 4, 7, 11 and 14 to Châtelet. A single journey costs €1.40. Check www.ratp.info for various types of tickets.

Car Parking: There is parking located nearby at Alma-Geaorge V.

The adjacent, and identical Theatre de la Ville is a venue for jazz, world music and contemporary dance.

STRASBOURG

Théâtre Municipal – Opéra du Rhin

Internationally renowned and culturally diverse, the Opéra National du Rhin provides its audiences with a wide variety of operas, dance, recitals, concerts, and shows, ensuring visitors both young and old get an opportunity to witness one of over 140 performances a year. Over the years, the Opéra National du Rhin has acquired a first-class reputation on the international opera scene, thanks to the work of renowned producers such as Jean-Pierre Ponnelle, with productions including 'The Magic Flute', 'La Bohème' and 'Turandot' together with more recently, Achim Freyer, Philippe Arlaud, Alfred Kirchner, Georges Lavaudant and Michael Grüber. In addition, singing greats such as Teresa Berganza, José Van Dam and Sir John Tomlinson are joined by a list of exceptional conductors such as Alain Lombard and Carlo Rizzi in a roll-call that is as rich in quality as it is wide in variety. The Opéra National du Rhin

19 Pl.Broglie
Strasbourg
F-67008
France
Tel: +33 (0)3 88 75 48 00
Fax: +33 (0)3 88 24 09 34
www.opéranationaldurhin.fr

continues to collaborate with venues around the world, with partnerships including that with the Deutsche Staatsoper in Berlin, the Royal de la Monnaie in Brussels and the Royal Opera House in London, to present and co-present some of the finest opera the world has ever seen.

TICKETING

Advance Sales: Tickets can be booked from the start of the season.

Price Range: Tickets generally range from €12.00 to €78.00.

Concessions: A 50% discount is available for people under 26, disabled patrons as well as their carers. With a special card, seniors can also obtain reductions of 50%.

Box Office

The Box Office is open Monday to Friday, 11.00 a.m.–6.00 p.m.; Saturday, 11.00 a.m.–4.00 p.m. When performances are held on Sundays, the Box Office opens from one hour before the performance commences.
Tel: +33 (0)388 754823
Fax: +33 (0)388 754 896
www.opéranationaldurhin.fr

PERFORMANCES

Events take place from September to July.

Times: 8.00 p.m. Matinees on Sunday at 3.00 p.m.

Programmes: Programmes are available, with selected descriptions provided in English and German, as well as French. Programmes generally range between €3.00 and €9.00.

Resident Groups: The Orchestre Philharmonique de Strasbourg and the Orchestre Symphonique de Mulhouse

SEATING

Capacity: 1,142

Organization: The auditorium is arranged into stalls and four balconies.

Best Seats: The best seats are located in the first balcony.

Good Seats on a Budget: Cheap seats are available on the first balcony for as little as €11.00.

Seats to Avoid: Some seats have restricted views.

FACILITIES

Dining

A café serving both hot and cold meals is located on-site.

Services

Guide dogs welcome.

There are two designated disabled places in the auditorium.

HOW TO GET THERE

Overground: Plaza Droglie

Strasbourg features a large number of attractive parks, including the Parc de l'Orangerie, now displaying noteworthy French gardens, a Neo-Classical castle, and a small zoo; the Parc de la Citadelle, built around the remains of a seventeenth-century fortress; the Parc de Pourtalès, laid out in English style around a Baroque castle; the Jardin Botanique (botanical garden); the futuristic Parc des Poteries from the late 1990s; and the Jardin des deux Rives, which is spread over Strasbourg and Kehl on both sides of the Rhine.

TOULON

Opéra de Toulon

Opéra de Toulon is often referred to as one of the most beautiful and largest theatres in France. It has been considered a national treasure since its inauguration in 1862, the building itself being notorious for its magnificent acoustic powers. It now has a prominent place in the heart of its local community which now manages the theatre's variable repertoire, welcoming amateur productions as well as innovative ballet, dance and opera. Toulon, which was made famous by its appearance in Victor Hugo's 'Les Miserables', pays homage to its literary notoriety with the grand entrance of the opera house being dedicated to Hugo. The architecture celebrates other local talents including sculptor Toulonnais Mountain and poet Louis Daumas, their works being on display around the grounds of the theatre. The interior, and

Boulevard de Strasbourg
Toulon
F-83000
France
Tel: +33 (0)4 9493 0376
Fax: +33 (0)4 9409 3029
URL: www.operadetoulon.fr

TOULOUSE

Théâtre du Capitole

The Théâtre du Capitole started life in the early nineteenth century, and was launched within the site of the Toulouse Town Hall. To accompany the Théâtre du Capitole during its operatic seasons, Orchestre du Capitole de Toulouse was created at the beginning of the nineteenth in particular the ceiling of the theatre is richly decorated by the works of John Louis Duveau, which adds to the splendour of this rare architectural treasure.

TICKETING

Concessions: 50% discount for students and the unemployed. 15% discount for groups of 10 or more.

Box Office

The Box Office is located on-site and is open Tuesday to Saturday, 9.30 a.m.–12.30 p.m. and 2.00 p.m.–6.00 p.m.
Tel: +33 (0)4 9492 7078

Pl.du Capitole
Toluse
F-31000
France
Tel: +33 (0)561 22 31 31
Fax: +33 (0)561 62 70 77
www.theatre-du-capitole.org

century. It received recognition as a symphonic orchestra in 1945. Unfortunately, the building which was inaugurated in 1818 was damaged by a fire, and was rebuilt and decorated by Paul Pujol in a Neo-Baroque style. Today, after another renovation in 1996, the Orchestre du Capitole provides audiences with delightful seats and quality performances, all set in a classic yet contemporary style.

TICKETING

Price Range: Tickets generally range from €9.10 to €93.00.

Box Office

Tel: +33 (0)561 63 1313
Lines are open Tuesday to Saturday, 9.00 a.m.–12.30 p.m. and 2.30 p.m.–5.45 p.m.

PERFORMANCES

Events take place from October to June.

Resident Groups: Orchestre national du Capitole de Toulouse

SEATING

Capacity: 1,200

Organization: The auditorium is arranged into stalls and four balconies, with boxes.

Best Seats: stalls and first balcony

Good Seats on a Budget: Other balconies and boxes have fairly cheap seats.

Seats to Avoid: Some seats in the top balcony, and some boxes in all balconies except the first have restricted views.

HOW TO GET THERE

Bus: 10

Underground: Capitole Station is five minutes from the venue. €1.20 for a single ticket.

GERMANY

BADEN

Festspielhaus Baden-Baden

Opened in 1998, incorporating the Baden-Baden train station, the Festspielhaus Baden-Baden has the distinction of being Europe's only exclusively privately funded opera house,

Beim Alten Bahnhof 2
Baden–Baden
D-76530
Germany
Tel: +49 (0)72 21 30 13 101
Fax: +49 (0)72 21 30 13 211
www.festspielhaus.de

a distinction all the more extraordinary as it is Europe's second largest opera house. It was designed by Wilhelm Holzbauer, who integrated the Neo-Classical style of the train station with the modernist design of the Festival Hall, with the train station used as an entrance. The opera house has world-class acoustics; and although its programme concentrates on classics such as 'La Traviata' and 'Der Ring des Nibelungen', it welcomes performances from promising newcomers. It sponsors young people to attend classical music concerts, introducing them progressively to the joys of opera. In support of this idea, every year it awards the Herbert von Karajan Music Prize to a musician of international repute, which includes a grant of €50,000, to be used to support promising musicians.

TICKETING

Advance Sales: Tickets go on sale at various times of the year, check website for details.

Price Range: Tickets generally range from €24.00 to €95.00.

Concessions: Reduced rates are available for students, seniors, disabled patrons and holders of the Baden-Baden family pass.

Box Office

> The Box Office is open Monday to Friday, 10.00 a.m.–6.00 p.m.; weekends and public holidays, 10.00 a.m.–2.00 p.m. There are no additional booking fees levied.
> Tel: +49 (0)72 21 30 13 101
> Fax: +49 (0)72 21 30 13 211
> www.festspielhaus.de

PERFORMANCES

The season is structured around four annual festivals: Whitsun, Summer, Autumn and Winter.

Times: A typical concert can start at 6.00 p.m., 7.00 p.m. or 8.00 p.m.

Programmes: Programmes can be downloaded from the website free of charge.

Annual Festivals/Special Events: In conjunction with the structure of the season, the festivals in Whitsun, Summer, Autumn and Winter earmark each of the four seasons.

SEATING

Capacity: 2,500

Organization: A flat floor, two balconies; all with side views.

Best Seats: stalls and first balcony

Good Seats on a Budget: Second balcony

Seats to Avoid: All have good views.

EDUCATION

Guided Tours

Tours with the venue can be arranged in advance. Tours take place at 11.00 a.m. from Monday to Friday and 2.00 p.m. on weekends and public holidays.

Tel: +49 (0) 72 2130 13 101 or see the website for further details.

Cost: €7.00

Concessions: €5.00 for students and visitor card holders.

FACILITIES

Dining

The Festspielhaus kitchen serves a range of food and refreshments. Tel: +49 (0)72 2130 130 for reservations.

Services

The building is wheelchair accessible; however, wheelchair spaces can only be purchased at the Box Office.

HOW TO GET THERE

Bus: 201

Baden-Baden is a town of great natural beauty and cultural interest, a noted wine region with Europe's oldest casino.

BAYREUTH

Festspielhaus

Built specifically to host the Annual Bayreuth Festival, which is devoted principally to performing the works of Richard Wagner, the Festspielhaus was inaugurated in 1876 with a performance of his opera cycle, 'Der Ring des Nibelungen' (The Ring of the Nibelungs), more popularly known as 'The Ring Cycle'. The Festspielhaus is noted for having a pitch black pit, forcing the audience to concentrate on the drama onstage rather than the orchestra. However, this renders the work of the conductor extremely challenging. The double proscenium has the effect of making the orchestra appear further away than it actually is, giving the stage an almost mythical character. It goes without saying that this is an absolute must for devotees of Wagner. However, tickets sell out very quickly, and for many

Bayreuther Festspiele GmbH
Festspielhügel 1–2
Bayreuth
D-95445
Germany
Tel: +49 (0)921 78 78 0
www.bayreuther-festspiele.de

performances, visitors must book years in advance to obtain a ticket.

TICKETING

Price Range: Tickets generally range from €13.00 to €208.00.

Box Office

During festival days tickets are sold at the Box Office on performance days between 1.30 p.m.–4.00 p.m. The Festspielhaus does not operate an online ordering system, and visitors wishing to purchase a ticket must reserve them via their mailing system. Visitors interested in purchasing a ticket are asked to write a written request to Bayreuther Festspiele, Kartenbüro, Postfach 10 02 62, D-95402, Bayreuth, Germany. They are then sent a booking form which must be returned by the date specified. If successful, tickets are then allocated accordingly.
Tel: +49 (0)921 78 78 0
Lines are open Monday to Friday, 11.00 a.m.–noon.

PERFORMANCES

Annual Festivals/Special Events:
The Annual Beyreuth Festival takes place every summer for one month.

SEATING

Organization: The auditorium is arranged into stalls, two balconies and a gallery section.

EDUCATION

Guided Tours

Regular guided tours take place at the Festspielhaus, allowing visitors an insight into how the venue is run, together with its historical background. Tours are conducted daily except Mondays at 10.00 a.m. and 2.00 p.m. Please note that these tours are only available in German and tours are generally not available during the festival period.
Tel: +49 (0)921 78 78 0 for further information. Groups are asked to notify the venue prior to visiting.

Cost: €3.00

Concessions: €2.50 per person for groups of 12 or more.

BERLIN

Deutsche Oper

The first Operhaus opened in 1912, but had the misfortune of being bombed to destruction in 1943. After some years in exile, it returned to the Bismarckstrasse in 1961 with a performance of Don Giovanni, the new building having been designed by Fritz Bornemann. It also had the distinction of being the only opera house open in West Berlin during the period of the city's partition by the Berlin Wall. Bornemann's building is a masterpiece of modernist style, built around 88 slabs of whitened concrete; its purpose is not the collective engagement in an artistic performance, but rather an individual experience. To this end, each seat directly facing the stage, and interaction with other audience members is impossible inside the auditorium – devotees of Wagner will note these parallels between the Oper and the Festspeilhaus. As can be expected, the Oper's programme is radical, even controversial, with protests breaking out recently over its staging of Mozart's

Bismarckstraße 35
Berlin
D-10627
Germany
Tel: +49 (0)303 43 84 1
Fax: +49 (0)303 43 84 232
www.deutscheoperberlin.de

'Idomenio', which portrayed the executed heads of Buddha, Christ and Mohammed.

TICKETING

Advance Sales: Tickets for the entire season go on sale at the start of May.

Box Office

> The Box Office is open Monday to Saturday, 11.00 a.m. to one hour before performance; after this period, the Box Office sells tickets solely for the upcoming performance, or, if there is no performance, closes at 7.00 p.m. Sunday, 10.00 a.m.–2.00 p.m.; also opens an hour before performance. There is a €2.00 per ticket transaction charge for remote bookings. Tel: Tel: +49 (0)30 343 84 343 Fax: +49 (0)303 43 84 55 www.deutscheoperberlin.de/tickets

PERFORMANCES

Events take place from September to June.

Times: Performance times vary and can take place anytime from 6.00 p.m.–10.00 p.m. Some matinee shows are available.

Resident Groups: Staatsballett Berlin

Annual Festivals/Special Events: The Puccini Festival and Strauss Festival are held annually during January and February.

SEATING

Capacity: 1,885

Organization: The auditorium is arranged into an orchestra pit with two galleries, side views and boxes available for galleries.

Best Seats: The best seats are in the orchestra pit, the front first gallery and the boxes.

Good Seats on a Budget: The back of the pit and second gallery provide the cheapest seating.

Seats to Avoid: No seats have severely restricted views.

EDUCATION

Guided Tours

Guided tours are conducted once a month. See the website for specific dates. Tel: +49 (0)303 43 84 225 or email: jenss@deutscheoperberlin.de for further enquiries.

Cost: €5.00

Concessions: Group discount is available.

FACILITIES

Dining

The site is equipped with a restaurant, cafés and a bar.

Services

♿ Disabled access.

HOW TO GET THERE

Bus: 101 and 109

Underground: U-Bahn line U2 to Deutsche Oper; U7 to Bismarckstraße. Single journey costs €2.20 onwards.

Car Parking: 300 parking spaces are available on-site.

Deutsche Staatsoper unter den Linden

Commissioned by Frederick II as 'The Court Opera', and designed by Georg Wenzeslas von Knobelsdorff as 'the enchanted castle', the Staatsoper saw its debut performance in 1742, ten months before its completion. The building was badly burnt in 1843 and was redesigned by Carl Ferdinand Langhans, reopening in 1844. During World War II, it was heavily destroyed by bombing, rebuilt and bombed again. Even during its isolation behind the Berlin Wall, it was able to maintain an international reputation; and since reunification, it has been recognized as one of the world's leading opera houses. Daniel Barenboim currently serves as its General Music Director.

Unter den Linden 7
Berlin
D-10117
Germany
Tel: +49 (0)30 20 35 40
Fax: +49 (0)30 20 35 44 80
www.staatsoper-berlin.org

TICKETING

Advance Sales: The first tickets go on sale from 13 March for performances of the Staatskapelle Berlin; opera tickets go on sale on 18 April for Friends of Staatsoper and on 25 April for others.

Price Range: Tickets generally range from €5.00 to €160.00.

Concessions: A discount of 50% for seats of category V–VII seats is offered to children, students and the unemployed. In addition, any unsold seat will be offered at €12.00, 30 minutes before the performance. Holders of Staatsoper Card save 20% off symphony concerts and 25% off opera performances; the Staatsoper card costs €15.00 for children under 16, students under 30, trainees, those on national service, those on welfare and the unemployed. A 25% discount on seats in stalls rows 17 and 18 is offered to disabled patrons with an aG card. Disabled persons with a category 'B' card will be able to obtain a free ticket in all price categories for their escort on production of their disability card. Contact for further information.

Box Office

The Box Office is open Monday to Friday, 11.00 a.m.–7.00 p.m.; Saturday, Sunday and Public Holidays, 2.00 p.m.–7.00 p.m.
Tel: +49 (0)30 20 35 45 55

Lines are open Monday to Saturday, 10.00 a.m.–8.00 p.m., Sunday and bank holidays, 2.00 p.m.–8.00 p.m.
Fax: +49 (0)30 20 35 44 83
www.staatsoper-berlin.org

PERFORMANCES

Events occur all year round. Up-to-date information is available from the website.

Times: Varies. Typically 7.00 p.m., 7.30 p.m. or 8.00 p.m.; some matinee shows are also available.

Programmes: The Season Guide, Monthly Schedule or Concert Guide can be downloaded free of charge from the website, collected from the Box Office or can be sent via post if the Visitor Centre is contacted.

Resident Groups: Staatskapelle Berlin

Annual Festivals/Special Events: The Cadenza Baroque Festival during the new year is devoted to Baroque music. The Festtage Festival in April is dedicated to the works of Mahler.

SEATING

Capacity: 1,400

Organization: The auditorium consists of an orchestra pit and three galleries.

Best Seats: The best seats are located in the orchestra pit or the first gallery.

Good Seats on a Budget: The cheapest seats are situated on the sides of the third and second gallery; those at centre-back of third gallery are also inexpensive.

EDUCATION

Guided Tours

Guided tours of the venue can be arranged in advance.
Tel: +49 (0)30 20 35 44 38 or email: contact@staatsoper-berlin.de to arrange.

FACILITIES

Dining

Pastries and canapes are available from an hour before the performance and during the interval.

Services

Disabled access.

HOW TO GET THERE

Bus: 100, 147, 200, TXL and N5

Underground: U-Bahn line U2 to Hausvogteiplatz, U6 to Französische Straße, U2 or U6 to Stadtmitte; or U6 to Friedrichstraße. Single journey costs €2.20 onwards.

Car Parking: There is an underground car park located in Bebelplatz. The cost of parking is €4.00, valid from one hour before the concert to 11.59 p.m.

> Unter den Linden is one of the most beautiful streets in Berlin, and boasts, amongst other attractions, the Berlin State Library and St Hedwig's Cathedral.

Komische Oper

Built in 1892 by the architects Ferdinand Fellner and Hermann Helmer as a vehicle for light operetta, the Theater Unter den Linden, as it was then known, was forced to close less than five years later in 1896 after going bankrupt. Reincarnated as the Metropol-Theater in 1898, for several years the venue played host to the famous Metropole Revues. It was nationalized in 1934 and used by the Nazis to show operetta, however, it was badly damaged during World War II, with a bomb completely destroying the entrance area and the ceiling painting. Hope did arise from this disaster, as the auditorium managed to survive the attack intact. Rebuilt after the war, the Komische Oper was founded by the Austrian director Walter Felsenstein and opened on 23 December with his production of 'Die Fledermaus' by Johann Strauß. The name of the house came from the French opera comique tradition of the late eighteenth century and from Berlin's first Komische Oper under Hans Gregor on Weidendammer Brücke, which was also inspired by this tradition. The site was then completely rebuilt by Kunz Nierade in 1966, opening to Don Giovanni. Despite this, it has retained its late Viennese Baroque style,

> Stiftung Oper in Berlin
> Behrenstraße 55–57
> Berlin
> D-10117
> Germany
> Tel: +49 (0)30 20 26 00
> Fax: +49 (0)30 20 26 04 05
> www.komische-oper-berlin.com

and is still the place to be if comic opera is to your taste.

TICKETING

Price Range: Tickets generally range from €8.00 to €93.00 for premiers, €62.00 otherwise.

Concessions: Children pay a special rate of €8.00 for any ticket. Students receive a 25% discount for price segments I–IV, seniors are eligible for a 5% reduction for prices in segments III–V. In certain circumstances, carers of disabled patrons get a free ticket. The unemployed receive a 25% discount for price segments I–IV; owners of a social welfare card receive €3.00 tickets at the Box Office 15 minutes before the beginning of the performance. These tickets are valid for all performances of the repertoire, symphony concerts and cinema-concerts.

Box Office

The Box Office is open Monday to Saturday, 9.00 a.m.–8.00 p.m.; Sundays and holidays, 2.00 p.m.–8.00 p.m. Please note, reduced price tickets cannot be purchased online.
Tel: +49 (0)30 47 99 74 00
www.komische-oper-berlin.de

PERFORMANCES

Events take place from October to July. Up-to-date information is available from the website.

Times: A typical performance starts at 7.00 p.m. or 8.00 p.m.; however this can vary.

EDUCATION

Guided Tours

Special tours of the venue are conducted for both adult visitors and schoolgroups, allowing visitors a glimpse behind the scenes at the Oper. Tours require advance registration. For further information, contact the venue at: +49 (0)30 47 99 74 00.

Cost: €5.00

Concessions: From €2.5 onwards.

FACILITIES

Dining

Run by Andreas Gaul, a special dining area opens to guests an hour before performances and during the interval.

HOW TO GET THERE

Bus: TXL, 100, 147, 200, 348

Overground: S1, 2, 3, 5, 9, 25 and 75 to Friedrichstraße.

Underground: U-Bahn line U6 to Französische Str. Single journey costs €2.20 onwards.

Konzerthaus Berlin [Schauspielhaus am Gendarmenmarkt]

Formerly known as the Schauspielhaus, what visitors now know as the Konzerthaus Berlin was constructed by the architect Karl Friedrich between 1818 and 1821, and represents a prime example of classicism in German architecture. Among other accolades, the Konzerthaus was the location where Carl Maria von Weber successfully premiered his opera, 'Der Freischütz', where Wagner conducted his

Gendarmenmarkt
Berlin-Mitte
Berlin
D-10117
Germany
Tel: +49 (0)30 20 30 92 378
www.Konzerthaus.de

'Fliegender Holländer' (The Flying Dutchman), and where Beethoven's Symphony No. 9 had its Berlin premiere. Like so many of its contemporaries, much of the venue was destroyed during World War II, and the site was not reopened as a concert house until 1 October 1984. Today, the Konzerthaus Berlin has four halls; the Great and Small Hall, the Werner Otto Hall, and the Musiklub, which together play host to over 550 events every year, serving to delight and intrigue audiences in equal measure.

TICKETING

Price Range: Tickets generally range from €11.00 to €99.00.

Concessions: A 25% discount is offered for students up to 27 years, senior citizens and the unemployed. For disabled patrons selected seats are available for between €10.00–€15.00.

Box Office

The Box Office is open Monday to Saturday, noon–7.00 p.m.; Sunday, noon–4.00 p.m. Visitors are advised that orders made via the post or

fax can take up to four weeks to process.
Tel: +49 (0)30 20 30 92 101
Lines are open Monday to Saturday, 9.00 a.m.–8.00 p.m., Sunday and public holidays, noon–8.00 p.m.
Fax: +49 (0)30 20 30 92 233
www.konzerthaus.de under 'Programme'.

PERFORMANCES

Times: Evening performances generally commence at 8.00 p.m. However, the Konzerthaus showcases a range of performances, including matinees and special performances for children, details of which can be found on the website.

Programmes: Preview programmes for selected shows can be downloaded from the website. See individual performances for availability.

Resident Groups: The Konzerthausorchester

SEATING

Capacity: Capacity and seating arrangements vary according to the hall visited. Contact the Box Office for details.

EDUCATION

Guided Tours

Visitors can participate in a guided tour of the venue which is conducted every Saturday at 1.00 p.m. Tours can be conducted in a variety of languages and visitors are asked to contact the venue in advance to make arrangements. Alternatively, visitors can also take part in a special free 'round tour' of the Koncerthaus Berlin. Run by volunteers, the tour provides guests with a 30 minute insight into the venue. Dates are published on the website and the 'Besucherservice' area at the Box Office. Tel: +49 (0)30 20 30 92 343 or email: press@konzerthaus.de for further information. Further details can also be found on the website.

Cost: €3.00

FACILITIES

Services

Wheelchair facilities and seats for escorts are available at all halls of the Konzerthaus Berlin. There are eight seats available in the Great Hall, four seats in the Small Hall and Werner Otto Hall, and two seats in the Musikclub. Visitors with mobility impairments are advised to use the entrance located on Charlottenstraße at the rear of the Konzerthaus for easier access to the venue.

HOW TO GET THERE

Underground: Französische Straße, Stadtmitte or Hausvogteiplatz stations. Single journey costs €2.20 onwards.

Philharmonie & Kammermusiksaal der Philharmonie

Two examples of architectural innovation represent the venues that are the Philharmonie & Kammermusiksaal der Philharmonie. The main building was designed and built by architect Hans Scharoun between 1960–63. Shaped in the form of a pentagon, the arrangement involves irregularly ascending seats which surround the main stage. Such an unusual design of the concert hall has proven surprisingly fortunate for the Philharmonie, with all seats having equally excellent acoustics, and even the tiniest of details being audible from the furthest seats. The main hall plays host to approximately 270 concerts every year, and is where the Berlin Philharmonic and other guest orchestras give their concerts. The smaller Kammermusiksaal der Philharmonie, or Chamber Music Hall is no less popular. Constructed between 1984–87 as Scharoun's second project, the hall plays host to some 240 performances a year, providing audiences with a more intimate environment ranging from smaller orchestral formations to recitals.

Stiftung Berliner Philharmoniker
Herbert-von-Karajan Street 1
Berlin
D-10785
Germany
Tel: +49 (0)30 254 880
Fax: +49 (0)30 254 88323
www.berliner-philharmoniker.de

TICKETING

Advance Sales: Tickets go on sale at various times of the year, although they are always first sold on Sundays. Check the website for details.

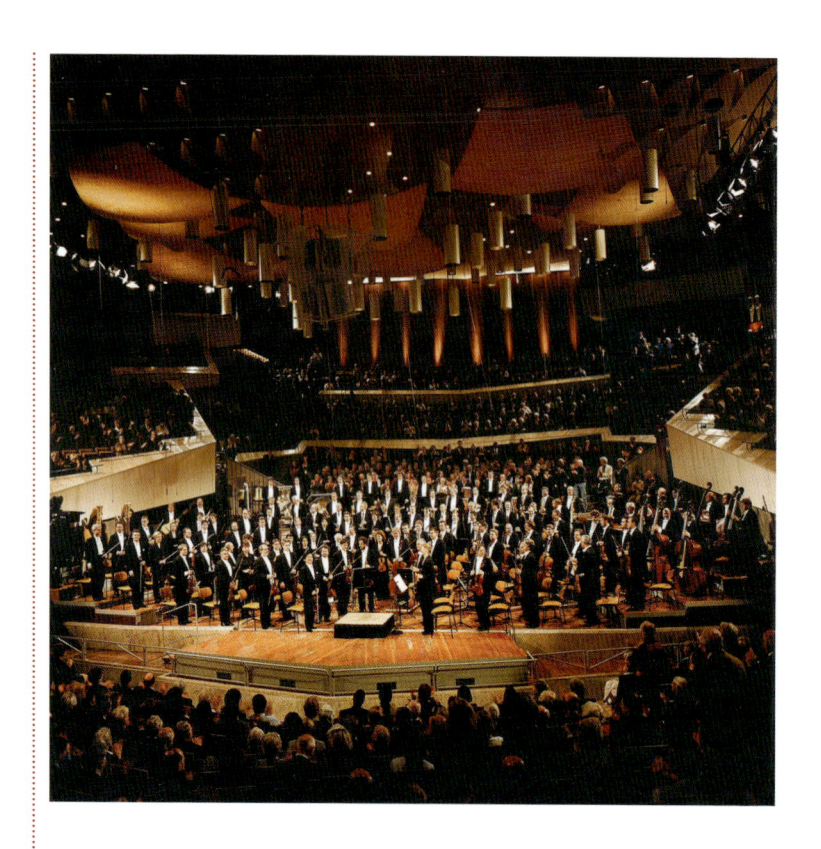

Price Range: Tickets generally range from €7.00 to €297.00.

Concessions: A 50% discount for unsold seats is available for tickets purchased at the evening Box Office for children and students. For disabled patrons, a free ticket is issued for an accompanying escort.

Box Office

The Box Office is open Monday to Friday, 3.00 p.m.–6.00 p.m.; weekends and holidays, 11.00 a.m.–2.00 p.m. There is a transaction charge of €2.00 per ticket for remote bookings. Tel: +49 (0)30 254 880
www.berliner-philharmoniker.de/en/tickets

PERFORMANCES

Events take place from September to June.

Times: Performances typically start at 8.00 p.m., but can vary.

Programmes: A programme for the event is enclosed with ticket.

Resident Groups: Berlin Philharmonic Orchestra

Annual Festivals/Special Events: The Salzburg Easter Festival takes place from March to April.

SEATING

Capacity: Main Hall – 2,440; Chamber Music Hall – 1,180.

Organization: The auditorium is arranged in a pentagonal shape around the central podium where the orchestra plays, the seats rising in irregular heights.

Best Seats: All seats have a consistently excellent sound, however those in row A have the closest view to the podium.

Good Seats on a Budget: Standing room can be obtained for as little as €7.00; cheap seats are available behind the orchestra and at the back of the concert hall; all seats have excellent acoustics.

EDUCATION

Guided Tours

Guided tours are conducted daily at 1.00 p.m. The venue also offers a special group tour to its visitors. Designed for groups of ten or more, the tour is offered in a variety of languages, including German, English, French, Italian and Spanish. Tours cost €30.00 in German and €40.00 in all other languages. Special discounts are available for schoolgroups. All tours last approximately an hour. Those wishing to book a group tour should contact the Philharmonic in advance.
Tel: +49 (0)30 254 881 56 or email: tour@berliner-philharmoniker.de. Further details can also be found on the website.

Cost: €3.00

Concessions: €2.00 for students, unemployed, retired, and disabled persons.

FACILITIES

Services

♿ Eight spaces are available in the main hall, four in chamber music hall.

HOW TO GET THERE

Bus: M41 and 200 to Philharmonic, 148 to Kulturforum, M29 to Potzdamer Brucke.

Overground: S1, S2, S25 and S26 to Potzdamer Platz.

Underground: U-Bahn line U2 to Plotzdamer Platz. Single journey costs €2.20 onwards.

Car Parking: Some parking is available within the complex; numerous parking facilities nearby, including the Sony Centre and Potzdamer Platz Arcades.

> The Herbert-von-Karajan-Straße boasts the Neue Nationalgalerie and the Gemäldegalerie, for lovers of modern and classical art respectively.

BONN

Beethovenhalle

Named after the famous composer Beethoven, the Beethovenhalle in Bonn serves as a complex for international classical music, and has a range of halls, seminar rooms and studios, providing the finest facilities for a range of musical greats. The first Beethovenhalle was initiated by Franz Liszt in 1845. Unfortunately, due to the wooden structure, the building was decommissioned a short while later for fear of a fire destroying the building. The building finally succumbed in October 1944, following one of the largest bomb attacks on the city during World War II. Fortunately, hope arose from these many setbacks, eventually leading to the formation of the Beethovenhalle as audiences know it today. In 1985, the hall was forced to close as the building was damaged by an arson

> Wachsbleiche 16
> Bonn
> D-53111
> Germany
> Tel: +49 (0) 228 / 7222–0
> Fax: +49 (0)228 7222 111
> www.beethovenhalle.de

attack. After further modernization and reopening in 1997, the site now offers a diverse range of possibilities, with halls able to cater for audiences from 90 to 2,000. Whether a classical music concert, a celebratory festival or commemorative event, the Beethovenhalle provides visitors with a flexible yet classy arrangement.

TICKETING

Advance Sales:
Tickets cannot be booked via the website and generally need to be booked in person either at the Beethovenhalle or via a range of outlets in Bonn.

SEATING

Capacity: The main hall has a capacity of 1,980.

FACILITIES

Dining

DACAPO provides visitors with a wide range of food and refreshments. Full menus and booking and information can be found on the website www.dacapo-bonn.de.

Services

The venue is fully wheelchair accessible, with special entrances designed for mobility impaired individuals.

HOW TO GET THERE

Bus: 537, 551, 628 and 638 from Bonn Main Station all go to the Beethovenhalle. A single ticket costs €1.80; Day ticket costs €4.70.

COLOGNE

Kölner Philharmonie

Opening in 1986, the Philharmonie has become one of Germany's most important classical music venues. The Philharmonie's podium is at the centre of the hall, with seats surrounding it in a circle, like an amphitheatre. Continuing a well deserved reputation of being an extremely beautiful and well engineered concert hall, the venue hosts performances that are astonishingly diverse, including classical, jazz, opera, world and children's music having an excellent representation here. The Philharmonie is dedicated to promoting innovative new music, and continues to promote young artists whilst simultaneously reaching out to young audiences.

Köln Music GmBh
Bischofsgardenstrasse 1
Köln
D-50667
Germany
Tel: +49 (0)221 204 080
Fax: +49 (0)221 204 08222
www.koelner-philharmonie.de

TICKETING

Advance Sales: Advance sales vary, with tickets generally being released from four months in advance.

Price Range: Tickets generally range from €10.00 to €110.00.

Concessions: A 25% reduction on the ticket price is available for children, students, senior citizens and disabled patrons.

Box Office

Two outlets, KölnMusik Ticket, located directly adjacent to Köln Cathedral and KölnMusik Event in the bookstore Mayersche Buchhandlung at Neumarkt sell tickets for the Kölner Philharmonie.
KölnMusik Ticket opening hours are Monday to Friday, 10.00 a.m.–7.00 p.m., Saturday, 10.00 a.m.–4.00 p.m.; for the KölnMusik Event: Monday to Saturday, 9.00 a.m.–8.00 p.m. A 10% service charge applies to remote bookings.

Tel: KölnMusik Ticket: +49 (0)221 2040 8160; KölnMusik Event: +49 (0)221 2040 8333
www.koelner-philharmonie.de

PERFORMANCES

Performances take place all year round.

Times: Performances typically start at 8.00 p.m., some matinees and morning concerts are also available.

Programmes: Programmes for selected events can be ordered from the website. Programmes cost approximately €2.50, with a €2.50 booking/delivery fee. English programmes are available.

Resident Groups: The Kölner Philharmonie, the Gürzenich-Orchestra Cologne and the WDR Symphony Orchestra Cologne

Annual Festivals/Special Events: Triennale, the classical music festival takes place annually between April and May.

SEATING

Capacity: 2,100

Organization: The auditorium consists of a circular podium in centre of hall, in front of the podium is an ascending semicircle of seats, behind the podium is a choir gallery and two balconies.

Best Seats: Blocks A, B, D, E, Z are closest to the podium.

Good Seats on a Budget: Blocks R, S, U, X have the cheapest seats, and have excellent acoustics.

EDUCATION

Guided Tours

Tours can be arranged, although the venue only caters for groups. Email: feedback@koelnmusik.de for further information.

FACILITIES

Dining

The Kölner's Bar sell a range of drinks and snacks.

Services

The seats in blocks R, S and Z are available to wheelchair users.

Guide dogs are welcomed in the auditorium; however, the number of seats are restricted and it is wise to phone ahead. The website gives detailed information for the blind to navigate the theatre.

HOW TO GET THERE

Overground: Köln main railway station is located 5 minutes walking distance from the venue.

Underground: Dom/Hauptbahnhof or Heumarkt. An admissions ticket allows you to travel on all buses, trams and trains in the Rhein-Seig region for up to four hours before and after a concert.

Car Parking: The Philharmonie Car Park is available for patrons and costs €2.50, allowing visitors to park 90 minutes before the performance, and up to 150 minutes after.

Oper der Stadt Köln

Controversial on its opening, the Oper der Stadt Köln came under fire in 1957 by some because of its five jutting balconies, encapsulated in a trapeze-shaped building made from a combination of concrete, glass and brick. Despite the initial criticism, today the venue is a popular choice for opera goers, featuring a diverse range of artists, and tickets are sold fast due to some rare appearances by more famous names. Nevertheless, this large, modern opera house offers a complete repertoire with works of classical and Romantic opera literature, as well as remarkable contemporary works.

TICKETING

Advance Sales: Tickets for the entire season go on sale on its commencement in September.

Price Range: Tickets generally range from €10.00 to €66.00.

Offenbachplatz
Köln
D-50677
Germany
Tel: +49 (0)221 221 2 8256
Fax: +49 (0)221 221 2 2211
www.buehnenkoeln.de

Concessions: A 50% discount is offered to children and students.

Box Office

> The Box Office is open Monday to Friday, 9.00 a.m.–6.00 p.m.; Saturday, 9.00 a.m.–2.00 p.m. For remote bookings, there is a transaction charge of €1.20 per ticket.
> Tel: +49 (0)221 221 2 8204
> Fax: +49 (0)221 221 2 8249

PERFORMANCES

Events take place from September to June.

Times: 7.30 p.m.

Resident Groups: The Guerzenich Orchestra

SEATING

Capacity: 1,330

Organization: The auditorium is divided in four parquets and two balconies.

Best Seats: The best seats are located in the parquet and the first balcony.

Good Seats on a Budget: Second balcony

Seats to Avoid: The left and right side of both balconies have poor views.

EDUCATION

Guided Tours

Tours of the venue can be arranged, though the venue only caters for groups.
Tel: +49 (0)221 221 2 8295 to arrange a tour.

FACILITIES

Services

Four designated wheelchair spaces are available. Please contact in advance as these seats are in high demand.

HOW TO GET THERE

Bus: 136, 146, 106

Underground: Neumarket. Single tickets range from €1.20 to €2.40 depending on distance travelled.

DRESDEN

Staatsoper Dresden – Semperoper

A picturesque scene on the banks of the River Elbe, the Semperoper in Dresden is one of the most famous opera houses in the world. Constructed in 1841 by Gottfried Semper in the early Renaissance style, it was rebuilt in 1869 after a fire destroyed much of the building. The Semperoper is considered to be a prime example of Dresden-Baroque architecture, with the interior created by famous architects of the time such as Johannes Schilling. Monuments on the portal depict famous figures such as Johann Wolfgang von Goethe, William Shakespeare, Sophocles, Molière and Euripides. The second building was constructed in 1878, with the plans led by Gottfried's son, Manfred Semper. In the pre-war years, the building premiered many of the works of Richard Strauss,

Theaterplatz 2
Dresden
D-01067
Germany
Tel: +49 (0)351 49 110
Fax: +49 (0)351 49 11 698
www.semperoper.de

only to be sadly destroyed again in World War II by Allied bombing and subsequent fire storms. Exactly 40 years later, on 13 February 1985, the opera was rebuilt almost the same as it was before the war. It reopened with the same opera that was performed last before the destruction in 1945 – Weber's 'Der Freischütz'. Today, most operas are accompanied by the Sächsische Staatskapelle Dresden, an orchestra which has bred world famous chief conductors such as Carl Maria von Weber, Richard Wagner and Giuseppe Sinopoli – unsurprisingly, the glittering array of talent ensures performances are nearly always sold out.

TICKETING

Price Range: Tickets generally range from €3.00 to €116.60.

Box Office

The daytime Box Office is located in the Schinkelwache, directly opposite to the Semperoper. The evening Box Office, located on-site opens one hour before performances. The Box Office is open Monday to Friday, 10.00 a.m.–6.00 p.m.; weekends and holidays, 10.00 a.m.–4.00 p.m.
Tel: +49 (0)351 4911 705. For group reservations,
Tel: +49 (0)351 4911 718.

PERFORMANCES

Events occur all year round.

Resident Groups: Sächsische Staatskapelle Dresden

SEATING

Capacity: 1,323

Organization: The auditorium is arranged into stalls and four balconies.

Best Seats: The best seats are located in the stalls and first balcony.

EDUCATION

Guided Tours

The Semperoper conducts tours when performances are not being held, with a full list of available times published on the website. Individuals are able to join a tour on the day, though groups of ten or more are advised to book their tour in advance, where they will have the opportunity to choose a tour in a variety of languages including English, French, Spanish and Italian. Those expressing interest in a tour are invited to fill in an online form on the guidance website. Tel: +49 (0)351 4911 496 for further information.

Times: Monday to Thursday, 10.00 a.m.–4.30 p.m.; Friday, 10.00 a.m.–2.30 p.m.

Cost: €7.00. Private group tours cost €175.00 (max. 25 persons), with a €15.00 supplement payable for groups requiring a tour in a foreign language.

Concessions: €3.50 for students up to 27 years. Family ticket, (two adults and children up to 17 years) €12.00.

FACILITIES

Dining

The theatre's in-house restaurant/café provides visitors a wide range of light refreshments, including coffee, cold beverages, and small snacks. The restaurant opens one hour before performances, and also takes reservations for sitdown meals. Alternatively, the Italienischen Dörfchens restaurant, located near the Semperoper provides equal variety and quality in its meals and refreshments.

Services

Wheelchair access and special seating arrangements are available.

HOW TO GET THERE

Bus: S-Bahn line 8 to Hellerau or line 11 to Postplatz. Single ticket costs €1.70 onwards. Day DVB pass costs €4.50. A family pass for up to 6 people, including 2 adults costs €5.50.

Car Parking: The Semperoper provides its guests with an underground parking facility.

DUISBURG

Theater Duisburg

Theater Duisburg is one of two Opera Houses where performances are given by the Deutsche Oper am Rhein. The original Theater Duisburg was built in 1912, following the footsteps of its older sibling, the Opernhaus Düsseldorf, but was destroyed during the World War II and subsequently rebuilt in 1950. The Deutsche Oper am Rhein is one of the leading opera companies in Germany. After the 1875 construction of what later became known as the Opernhaus Düsseldorf, a strong connection between the two cities' opera houses was formed that continued from 1887 to 1920. It was re-established in 1955 with the creation of Oper am Rhein. Owing to the refurbishment of the Düsseldorf opera houses, the fiftieth anniversary celebration of the company's resumption after the war, took place in Duisburg with a performance of Richard Strauss' 'Elektra', the crowning performance of which was presented on 29 September 1956.

TICKETING

Advance Sales: Tickets are released two months before the performance date.

Price Range: Tickets generally range from €8.40 to €42.90.

Concessions: Children, students, disabled visitors, carers and the unemployed qualify for a 50% discount on ticket prices.

Neckarstraße 1
Duisburg
D-47051
Germany
Tel: +49 (0)203 3009 100
Fax: +49 (0)203 3009 210
www.duisburg.de/theater

Box Office

The Box Office is open Monday to Friday, 10.00 a.m.–6.30 p.m.; Saturday, 10.00 a.m.–1.00 p.m. A €2.50 transaction charge applies to all remote bookings.
Tel: +49 (0)300 9100
Fax: +49 (0)300 9210

PERFORMANCES

Events occur all year round, apart from a two weeks closure during the summer.

Times: 7.30 p.m.

Resident Groups: The Duisburg Philharmoniker and the Deutsche Oper am Rhein

Annual Festivals/Special Events: The Akzinti Festival takes place each May.

SEATING

Capacity: 1,069

Organization: The auditorium consists of a parquet and two balconies.

Best Seats: The best seats can be found in the parquet and in the first balcony.

Good Seats on a Budget:
The second balcony provides visitors with inexpensive seats.

FACILITIES

Dining

There is a Chinese restaurant located on-site.

Services

Disabled access.

HOW TO GET THERE

Bus: 934

Underground: Koenig Heinrich Platz

One of Duisburg's key attractions is the Anne Frank Memorial, which stands in a field of rubble. It is not possible to enter the field, and this gives an effect of distance. The black granite is irregularly smoothed and portrays an almost glassy, impenetrable depth, to signify mourning and pain. An unusual yet fitting tribute, well worth a visit.

DÜSSELDORF

Opernhaus Düsseldorf

The Opernhaus Düsseldorf forms the older of two venues where performances are given by the Deutsche Oper am Rhein. Constructed between 1873 and 1875, initial setbacks and budget overruns meant that on its inauguration day it was left partially completed. By 1921 the city had transferred the ownership of the theatre to the opera company and, in 1925, it was renamed as the Opernhaus to distinguish it from other theatres presenting operettas. After bombs during World War II destroyed much of the auditorium, some performances did proceed for several months in an auditorium reduced to 1,000 seats. However, by September 1944 all theatres were closed, and regular performances did not begin again until October 1945 with Bizet's 'Carmen'. Major renovations began after

---

Heinrich Heine Allee 24
Düsseldorf
D-40213
Germany
Tel: +49 (0)211 89 25 211
Fax: +49 (0)89 25365
www.rheinoper.de

the war in 1954 to improve what had been temporal repairs to the building. Between 1954 and its reopening on 22 April 1956, the house was restored and inaugurated with a performance of Beethoven's 'Fidelio'. Also restored was the link between the Düsseldorf and Duisberg opera houses in the form of a joint company, the Deutsche Oper am Rhein, which continues to this day to provide audiences in both Düsseldorf and Duisburg with the best in classical opera.

TICKETING

Advance Sales: Tickets are released two months before the performance date. In the case of premieres, tickets can be purchased from one month before the performance.

Price Range: Tickets generally range from €7.70 to €94.60.

Concessions: A 50% discount is offered to students and pupils under 27. Disabled patrons are also entitled to a 50% discount. Please note that premieres are excluded from all concession prices.

Box Office

The Box Office is open Monday to Friday, 10.00 a.m.–8.00 p.m.; Saturday, 10.00 a.m.–6.00 p.m. For remote bookings, a 15% reservation fee is added to the ticket price.
Tel: +49 (0)211 89 25 211
Lines are open Monday to Friday, 9.00 a.m.–5.00 p.m. Saturday, noon–4.00 p.m.
www.rheinoper.de

PERFORMANCES

Events occur all year round.

Times: Evening performances generally start at 7.30 p.m., although with matinee performances and other events taken into consideration, this can vary.

Resident Groups: Deutsche Oper am Rhein

SEATING

Capacity: 1,342

Organization: The auditorium is arranged into stalls and three balconies. A seating plan can be found on the website.

EDUCATION

Guided Tours

Although there are no specific tour programmes in place, the venue offers an exciting programme for children and school pupils, details of which can be found on the website under 'Junge Oper' (German only).

HOW TO GET THERE

Bus: Straßenbahnlinien lines 704 and 709 to the Landtag/Kniebrücke stop or lines 725, 726 and 835. Single tickets are dependent on zone. Short trip costs from €1.10. Day ticket costs from €4.90.

Car Parking: There is a car park located at Stadttor, full details of which (including a map) can be found on the website under 'Anfahrt'. For a special price of €4.00, visitors can park at the venue from 75 minutes before the performance up until 11.30 p.m. for evening performances, and from 1.45 p.m.–7.00 p.m. for Sunday matinee performances.

FRANKFURT

Alte Oper Frankfurt

Financed by Frankfurt's own citizens and designed by Berlin architect Richard Lucae, the Alte Oper is one of Frankfurt's major concert halls, premiering many important works throughout a history which has spanned more than 100 years. The building was inaugurated on 20 October 1880 in front of an audience which included Kaiser Wilhelm I of Germany. World War II bombings in 1944 all but destroyed the building, and the venue was not reopened until 1981, to a performance of Benjamin Britten's aptly titled 'War Requiem'. Today, the Alte Oper consists of the Grosse Saal, the Mozart Saal and several small halls used for conventions. Because the newer Frankfurt Oper had already been built in 1951, the rebuilt Alte Oper was designed for use as a concert hall from the beginning of its

Opernplatz 1
Frankfurt
D-60313
Germany
Tel: +49 (0)69 134 0218
Fax: +49 (0)69 134 0537
www.alteoper.de

reconstruction, continuing its wide repertoire of concerts and plays.

TICKETING

Price Range: Tickets generally range from €12.00 to €150.00.

Concessions: Discounted tickets are sold at the evening Box Office generally on the day of the performance and provide special discounted rates for students, senior citizens, the disabled, the unemployed and some other concession groups. For further information, contact the Box Office.

Box Office

The Box Office is open Monday to Friday, 10.00 a.m.–6.30 p.m.; Saturday, 10.00 a.m.–2.00 p.m. and from one hour before performances. For tickets booked via www.frankfurt-ticket.de there is a service charge of €1.10 per ticket.
Tel: +49 (0)69 134 0400
Lines are open Monday to Friday, 8.00 a.m.–8.00 p.m.; Saturday, 8.00 a.m.–7.00 p.m.; Sunday, 10.00 a.m.–6.30 p.m.
www.frankfurt-ticket.de

PERFORMANCES

Events take place from mid-August to mid-July.

SEATING

Capacity: 2,450

Best Seats: All seats provide excellent acoustics and good views.

EDUCATION

Guided Tours

Tours of the venue can be arranged in advance providing the group consists of 12 or more visitors. Those interested are asked to fill up an online form on the website under 'Alte Oper Frankfurt/Führungen', or contact the education department directly. Tel: +49 (0)69 1340 341

FACILITIES

Dining

The Alte Oper has several restaurants and cafés on-site, allowing visitors to pick up refreshments or sit down for a meal at their convenience.

Services

There are four designated places for wheelchairs.

Visitors with guide dogs are asked to inform the venue prior to their visit.

HOW TO GET THERE

Overground: Station Taunusanlage

Underground: U-Bahn lines U6, U7 to Alte Oper. Single prices dependent on route taken. Short trip costs €1.55 onwards. Tageskarte (day pass) costs from €4.90.

Städtische Bühnen – Oper Frankfurt

The recipient of numerous awards, the Frankfurt Oper is an important European opera house located in the city of Frankfurt which continues to lead the way in classical music. The venue has nurtured several

Untermainanlage 11
Frankfurt
D-60311
Germany
Tel: +49 (0)69 212 02
Fax: +49 (0)69 212 37 499
www.oper-frankfurt.de

famous singers, including the soprano Cheryl Studer and Diana Damrau, and is never short of a long roll-call of accomplished singers. In addition, during the 2005–06 season, the Oper played host to no less than twelve premieres, a number that no other venue has been able to match. In addition to supporting the existing performers of highest standard, the Oper continues to encourage younger visitors to develop interest in classical music through its special concerts designed for children. Concurrently, it fosters musicians of the future through the various workshops and projects, ensuring all have the opportunity to experience the unique and distinctive atmosphere at the Frankfurt Oper.

TICKETING

Advance Sales: Tickets are released three months before the performance date.

Price Range: Tickets generally range from €9.00 to €115.00.

Concessions: There are many offers available, although discounts depend on individual performances. Students pay a flat €11.00 for any performance. Disabled visitors and carers pay a €5.00 flat fee for tickets.

Box Office

The Box Office is open Monday to Friday, 10.00 a.m.–6.00 p.m.; Saturday, 10.00 a.m.–2.00 p.m.
Tel: +49 (0)69 2123 7333
Fax: +49 (0)69 1340 444
www.ticketcorner.de

PERFORMANCES

Events take place from September to June.

Times: 7.30 p.m.

Programmes: Programmes are usually available at the box office for €4.50.

Resident Groups: Frankfurt Muzeum Orchestra

SEATING

Capacity: 1,364

Organization: The auditorium is arranged into a parquet and three balconies.

Best Seats: The best seats are located in the parquet and first balcony.

Good Seats on a Budget: Category 5 seats in the middle of the second balcony provide the best value for money.

Seats to Avoid: The sides of the second and third balconies have restricted views.

EDUCATION

Guided Tours

Once a month, tours can be arranged for groups. In addition, Frankfurt Oper's dramaturges offer free introductory talks (about the synopsis, context and production) half an hour before every performance begins. These take place in the opera house's Chagallsaal on the first floor. For further enquiries, email: info@oper-frankfurt.de

Cost: €6.00

FACILITIES

Dining

There is a restaurant, café and a bar located on-site.

Services

Disabled access.

HOW TO GET THERE

Bus: N8. Single prices dependent on route taken. Short trip from €1.55. Tageskarte (day pass) costs from €4.90.

Underground: U-Bahn Lines U1, U2, U3, U4, U5 to Willy-Brandtplatz. For visitors to the Frankfurt Oper, a purchased ticket entitles the holder to use all local transport on the day of the performance and is valid from five hours before the performance begins and, afterwards, until the public transport system closes down.

HAMBURG

Hamburgische Staatsoper

The Staatsoper opened in 1678 as Germany's first people's theatre, and was one of the first music houses opened to the public which was not devoted to sacred music. With the addition of a comedy house and a new opera theatre, it quickly blossomed into one of Germany's premier theatre and concert halls, with Handel, Goethe, Schiller, Paganini and Mahler all having a significant part to play in its history. After being partly destroyed in World War II, the citizens of Hamburg were able to donate enough money to be able to open a new opera house. It now concentrates on maintaining a modern repetoire with full attention being paid to the classics.

Grosse Theaterstrasse 25
Hamburg
D-20354
Germany
Tel: +49 (0)40 35 6868
Fax: +49 (0)40 356 8610
www.hamburgische-staatsoper.de

TICKETING

Price Range: Tickets generally range from €5.00 to €146.00.

Concessions: Disabled patrons pay a €10.00 flat fee for tickets to performances.

Box Office

The Box Office is open Monday to Saturday, 10.00 a.m.–6.30 p.m. The season Ticket Office opens on Friday from 10.00 a.m.–4.30 p.m.
Tel: +49 (0)40 35 6868

PERFORMANCES

Events take place from September to July.

Times: Varies. Evening, morning and matinee productions are available.

Resident Groups: The Hamburg Philharmonic State Orchestra and the State Opera Chorus

SEATING

Capacity: 1,672

Organization: The auditorium is arranged into stalls, four rows of balconies and boxes.

Best Seats: The best seats can be found in the centre of rows 11 to 14.

Good Seats on a Budget: The best seats for a low budget are seats in the second and third balcony, which are sold 28 days before every performance.

Seats to Avoid: The worst seats are those in the balcony near the stage, which offer a restricted view of the stage. Subtitles (in German) are not visible from these seats.

EDUCATION

Guided Tours

Guided tours can be arranged on demand, and are available in German as well as English. Contact Ms Schuller to arrange a tour. Tel: +49 (0)49 356 8301.

FACILITIES

Services

Four places are available in the last row of the stalls for disabled audiences.

HOW TO GET THERE

Bus: 4, 5, 34, 36 and 109. Visitor's opera tickets act as free transport pass on the day of the performance.

Overground: S11, S21 and S31 to Dammtorbahnhof; or S1, S2 and S3 to Jungfernstieg.

Underground: U-Bahn line U1 to Stephansplatz; line U2 to Gänsemarkt. Single City/Town ticket costs from €1.10. Day ticket costs from €5.80 inclusive of three children under 15 travelling with an adult.

Laeiszhalle

Constructed through a donation bequeathed by the ship owner Carl Heinrich Laeisz, the Laeiszhalle in Hamburg was built between 1904 and 1908 by architects Martin Haller and Wilhelm Emil Meerwein. A prime example of Neo-Baroque architecture, the building was constructed to blend in with the rest of the city, providing a representative example of the Baroque-built architecture of Hamburg. Today, the Laeiszhalle stands as one of the few concert venues to survive World War II undamaged. The building was however renovated in 1983, rejuvenating the site and providing new technical equipment and brand new facilities. Today, the venue continues its grand theme. Proudly displaying a picture of the venue's founders in the form of a relief in the main staircase, and possessing a foyer flanked by busts honouring the composers Johannes Brahms and Tchaikovsky, the busts serve as a reminder to all who visit of the excellent classical repertoire which reverberates through the venue's walls.

TICKETING

Box Office

Musikhalle Hamburg
Johannes-Brahms-Platz
Hamburg
D-20355
Germany
Tel: +49 (0)40 357 6660
Fax: +49 (0)40 348 0168
www.laeiszhalle.de

Tickets are sold via popular ticket outlets spread all across Hamburg. See the website for a full listing.
Tel: +49 (0)40 34 6920
Lines are open Monday to Friday, 10.00 a.m. 6.00 p.m. The evening Box Office also opens an hour before performances.
Fax: +49 (0)40 35 71 9036
www.laeiszhalle.de Online reservations are only available for selected performances, see the website for further information.

SEATING

Capacity: Large Hall – 2,023; Small Hall – 639.

FACILITIES

Dining

For ideas on dining in the vicinity, the website lists a range of outlets which serve a variety of meals and refreshments.

Services

The Large Hall has space for six wheelchairs in the parquet left, side row; and the Small Hall includes space for four wheelchairs behind row 20.

HOW TO GET THERE

Bus: 35, 36, 111, 112

Underground: U-Bahn line U1 to Stephansplatz; line U2 to Gänsemarkt/Messehallen. Single City/Town Ticket costs from €1.10. Day ticket costs from €5.80 inclusive of three children under 15 travelling with an adult.

Car Parking: In Gänsemarkt there is a multi-storey car park available for visitors to use. Entrance via Dammtorwall/Welckerstraße.

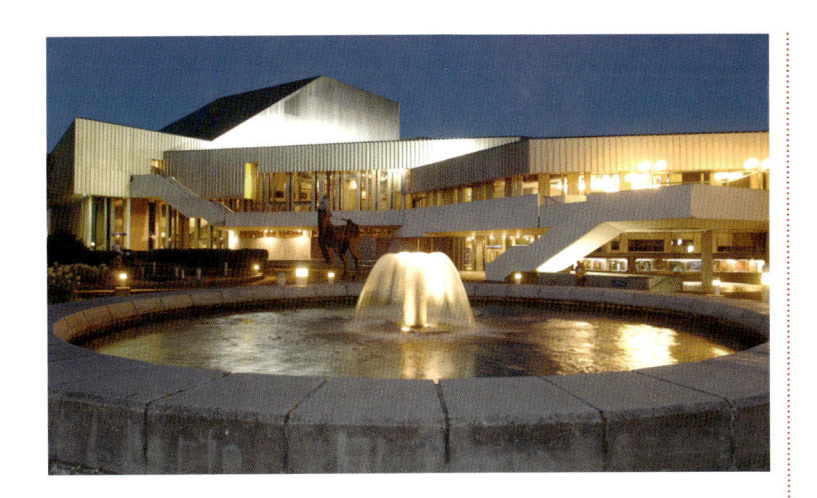

KARLSRUHE

Badisches Staatstheater

The Badisches Staatstheater is the main venue in Karlsruhe for opera, drama and ballet. The current building opened in 1975, after the original venue was completely destroyed by fire during the nineteenth century and devastated by bombs during World War II. What emerged in its place however, was a fine venue, with excellent acoustics enabling all visitors to enjoy performances to their full potential. Some may find the interior stark, as the inside walls are made of concrete, a far cry from the ornate decoration found in many other concert halls. However, this should not distract visitors from the real purpose of the hall. Equipped with excellent facilities, including a revolving stage, the Badisches Staatstheater leads the way in its ability to produce visual effects and rapid scene changes, while never forgetting the fundamentals of good, clean acoustics.

Baumeisterstr.11
Karlsruhe
D-76137
Germany
Tel: +49 (0)721 35 57 0
Fax: +49 (0)721 37 32 23
www.staatstheater.karlsruhe.de

TICKETING

Price Range: Tickets generally range from €8.00 to €84.50.

Concessions: A 50% discount on ticket prices is offered to children, students and disabled visitors. Please note that these reductions exclude premieres and other special concerts. In addition, starting 20 minutes before the performance, pupils and students can purchase tickets in price groups I–III for only €6.00.

Box Office

The Box Office is open Monday to Friday, 10.00 a.m.–1.00 p.m. and 4.00 p.m.–6.30 p.m.; Saturday, 10.00 a.m.–1.00 p.m. Please note that reduced tickets cannot be purchased online.
Tel: +49 (0)721 93 33 33
Lines are open Monday to Friday, 10.00 a.m.–6.30 p.m. and/or up to the beginning of the evening performance; Saturday, 10.00 a.m.–1.00 p.m.
Fax: +49 (0)721 35 57 346
www.staatstheater.karlsruhe.de

PERFORMANCES

Events take place from September to July.

SEATING

Capacity: The Main Hall has a capacity of 1,002 seats, the Small Hall has a capacity of 330 seats, with room for 100 standing.

Organization: The main auditorium is arranged into a parquet, stalls and a balcony.

EDUCATION

Guided Tours

Although there are no specific general tours, the venue runs an extensive education programme, with activities designed especially for schools, pupils, families and seniors. For further information on specific programmes, contact the theatre directly. Tel: +49 (0)721 35 57 410 or email: daniela.voege@staatstheater-karlsruhe.de.

FACILITIES

Services

Disabled access.

HOW TO GET THERE

Bus: Visitors who purchase a ticket to the Badisches-Staatstheater are entitled to free transport using the KVV lines in Karlsruhe from three hours before the performance, and until the end of the day. Contact the venue for further information.

Car Parking: There is an underground car park on-site, which visitors to the Badisches Staatstheater can use at a special rate. Those arriving from an hour before the performance pay only €3.00 for the whole evening. Those arriving without a ticket can purchase one on the day and still qualify for these special rates.

LEIPZIG
Oper Leipzig

With roots that date back to the seventeenth century, the first Oper Leipzig House was opened in 1693 by the violinist Nikolaus Adam Strungk, a figure who was to be followed by successors such as Johann Sebastian Bach, who ran the Collegium Musicum at the venue. The Oper continued to develop throughout the centuries, expanding in size and growing its repertoire. Unfortunately, the twentieth century brought a particular blow to the site, when all the Leipzig theatres were destroyed in an air raid during World War II, just after the curtain had risen in the Neuen Theater for Richard Wagner's 'Die Walküre'. This event forced the theatres to compress their programme of shows, and in the coming years the sites were not able to play as much as they wished. Building work for a new opera house began in 1956, with a brand new opera house unveiled on 8 October 1960. The Gewandhaus Orchestra, which had been the opera orchestra since 1840, returned with the curtain rising in the evening for Richard Wagner's 'The Mastersingers of Nuremberg', unveiling to audiences the venue which still stands proudly on Augustusplatz to this day. The current Oper is built in a very Spartan style, as befitted its location in East Germany; however, its acoustics are truly excellent.

TICKETING

Advance Sales: Tickets go on sale from 1 August.

Price Range: Tickets generally range from €10.00 to €65.00.

Concessions: A 30% discount is offered to children, students and disabled visitors. Discounts exclude tickets for premiers,

Augustusplatz 12
Leipzig
D-04109
Germany
Tel: +49 (0) 341 12 61 352
www.oper-leipzig.de

Christmas events, Silvester events and guest performances.

Box Office

The Box Office is open Monday to Friday, 10.00 a.m.–8.00 p.m.; Saturday, 10.00 a.m.–4.00 p.m. Transaction charges vary.
Tel: +49 (0)341 12 61 261
Fax: +49 (0)341 12 61 300
www.oper-leipzig.de

PERFORMANCES

Events occur all year round.

Times: Varies, typically at 7.30 p.m.

Resident Groups: Gewandhaus Orchestra

SEATING

Capacity: 1,417

Organization: The auditorium is arranged into stalls, boxes and a balcony.

Best Seats: The best seats are located in the stalls and front of the balcony, together with the royal boxes.

Good Seats on a Budget: Zones IV and V have good budget seats.

FACILITIES

Services

♿ There are two designated spaces in Haus Drelinden and eight spaces in the opera house.

HOW TO GET THERE

Overground: Tram lines 4, 7, 8, 10, 11, 12, 15, 16; Autoplatz Station.

Car Parking: Parking is available in Augustplatz. There is a €2.00 discount offered on parking with tickets brought from visitor centre; or a €2.50 discount with tickets bought prior to the performance.

To round off your experience, why not visit the Bach Museum? The Archive is widely recognized as the world's pre-eminent centre of Bach scholarship. Comprising a research institute, a library, a museum, and an events department, the Bach Archive today occupies the historic Bosehaus complex at St Thomas Square, opposite the church where Johann Sebastian Bach served as cantor for twenty-seven years. Visit www.bach-leipzig.de for more information.

Neues Gewandhaus zu Leipzig

'Res Severa Verum Gaudium' ('True Pleasure is Serious Business'), the Latin motto inscribed on the Gewandhaus zu Leipzig's majestic organ inside its Great Hall. Today, this motto lives on through the venue's performances, standing on the site where the Museum of Fine Arts once displayed its treasures. Many former artistic themes have followed through into the Gewandhaus, with the Klinger Foyer boasting a magnificent sculpture of Ludwig van Beethoven by the artist Max Klinger, after whom the foyer was named. In addition, busts of many famous composers line the venue, all of whom hold a firm place in the history of the Gewandhaus. Each year, the site puts on around 180 events, of which approximately 70 are concerts with the resident Gewandhaus Orchestra.

Augustusplatz 8
Leipzig
D-04109
Germany
Tel: +49 (0)34 11 27 02 80
Fax: +49 (0)34 11 27 02 22
www.gewandhaus.de

Variable seating, a sound studio, projection areas, multi-media facilities and interpreters' booths all guarantee suitably high flexibility and a unique experience for each performance. The building is rounded off perfectly with the dazzling ceiling painting 'Song of Life' by Leipzig artist Sighard Gille. Spread over 712 square metres, and illuminated by spotlights at night to shine through the glass façade to the square outside, the painting serves to round off a venue that provides true pleasure both visually and acoustically.

TICKETING

Advance Sales: Tickets go on sale for entire season on 1 September.

Price Range: Tickets generally range from €9.00 to €60.00.

Concessions: Discounts vary according to the performance. Children and disabled visitors qualify for a 20% off if the orchestra is playing, otherwise discounts vary.

Box Office

The Box Office is open Monday to Friday, 10.00 a.m.–6.00 p.m., Saturday, 10.00 a.m.–2.00 p.m. The Box Office is closed on Sundays, unless a concert is taking place.
Tel: +49 (0)34 11 27 02 80
Lines are open Monday to Friday, 10.00 a.m.– 6.00 p.m.
Fax: +49 (0)34 11 27 02 22
Tickets can be obtained from website under 'schedule'.

PERFORMANCES

Events take place from September to July.

Times: Typically 8.00 p.m.

Resident Groups: The Gewendhaus Orchestra, the Gewendhaus Choir, the Gewandhaus Chamber Chorus and the Gewandhaus Children's Chorus

Annual Festivals/Special Events: Mendelssohn Festival.

SEATING

Capacity: 1,900–1,500

Organization: The auditorium is arranged into stalls and two balconies.

Best Seats: The best seats are located in the stalls and first balcony.

Good Seats on a Budget: Seats in the parquet provide good value for money.

EDUCATION

Guided Tours

Tours of the venue take place on Saturday and Thursday. Further information can be found on the website.

Times: Thursday at 12.30 p.m.; Saturday at 3.00 p.m. Other tour dates are available on the website.

Cost: €3.50

FACILITIES

Dining

The Nikisch Café is located in the foyer.

Services

Disabled access.

There is an induction loop fitted in both halls.

179

HOW TO GET THERE

Overground: Leipzig Main Station is five minutes walk from the venue.

MUNICH

Münchner Philharmonie

Founded by Franz Kaim, the son of a piano manufacturer, in 1893, the Münchner Philharmoniker and its venue have been playing host to some of the finest classical music performances Europe has seen for over 100 years. Inaugurated initially as the Kaim, the venue's philosophy has always been inclusive: right from the beginning the Philharmoniker structured its programmes and prices to allow people from all levels of society access to concerts. World War II saw the Philharmoniker's Tonhalle on the Türkenstrasse completely destroyed, forcing the orchestra to move into a temporary home at the Munich Herkulessaal, where it remained for the next forty years. The first concert after the World War II was opened by Eugen Jochum with the overture to Shakespeare's 'A Midsummer Night's Dream' by Felix Mendelssohn Bartholdy, whose music had been ostracized during the Nazi era. In 1985, the orchestra once again acquired its own concert hall with the Philharmonie in the Gasteig, Munich's municipal cultural centre, where it remains to this day a popular and welcoming choice for all who visit.

TICKETING

Price Range: Tickets generally range from €11.10 to €54.20.

Concessions: Concessions are generally available for children and students, although this is dependent on the performance and can only be ordered via selected Box Offices and online facilities. Contact the venue for further information. Disabled visitors qualify for concession prices as outlined above, with tickets generally sold at a 50% discount.

Kellerstrasse 4/III
Munich
D-81667
Germany
Tel: +49 (0)89 480 98 55 00
Fax: +49 (0)89 480 98 54 00
www.mphil.de and
www.gasteig.de

Box Office

The Münchner Philharmoniker has four main booking offices, as well as several outlets which sell tickets for events at the venue. A comprehensive list of these sites, together with individual opening times can be found on the website under 'Servce/Ticket Service'. In some cases, visitors can also receive their tickets via a system called 'PicTicket', where an e-ticket is sent via email or to a mobile phone. See the website or contact the venue directly for further details.
Tel: +49 (0)89 54 81 8181
Lines are open Monday to Friday, 9.00 a.m.–8.00 p.m.; Saturday, 9.00 a.m.–4.00 p.m.
Fax: +49 (0)89 54 81 8154
www.muenchenticket.de

PERFORMANCES

Events take place from September to July.

Times: Performances generally begin at 7.00 p.m. or 8.00 p.m.

Resident Groups: Münchner Philharmoniker

SEATING

Capacity: 2,387

Best Seats: The best seats are located in the sections B, C, G, H, I and J.

Seats to Avoid: The seats in sections M and R have poor views compared to the rest of the auditorium.

FACILITIES

Services

Wheelchair access and special seating is available, with 15 special seats available to accommodation wheelchair users and their carers.

HOW TO GET THERE

Bus: S-Bahn lines 15, 25 to Rosenheimer Platz or line 18 to Am Gasteig. Each concert ticket entitles the holder to use MVV transportation free of charge within the entire area served by the MVV. Tickets are valid from three hours before the start of performances and are valid until the last bus/tram that evening.

Car Parking: There is a parking garage located by Rosenheimer Strasse which is open for parking between 6.30 a.m.–12.30 a.m.

Nationaltheater – Bayerische Staatsoper

The Munich Nationaltheater found its roots when the then Elector of Bavaria, Ferdinand Maria decided to construct Germany's first free-standing opera house in what was then a disused grain storage. The cornerstone for the new Nationaltheater was laid in 1811, and was designed by Carl von Fischer. Unfortunately, the building was burned down in 1823, although it was quickly reopened under the designs of Leo von Klenze. The theatre had moved from staging Italian operas to staging German productions, and in 1864, King Ludwig II brought Wagner to this theatre, where 'Tristan und Isolde', 'Die Meistersinger von Nürnberg', 'Das Rheingold', 'Die Walküre' and 'Die Feen' all premiered, and composers such as Mozart and Richard Strauss were given prominence. The site was

Max-Joseph-Platz 2
Munich
D-80539
Germany
Tel: +49 (0)89 21 85 01
Fax: +49 (0)89 21 85 11 33
www.bayerische.staatsoper.de

bombarded in 1942 during World War II, but was rebuilt and staged its first festival in 1950. The theatre was given a real lease of life by the appointment of Günther Rennert, who decided to move the theatre in a modernist direction, while retaining the 'holy trinity' of Strauss, Wagner and Mozart. The current director, Sir Peter Jonas, has had great success in bringing Baroque music to this stage.

TICKETING

Advance Sales: Tickets go on sale up to three months in advance.

Price Range: Tickets generally range from €4.00 to €243.00.

Concessions: For younger visitors in possession of a 'young audience' card, some tickets can be bought for €8.00. Students and the unemployed are eligible for a 50% discount on selected tickets. In addition, reduced price standing tickets for performances are available from the first weekday following the release of tickets at the Box Office and provide visitors with a 50% reduction on the normal ticket price. Many standing room places are not standing room at all, but equipped with little benches.

Box Office

The Box Office is open Monday to Saturday, 10.00 a.m.–7.00 p.m. There is a €1.50 per ticket transaction charge for remote bookings.
Tel: +49 (0)89 21 85 19 30
Fax: +49 (0)89 21 85 19 03
www.staatsoper.de

PERFORMANCES

Events take place from September to July.

Times: Performances start between 6.00 p.m.–8.00 p.m.

Resident Groups: The Bavarian State Orchestra and the Bavarian State Choir

Annual Festivals/Special Events: The Munich Opera Festival takes place from June to July.

SEATING

Capacity: 2,101

Organization: The auditorium is arranged into stalls and four balconies.

Best Seats: The best seats are located in the stalls and first balcony.

Good Seats on a Budget: Seats located in the middle of the gallery provide good value for money.

Seats to Avoid: Some seats have a very restricted view of the stage. Ask at the Box Office for further details.

EDUCATION

Guided Tours

Tours of the Nationaltheater are conducted almost every day at 2.00 p.m. and last approximately 75 minutes. Tickets are available at the opera shop in the Box Office lobby, with the meeting point at the MarStallstraße, located by the North Entry Hall. Exact tour dates can be found on the website, and are in German only. For further information on group tours and tours in English, visitors are advised to contact the Nationaltheater to make arrangements.
Tel: +49 (0)21 85 10 25 or email: marketing@st-oper.diyern.de

Cost: €5.00

Concessions: €3.00 for students.

FACILITIES

Dining

Käfer's Theatre Catering provides guests with a range of meals and refreshments for visitors to enjoy. Guests are able to book a three-course meal, allowing them to enjoy a starter and main course before the performance, and a dessert during the interval. Located on-site on the ground floor, the restaurant opens one hour before each evening performance. Reservations can be made via: theatergastronomie@feinkost-kaefer.de; or Tel: +49 (0)89 416 88 10. Bars are also located on the parquet, first balcony and third balcony levels.

Services

HOW TO GET THERE

Overground: Tram line 18, Nationaltheater stop.

Underground: Marineplatz; Odeonplatz. Single ticket costs from €2.20 for one zone. Day ticket for inner district €4.80/€2.30 (child).

Car Parking: A nearby parking lot is located at Max Joseph-Platz, Maximillian Street. Parking costs €8.50, although there are limited spaces.

Staatstheater am Gärtnerplatz

Crowned with several names throughout its history, what is now known as the Staatstheater am Gärtnerplatz suffered from somewhat of a false start when M Schmidt, the establishment's first director quickly went bankrupt in his pursuit of the popular repertoire of the day. The theatre was then purchased by King Ludwig II of Bavaria who bought the premises and introduced the operettas of composers such as Johan Strauss and Karl Millöcker. For many years the theatre continued with its theme of operetta, although in recent years the company has focused mainly on

Gärtnerplatz 3
Munich
D-80469
Germany
Tel: +49 (0) 89 20 24 11
Fax: +49 (0) 89 20 24 1237
www.staatstheater-am-gaertnerplatz.de

opera, continuing its repertoire of operettas, musicals and ballet. The scope of its activities are similar to those of the Komische Oper in Berlin and the English National Opera in London. Today, with its classical architecture, the Staatstheater am Gärtnerplatz stands in the heart of Munich, perhaps less famous than the Nationaltheater, but nevertheless offers a vast repertoire from Mozart to Wilfried, alongside more contemporary pieces.

TICKETING

Advance Sales: Tickets can be reserved up to two months in advance. Fax orders can be reserved up to three months in advance.

Price Range: Tickets generally range from €3.00 to €115.00.

Concessions: Special group, family and student discounts are available for tickets booked on the day of the performance. Contact the venue for specific price lists. Reduced tickets are not available for online purchase. Disabled visitors are entitled to free entrance with carers qualifying for a 50% discount on tickets.

Box Office

The Box Office is open Monday to Friday, 10.00 a.m.–6.00 p.m.; Saturday, 10.00 a.m.–1.00 p.m. The Box Office also opens from one hour before performances. A €1.50 per ticket transaction charge applies to remote bookings.
Tel: +49 (0)89 21 85 1960
Lines are open Monday to Saturday, 10.00 a.m.–7.00 p.m.
www.staatstheater-tickets.bayern.de

PERFORMANCES

Events take place from September to July.

Times: Evening performances generally start between 7.00 p.m. and 8.00 p.m.

SEATING

Capacity: 893

Organization: The auditorium is arranged into stalls and four balconies.

FACILITIES

Dining

The Käfer Gastronomie provides an excellent catering service where visitors can enjoy some fine dishes and wines.
Tel: +49 (0)89 41 68 810 for reservations.

Services

The building is well equipped for disabled visitors, although access is limited in some places and tickets should be ordered in advance where possible. Special wheelchair places are located in the parquet row 6 and 13 (seat numbers: 136, 137, 346, 345).

There is an induction loop system fitted in the auditorium.

HOW TO GET THERE

Bus: Tram lines 17 and 18 to Reichenbachstraße, or line 27 to Fraunhoferstraße. Bus lines 52 and 152 to Gärtnerplatz, or line 131 to Fraunhoferstraße. Each concert ticket entitles the holder to use MVV transportation free of charge within the entire area served by the MVV. Tickets are valid from three hours before the start of performances and are valid until 6.00 a.m. the following day.

Underground: U-Bahn lines U1, U2, U7 and U8 to Fraunhoferstraße. Single ticket costs from €2.20 for one zone. Day ticket for inner district €4.30/€2.30 (child).

STUTTGART

Konzerthaus Stuttgarter Liederhalle

The Stuttgarter Liederhalle is located in the heart of Stuttgart, and is ideally positioned near many other cultural attractions. Boasting no less than five halls, the complex is equipped with state-of-the-art facilities, located across the site. The largest and most famous auditorium is probably the Beethoven Hall.

Berliner Platz 1
Stuttgart
D-70174
Germany
Tel: +49 (0)711 2027 710
Fax: +49 (0)711 2027 760
www.liederhalle-stuttgart.de

Characterized by its brilliant resonance, the hall seats over 2,000 people in an auditorium whose curved shape divides the hall elegantly and clearly. Seating some 750 people, the smaller Mozart Hall offers superb views of the stage and has excellent acoustics, with rising platforms placing both visitors and actors in the limelight. The crystalline pentagonal shape of this noble concert hall creates an unforgettable acoustic experience during concerts, all adding to a unique and edifying experience at Stuttgart's celebrated Liederhalle.

TICKETING

Box Office

The Box Office is open Monday to Saturday, 8.30 a.m.–8.00 p.m.
Tel: +49 (0)711 2555 555

PERFORMANCES

Performances are available all year round.

Times: Usually 8.00 p.m.

Resident Groups: The Stuttgart Phil and the Arizo Stuttgard

Annual Festivals/Special Events: The International Bach Academy hosts a special range of performances between mid-August to mid-September annually.

SEATING

Capacity:
Beethovenhalle – 2,108
Liederhalle – 1,869
Mozarthalle – 756
Schillerhalle – 406
Filchershalle – 320

FACILITIES

Dining

There is a restaurant located on-site.

Services

HOW TO GET THERE

Underground: Lines S2 or S3 to Haltestelle Stadtmitte. Single ticket costs from €1.80. Day pass costs from €5.10 for zones 1–2.

Car Parking: There are 2,000 parking spaces available on-site. Parking costs €15.00 daily; or €4.00 during special events.

Staatstheater Stuttgart

Known locally as the Grosses Haus, the Staatstheater Stuttgart was designed by renowned Munich architect Max Littmann and constructed between 1909 and 1912 under its initial name, the Königliche Hoftheater. The venue opened to an inaugural performance of Giacomo Puccini's 'Tosco' and was later renamed the Landestheater, and subsequently, the Staatstheater. The Staatstheater was one of the few venues not to be destroyed by World War II, and expanded in 1962 with the additional Kleines Haus, designed to host smaller concerts. During the 1980s, the Staatstheater Stuttgart underwent a renovation which restored it to its original lustre. An important centre for opera since the seventeenth century, Stuttgart has once again become an important and influential centre since the war, particularly for contemporary works. Three operas by Carl Orff received their premieres here and the company continues to be associated with several famous figures such as Wieland Wagner, Hans Werner Henze and Philip Glass.

Oberer Schloßgarten 6
Stuttgart
D-70173
Germany
Tel: +49 (0)711 20 32 0
Fax: +49 (0)711 20 32 389
www.staatstheater.stuttgart.de

TICKETING

Advance Sales: Tickets go on sale from one month before the performance.

Price Range: Tickets generally range from €8.00 to €126.00.

Concessions: Concessions are available for children and students under the age of 30 years, as well as disabled visitors and the unemployed. Tickets in advance are sold at the VII–VIII price range, although they are subject to availability and do not apply to premieres or special events. In the event of there being any remaining tickets for the performances, these are also sold at the reduced rates during the evening Box Office hours.

Box Office

The Box Office is open Monday to Friday, 10.00 a.m.–6.00 p.m.; Saturday, 10.00 a.m.–2.00 p.m. In addition, the Box Office opens from one hour before the performance.
Tel: +49 (0)711 20 20 90
Lines are open Monday to Friday, 10.00 a.m.–8.00 p.m.; Saturday, 10.00 a.m.–6.00 p.m.
www.staatstheater.stuttgart.de/karten_bestellen

PERFORMANCES

Events take place from September to July. The latest season's programme can be downloaded from the website, showing all upcoming performances for the coming year.

Times: Performance times vary. Check the website for full details.

Resident Groups: Staatsoper Stuttgart

SEATING

Capacity:
Opera House – 1,399
Schauspeilhaus – 851

HOW TO GET THERE

Bus: Visitors to the Wurttembergisches Staatstheater are entitled to free travel with VVS Public Transport on the day of the performance. The admission ticket serves as a transport ticket for second class travel three hours before and after the performance.

GREAT BRITAIN

BATH

The Assembly Rooms

The elegant Bath Assembly Rooms are located in the heart of the World Heritage City of Bath in England, now a visitor's attraction. The Assembly Rooms formed the hub of fashionable Georgian society in the city; people would gather in the rooms in the evening for balls and other public functions, or simply to play cards. Mothers and chaperones brought their daughters to Bath for the social season in the hope of marrying them off to a suitable husband, and would take their charge to such events where, very quickly, one might meet all the eligible young men in the city. Scenes such as this feature in the novels of Jane Austen, who lived in Bath from 1801 to 1805. Her two novels set in Bath, *Northanger Abbey* and *Persuasion* were published posthumously in 1818, and both mention the Assembly Rooms. The venue specializes in recitals and chamber music, with the bulk of performances taking place during the Bath Mozartfest and the Bath International Festival.

TICKETING

Price Range: Tickets generally range from £7.00 to £30.00.

Concessions: Under-16s receive half price tickets, but not for children's concerts. Students, seniors and the unemployed qualify for a £2.00 discount on a full price ticket. In addition, unsold tickets can be purchased at half price by those eligible for concessions, from 30 minutes before the event. Disabled carers qualify for a free ticket with proof of status.

Box Office

5 Bennett Street
Bath BA1 2QH
United Kingdom
Tel: +44 (0)122 547 77 89
Fax: +44 (0)122 542 81 84
www.nationaltrust.org.uk

The Bath Festival Box Office is located at 2 Church Street, Abbey Green, Bath, BA1 1NL. During the Bath Festival, opening hours are Monday to Saturday, 9.30 a.m.–5.30 p.m.; Sunday, 9.30 a.m.–5.30 p.m. There is a £1.00 per ticket transaction charge for remote bookings.
Tel: +44 (0)122 546 33 62
Fax: +44 (0)122 531 03 77
www.bathmusicfest.org.uk

PERFORMANCES

Events take place from March to October and November to February.

Times: Usually 7.30 p.m., but can vary.

Programmes: Programmes are available for purchase from the Box Office, although some programmes are included free with tickets.

Annual Festivals/Special Events: The Bath International Festival takes place between May and June and the Bath Mozartfest in November.

SEATING

Capacity: 500 in the Ball Room.

Seats to Avoid: All seats provide good views.

EDUCATION

Guided Tours

The Assembly Rooms form part of the National Trust and therefore have open access to the public. See the website for detailed information on events and points of interest.

FACILITIES

Dining

The Assembly Rooms Café is located in the Card Room and in the summer opens onto the garden. Open daily.
Tel: +44 (0)122 544 44 77 for reservations.

Services

Disabled access throughout the building. Contact in advance for further information.

Guide dogs welcome.

HOW TO GET THERE

Bus: 2, 6, 7, 20A and 20C. Adult return, £2.20; accompanied children under 16 go free; Adult day pass, £4.00; Child (unaccompanied) day pass, £2.60.

Car Parking: Charlotte Street car park is located in the city centre. Parking costs £2.50 for four hours; £6.00 per day.

The Guildhall

Situated in the very heart of Bath, the Guildhall is a sought-after venue for the filming of costume dramas. Its main rooms, the Banqueting Room and adjoining Aix-en-Provence Room, are masterpieces of Neo-Classical decoration, with sumptuous plasterwork and gilding, eighteenth century chandeliers by William Parker and a large collection of royal portraits from the Victoria Art Gallery. Within the building are smaller rooms, each with a character of its own, including the Brunswick, Kaposvar and Alkmaar Rooms, named after Bath's twin towns. Twice a year, the venue plays host to the Bath Mozartfest and Bath International Festival, two annual festivals which celebrate the best in classical music. Sharing the festivities with The Assembly Rooms, the events are well worth a visit, and have become an integral part of what makes Bath such a refined and cultured city.

High Street
Bath BA1 5AW
United Kingdom
Tel: +44 (0)122 547 70 68

TICKETING

Price Range: Tickets generally range from £8.00 to £15.00.

Concessions: Under-16s receive half price tickets, but not for children's concerts. Students, seniors and the unemployed qualify for a £2.00 discount off a full price ticket. In addition, unsold tickets can be purchased at half price by those eligible for concessions, from 30 minutes before the event. Disabled carers qualify for a free ticket with proof of status.

Box Office

The Bath Festival Box Office is located at 2 Church Street, Abbey Green, Bath, BA1 1NL. During the Bath Festival, opening hours are Monday to Saturday, 9.30 a.m.–5.30 p.m.; Sunday, 9.30 a.m.–5.30 p.m. There is a £1.00 per ticket transaction charge for remote bookings.
Tel: +44 (0)122 546 33 62
Fax: +44 (0)122 531 03 77
www.bathmusicfest.org.uk

PERFORMANCES

Events take place from March to October and November to February.

Times: Usually 7.30 p.m., but can vary.

Programmes: Programmes are available for purchase from the Box Office, although some programmes are included free with tickets.

Annual Festivals/Special Events: The Bath International Festival takes place between May and June and the Bath Mozartfest in November.

SEATING

Capacity: The Banqueting Room seats 360, the other rooms less than 100.

Good Seats on a Budget: All seats provide good views.

FACILITIES

Services

HOW TO GET THERE

Bus: 6, 13, 228, 231, 232, X71 and X72. Adult return, £2.20; accompanied children under 16 go free; Adult day pass, £4.00; Child (unaccompanied) day pass, £2.60.

Car Parking: Poulton car park on the High Street provides free parking.

> For further information on the Bath Mozartfest and Bath International Festival, see the respective websites: www.bathmozartfest.org.uk and www.bathmusicfest.org.uk

BELFAST

Ulster Hall

The Ulster Hall is one of the oldest buildings in Belfast. It was originally built in 1862 and was designed by W J Barre for the Ulster Hall Company. Sadly, the décor of the Hall is nowhere near as opulent as Barr intended. By 1862, the funds had been

> Bedford Street
> Belfast BT2 7FF
> Northern Ireland
> United Kingdom
> Tel: +44 (0)289 032 39 00
> Fax: +44 (0)289 024 71 99
> www.ulsterhall.co.uk

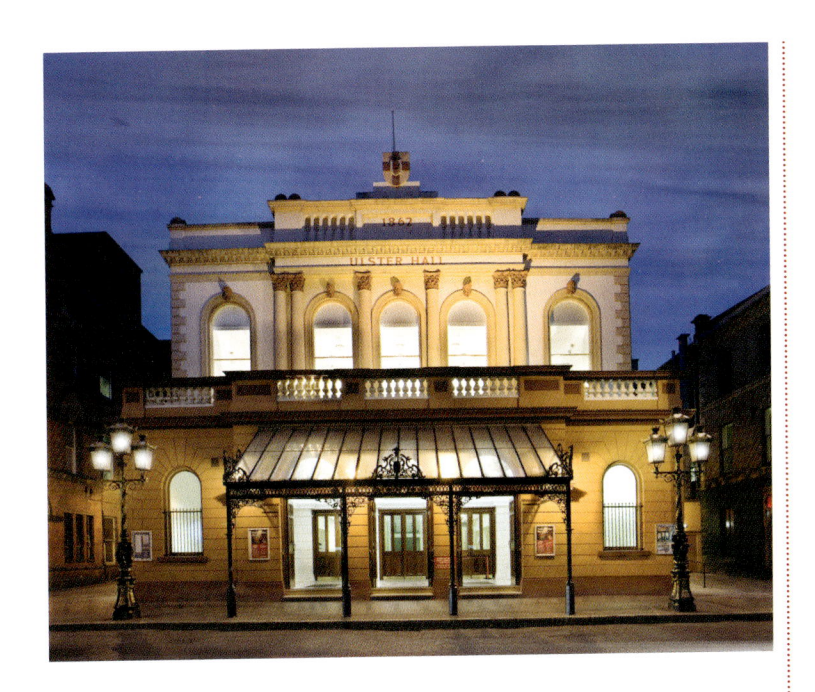

depleted and Ulster Hall opened with only a coat of whitewash. Over the years, various schemes have tried to glamourize the venue. However, the most recent renovation in 1984 returns to the venue's original design, making allowances for the 1903 ceiling and 1957 balcony front. The pride of the Hall is the Mulholland Grand Organ, which was built by William Hill and presented to the people of Belfast by Mr Andrew Mulholland, an ex-mayor of the city. As such, it is one of the oldest examples of classical English organ-building still in operation today. Between 1976 and 1978 the Mulholland was completely restored under the direction of the Rt Hon. Lord Dunleath, the great-grandson of the original donor. Ulster Hall features a year round programme of classical, rock and pop events, educational lectures and a range of activity days.

TICKETING

Price Range: Tickets generally range from £4.00 to £120.00.

Concessions: Prices vary according to promoter.

Box Office

The Ulster Hall does not have its own Box Office facility. Contact the venue or check online to book specific concerts.
Tel: +44 (0)289 032 39 00 (9.00 a.m.–5.00 p.m.)
email: ulsterhall@belfastcity.gov.uk

PERFORMANCES

Events take place all year round.

Times: 7.30 p.m. evenings; 3.00 p.m. matinees.

Resident Groups: The Ulster Orchestra plays regularly.

SEATING

Capacity: 2,000

Organization: The auditorium is divided into ten different seating blocks, which are in turn divided into four price bands.

Best Seats: Visitors looking for the best seats are advised to enquire at the venue, as it depends on the performance.

Seats to Avoid: Some seats are partially obscured by pillars.

FACILITIES

Dining

Snack and bar facilities may be available depending on the concert.

Services

Guide dogs welcome.

Seats can be removed to accommodate wheelchairs. Contact for further information.

HOW TO GET THERE

Bus: The Europa Bus Centre is 2 minutes walk from the venue. Adult single, £1.00; Child single, £0.50; Adult day pass, £3.50; Child day pass, £1.75.

Overground: Europa Station, Great Victoria Street is two minutes walk via the Galerie Ravenstein.

Car Parking: Secure car parks are located at Bedford Street, Ormeau Avenue and Dublin Road, although street parking in the area is free after 6.00 p.m. Parking costs £1.60 per hour.

Waterfront Hall

The Waterfront Hall is a state-of-the-art concert venue just ten minutes walk from the heart of Belfast's commercial centre. The Hall regularly hosts concerts by the Ulster Orchestra, as well as a variety of international artists. In addition to its music facilities, visual art, dance and theatre are also represented at the Waterfront, making it the cultural centre of Northern Ireland. Planning for the building began in 1989, with the hall being completed in 1997 for the sum of £32 million. The main circular auditorium is based on the Berlin Philharmonic Hall as designed by Hans Scharoun, however the flexible design of the auditorium allows the stalls seating to be moved to create a larger arena. An interesting architectural feature is the building's copper-coated dome, which will eventually turn green. At present, it reflects the dome of Belfast City Hall and other Victorian buildings in the city centre.

2 Lanyon Place
Belfast BT1 3WH
Northern Ireland
United Kingdom
Tel: +44 (0)289 033 44 00
Fax: +44 (0)289 024 98 62
www.waterfront.co.uk

TICKETING

Price Range: Tickets generally range from £10.00 to £35.00.

Concessions: A discount ranging from 5% to 15% is offered to children, students, senior citizens, disabled visitors and the unemployed.

Box Office

2 Lanyon Place
Belfast BT1 3WH
Northern Ireland
United Kingdom
Tel: +44 (0)289 033 44 00
Fax: +44 (0)289 024 98 62
www.waterfront.co.uk

PERFORMANCES

Events take place all year round.

Times: Usually 8.00 p.m., but can vary.

SEATING

Capacity: 2,241

Organization: Arena – 651; lower terrace – 452; upper terrace – 932; choir stalls – 206.

Best Seats: The online booking service allows visitors to see the view from different seats before buying tickets.

Good Seats on a Budget: The upper terrace provides good views at a budget price.

FACILITIES

Dining

The Arc Brasserie serves light refreshments from 10.00 a.m.–12.30 p.m. and 2.30 p.m.–5.00 p.m. The lunch menu is served from 12.30 p.m. to 2.00 p.m., and pre-performance dinner is available from 5.00 p.m.

Services

Guide dogs welcome.

Up to 22 spaces are available for patrons using wheelchairs and their companions in the main auditorium. They are situated in the arena block A, facing the stage with ramp access from the main concourse, and on the lower terrace at the rear of block.

Performance programmes are available on tape and in Braille, free of charge. Contact the Accessiblity Hotline on +44 (0)289 033 44 00.

HOW TO GET THERE

Bus: The Laganside Bus Centre is two minutes walk from the venue. Adult single, £1.00; Child single, £0.50; Adult day pass, £3.50; Child day pass, £1.75.

Overground: The Central Station on East Bridge Street is located five minutes from the venue.

Car Parking: The Lanyon and Hilton car parks are next to the venue. The total capacity is over 800 spaces, including 13 for Orange Badge Holders. Parking costs £1.60 per hour.

BIRMINGHAM

Symphony Hall

A global project for what is now an internationally recognized concert hall, the Symphony Hall in Birmingham opened in 1991 and was acknowledged almost immediately as one of the best of its kind in the world. Part of what makes the venue so unique is its moveable canopy, which can be raised or lowered in order to achieve the optimum sound for performers, and a reverberation chamber behind the Hall which increases its volume by 50%. In this way, the Symphony Hall, created by Artec Consultants in New York has provided a benchmark in modern design which many new concert halls now aspire to. Today, the Hall joins many other venues in this event-packed city which includes the nearby NEC, with a wide programme of events and guest orchestras that ensure a wide range of performances throughout the year.

Broad Street
Birmingham B1 2EA
United Kingdom
Tel: +44 (0)121 200 20 00
Fax: +44 (0)121 212 19 82
www.symphonyhall.co.uk

TICKETING

Advance Sales: Tickets can be purchased up to a year in advance.

Price Range: Tickets generally range from £5.00 to £40.00.

Concessions: One or two adults can each bring a child for free when they purchase a ticket. Additional children can purchase tickets at a rate of £7.00 each. A 50% discount is offered to those in full time education and young people aged 25 and under, (not available on £5.00 or choir seats). This discount also applies to concert packages. There is a limit of one ticket per student. Standby tickets are available on the day. Special discounts apply to those aged 60 or over. Ask at the Box Office for further information. For disabled patrons, a 10%–50% discount is available on full price tickets for disabled patrons and up to one companion on most concerts. Special standby tickets are available for those in receipt of benefits from 1.00 p.m. on the day of performance for evening concerts and from 10.00 a.m. for matinees. The tickets cost £4.00 and are subject to availability.

Box Office

Monday to Friday, 10.00 a.m.–6.00 p.m. (extended to 8.00 p.m. on concert nights); Saturday, 10.00 a.m.–8.00 p.m.; Sunday 2.00 p.m.–8.00 p.m. when there is an evening performance. Alternatively weekend opening is, 10.00 a.m.–5.00 p.m. when there is a morning performance and noon–5.00 p.m. when there is an afternoon or no performances. There is up to a £2.00 charge when tickets are sent via post. Alternatively tickets can be held at the Box Office for collection at no extra charge.

Tel: +44 (0)121 780 33 33 or for group bookings, Tel: 0800 358 7070 (Monday to Friday, 10.00 a.m.–5.00 p.m.) from the UK only.
www.symphonyhall.co.uk/how_to_book.asp

PERFORMANCES

Events occur all year round.

Times: Many evening performances commence at 7.30 p.m., although times vary from performance to performance.

Resident Groups: City of Birmingham Symphony Orchestra

SEATING

Capacity: 2,262

Organization: The Hall is arranged into a selection of stalls, a stalls terrace, a circle, upper circle and grand tier.

Best Seats: Although the acoustics are superb from anywhere in the Hall, visitors can get a great view from the central seats.

Good Seats on a Budget: Seat prices vary depending on the event, but for concerts in Symphony Hall's International Concert Season, tickets are available from £5.00, and seats in the Choir (behind the orchestra) are always a popular choice.

Seats to Avoid: Anyone who suffers from vertigo would probably be advised not to sit high up in the grand tier.

EDUCATION

Guided Tours

There are tours available of the Symphony Hall, tickets for which can be purchased at the Box Office. Tours last approximately an hour and a half.

Cost: £2.50

FACILITIES

Dining

The popular Strada Restaurant & Bar offers diners authentic Italian food in a stylish setting. Symphony Hall concert-goers can receive 10% off. Collect a card from the Box Office and present when dining. For reservations call: +44 (0)121 212 2661. In addition to this, Café Vite is a public restaurant located on-site which offers a variety of hot meals, snacks and drinks. Joining these are the foyer bars, which open an hour before the start of a concert and stay open for the interval and post concert on Level 3.

Services

The flexible arrangement of the Hall means that wheelchair users can be easily accomodated, with four special wheelchair spaces located in the stalls.

Guide dogs are welcome. Tactile signage is also fitted in the lifts.

The Symphony Hall is equipped with an infra-red hearing enhancement system, which can be used in conjunction with a hearing aid or with earphones. In both cases visitors will need a receiver to use the system and these are available to borrow, free of charge, from the 'Symphony Hall Gifts' stand on the ground floor outside Door 2. Visitors can obtain these by asking a steward on arrival.

Symphony Hall's Diary of Events is available on audio cassette, free of charge from: Vista, Margaret Road, Leicester, LE5 5FU. Tel: +44 (0)116 249 09 09

HOW TO GET THERE

Overground: Birmingham New Street and Snow Hill Stations are within easy walking distance of Symphony Hall. Moor Street and Five Ways are slightly further away but still within walking distance.

Car Parking: The main Pay & Display car park at the National Indoor Arena (NIA) has approximately 2,500 spaces, and is about ten minutes walk from the Hall. Additional spaces are available in the local Brindley Drive, Brindleyplace and Cambridge Street car park.

BRIGHTON

Brighton Dome

Consisting of three unique sites held together under one roof, the Brighton Dome encompasses the Concert Hall, Corn Exchange and Pavilion Theatre. It was originally built for the then Prince of Wales (later George IV) and forms part of the Royal Pavilion Estate located in the heart of Brighton. The Concert Hall itself was inspired by the Corn Exchange in Paris, and originally served as the Price Regent's riding stables when it was designed in the early nineteenth century. Later converted into a concert hall in 1866, it quickly grew to become one of the most culturally significant venues in the South. Recently, the Concert Hall's multi-million pound rebuilding and refurbishment project has restored the venue to its former glory, maintaining the integrity of both the Grade 1 listed Regency exterior

29 New Road
Brighton BN1 1UG
United Kingdom
Tel: +44 (0)127 370 07 47
www.brightondome.org

and the 1930s Grade 1 listed interior. Superb new facilities, comfortable seating and enhanced acoustics have transformed the Concert Hall into a major centre for live arts and entertainment, well equipped for the twenty-first century.

TICKETING

Advance Sales: Tickets are released six months before the performance date.

Price Range: Tickets generally range from £6.00 to £35.00.

Concessions: Classical concerts rarely have concessions, but if so they are usually £2.00 less than full price. Sunday morning children's events cost £5.00. A companion sitting in a neighbouring seat to a wheelchair user may be admitted free of charge.

Box Office

> The Box Office is open Monday to Saturday, 10.00 a.m.–6.00 p.m. Transaction charges for remote bookings vary.
> Tel: +44 (0)127 370 97 09
> www.brightondome.org

PERFORMANCES

Events occur all year round.

Times: 2.45 p.m. matinees; 7.45 p.m. evenings; 11.30 a.m. for Sunday morning performances.

Resident Groups: Brighton Philharmonic Orchestra

Annual Festivals/Special Events: The Annual Brighton Festival takes place every May.

SEATING

Capacity: 1,872

Organization: The auditorium has centre stalls, rear stalls and a dress circle.

Best Seats: Centre stalls

Good Seats on a Budget: row T in the rear stalls left and right

Seats to Avoid: Side stalls and behind the conductor in the rear stalls.

FACILITIES

Dining

Two fully licensed bars, including the stunning new Dome

foyer and the Dome Founder's Room (also available for hire for smallscale launches, events and gatherings) are available for guests to enjoy a range of food and refreshments.

Services

Guide dogs welcome.

There are several positions designed for wheelchair users in the stalls and circle areas of the Concert Hall, with lift access and toilets for wheelchair users at each entrance.

Both the Pavilion Theatre and Corn Exchange have induction loops in place. There is a Sennheiser infra-red assisted hearing system in the Concert Hall. Visitors should reserve their units when making their booking and check that their hearing aid is compatible with this system. A deposit is required.

Large print programmes are available from the Box Office.

HOW TO GET THERE

Bus: 1, 10, 10A, 12, 12A, 13, 14, 14A, 14B, 14C, 1A, 1B and 1C. Adult single, £1.50; under-14s, £0.75.

Car Parking: On-street parking is very limited, but improves after 6.00 p.m. and on Sundays. There are also NCP car parks nearby. The nearest of these is in Church Street. It is open 24 hours, and has 587 spaces. Parking costs £0.70 for 15 minutes; £14.00 per day.

CARDIFF

Canolfan Mileniwm Cymru

The Wales Millennium Centre is a vibrant, colourful centre with plenty of activities throughout the day and the night. Visitors to the Centre are reminded of the fact that the building was both designed and built in Wales. With a brief to the architect

Bute Place
Cardiff CF10 2AL
United Kingdom
Tel: +44 (0)870 040 20 00
www.wmc.org.uk

Percy Thomas that the building was to be 'unmistakably Welsh and internationally outstanding', the results produced a building with the front face incorporating a shell which leans out over the main entrance to the building. This important face of the building is emphasized by a spectacular set of windows, made in the form of letters, that read together as a poem. The idea of this monumental inscription came from Roman classical architecture. The Romans brought Christianity to these islands, along with the custom of engraving stone. The form of the Celtic Cross embodies the cross-fertilization of indigenous and Roman cultures, from which the Welsh nation first emerged. The poem reads–'Creu Gwir/Fel Gwydr/O Ffwrnais Awen' ('In These Stones/Horizons/Sing'), an idea which resonates through the rest of the building and through the Centre's many performances.

TICKETING

Advance Sales: Tickets are released three months before the performance date.

Price Range: Tickets generally range from £5.00 to £45.00.

Concessions: Children, students and seniors receive a 10% discount on ticket prices excluding opera performances.

Carers of disabled visitors are entitled to a free ticket.

Box Office

> The Ticket and Information Office is located in the foyer of Wales Millennium Centre and is straight in front of the main entrance doors. The Box Office is open Monday to Friday, 10.00 a.m.–7.00 p.m.
> Tel: +44 (0)870 040 2000
> www.wmc.org

PERFORMANCES

Events occur all year round.

Times: Evening performances generally commence at 7.30 p.m.

Resident Groups: Welsh National Opera

SEATING

Capacity: 1,650

EDUCATION

Guided Tours

Lasting approximately one hour, guided tours of the building run daily and allow visitors an insight into one of the biggest stages in Britain, even allowing visitors access to dressing rooms and other behind-the-scenes activities at the venue. Tel: 0870 040 20 00 or see the website for further information.

Cost: £5.00

Concessions: £4.00

FACILITIES

Dining

Brazz-Brasserie Bar Café, which was recently ranked as one of the top three theatre restaurants in the UK by The Telegraph, provides a casual eating environment which is transformed into a restuarant serving meals during the evening. It is open from 10.00 a.m.–midnight or approximately 10.00 p.m. if there is no performance in the Donald Gordon Theatre. This is accompanied by a range of other refreshment venues, further details of which can be found on the website under, 'Eat, drink, shop'.

Services

There are up to 22 spaces for wheelchair users in the main auditorium.

Audio Described Performances are preceded by a Touch Tour. This Tour is specifically intended for partially sighted patrons and it provides them with a tactile experience of the set, costumes, and props of the show.

HOW TO GET THERE

Bus: 1, 2, 6 (Bay Express), 8 and 35. Single fares £0.90 onwards (child £0.60). One day unlimited travel pass £3.00 (child £2.00).

Car Parking: There are several car parks in the area, including parks located on Mermaid Quay, Havannah Street (near Techniquest & St David's Spa Hotel) and Pierhead Street (near the Welsh Assembly behind the Wales Millennium Centre). For those wanting a personal service, there is also a Valet Parking Service available. Mermaid Quay and Havannah Street charge at a rate of £0.50 per hour; Pierhead Street car park charges £1.50 for two hours parking. The Valet Service costs £12.50 in advance and £15.00 on the night. See the website for further details on this service.

The Tesco stage offers free performances in afternoons and at lunchtimes.

St David's Hall

Situated in the heart of Cardiff, St David's Hall is the National Concert Hall and Conference Centre of Wales. With its wide range of live entertainment, free exhibitions, conferences, participation workshops, two bars and a range of places to eat, all encompassed within relaxing surroundings, St David's Hall is a building to be enjoyed both in day and at night. Home to the Annual Welsh Proms Cardiff, the world-class Orchestral Concert Series and the famous bi-annual BBC Cardiff Singer of the World competition, St David's Hall presents a multitude of live entertainment, including pop, rock, folk, jazz, rhythm and blues, together with comedy, lunchtime concerts,

The Hayes
Cardiff CF10 1SH
United Kingdom
Tel: +44 (0)292 087 84 44
Fax: +44 (0)292 087 85 99
www.stdavidshallcardiff.co.uk

musicals and, of course, classical music.

TICKETING

Price Range: Tickets generally range from £4.00 to £36.00.

Concessions: Children, students, senior citizens, disabled visitors, carers and the unemployed receive a discount between £1.00 and £5.00 on the full ticket price. Student tickets are also available at half price for orchestral concerts within the St David's Hall Orchestral Concert Series.

Box Office

The Box Office is open Monday to Saturday, 10.00 a.m.–6.00 p.m., or to 8.00 p.m. when there is an evening performance. The Box Office also opens on Sundays and Bank Holidays one hour prior to the performance.
Tel: +44 (0)292 087 84 44
Fax: +44 (0)292 087 85 99
www.stdavidshallcardiff.co.uk

PERFORMANCES

Events occur all year round.

SEATING

Capacity: The auditorium has a capacity of 1,500.

Organization: Seating is arranged into 12 separate blocks.

Best Seats: The best seats can be found in tier 1.

Good Seats on a Budget: The stalls provide good seats at a reasonable price.

FACILITIES

Dining

St David's Hall includes an Art Café, the Celebrity Restaurant and Gallery, where a superb evening menu of Welsh and European dishes includes a two-course 'Showsupper' with coffee or a two-course Carvery with coffee for just £12.00 per person, together with bars on levels 3 and 5.

Services

An infra-red system is now available throughout the auditorium, (except for tier 5). The system can be used with or without a hearing aid.

HOW TO GET THERE

Bus: Cardiff Central Bus Station is approximately five minutes walk from the Hall. Single fare £0.90 onwards (child £0.60). One day unlimited travel pass £3.00 (child £2.00).

Car Parking: Car parks are located in the area, with four NCP car parks nearby.

EDINBURGH

Edinburgh Festival Theatre

The Festival Theatre is the Scottish capital's arena for opera and ballet, and takes its place at the heart of the Edinburgh

13/29 Nicolson Street
Edinburgh EH8 9FT
United Kingdom
Tel: +44 (0)131 529 60 00
Fax: +44 (0)131 662 11 99
www.eft.co.uk

International Festival. The Theatre runs an annual contemporary dance season alongside large-scale musicals, international ballet companies and a variety of one-night musical events. The King's Theatre, which forms part of the Festival City Theatres Trust, houses visits from the Royal National Theatre and other major touring drama productions as well as being home to Edinburgh's annual pantomime and the productions of local amateur societies. The Edinburgh Festival Theatre as it is known today opened in 1994, this time with an impressive glass fronted structure created by architect Colin Ross as the new entrance to the former Empire Palace Theatre. The addition provides visitors with a return to the venue's former 1928 glory, a dramatic mix of art nouveau, beaux arts and Neo-Classicism, encompassing perfect acoustics within an intimate environment.

TICKETING

Advance Sales: Tickets are released up to nine months in advance.

Price Range: Tickets generally range from £16.00 to £28.00.

Concessions: Children, students, senior citizens and the unemployed qualify for a discount of £3.00–£5.00 on the full ticket price, although these discounts do not usually apply to

Friday and Saturday evening performances.

Box Office

The Box Office is open Monday to Saturday, 10.00 a.m.–8.00 p.m. (6.00 p.m. on nonperformance nights), and from 4.00 p.m. to curtain-up on performance Sundays.
Tel: +44 (0)131 529 60 00
Fax: +44 (0)131 662 11 99
www.eft.co.uk

PERFORMANCES

Events occur all year round.

Annual Festivals/Special Events: The Edinburgh Festival takes place every August.

SEATING

Capacity: 1,800

Organization: The auditorium consists of stalls seperated into three price bands (most expensive), a dress circle in three price bands, and an upper circle in four price bands.

Seats to Avoid: Certain price bands located within the auditorium have restricted viewing. The dress circle 3 and upper circle 4 have limited views; surtitles may not be visible from the stalls, prices 3 and 4. In addition, there is a handrail at the front of the upper circle which may obstruct the view in upper circle price 2.

FACILITIES

Dining

Café Lucia serves guests during the morning, lunchtime and afternoon. There are three other bars in the Festival Theatre: the Johnnie Walker Bar and Taittinger Bar on the dress circle level and the Scottish Power Gallery on the upper circle level. These bars open from one hour before the performance, and stay open until after the interval.

Services

Guide dogs welcome.

Eight wheelchair spaces are available in the stalls.

Although there are no specific facilities on-site, programmes of many performances can be sent on tape and in large print.

HOW TO GET THERE

Bus: 2, 3, 3A, 5, 7, 8, 14, 21, 29, 31, 33, 37, 37A, 42 and 49. Adult single, £1.00; Child, £0.60.

Overground: The nearest rail station to the Festival Theatre is Waverley Station, half a mile away.

Car Parking: There is limited street parking around the Festival Theatre. There is small car park located about five minutes walk from the Theatre on Niddry Street (Open daily, 7.00 a.m.– 11.00 p.m.).

Usher Hall

The Usher Hall is one of the most outstanding concert halls in the world. A landmark in the heart of Scotland's capital, it stands for the highest level of musical and civic participation, and for the better part of a century it has hosted some of the greatest concerts and events in the city. Andrew Usher was already known as a generous man when he made his historic offer to the City of Edinburgh in July 1896 to found a concert hall. The style of the project was part of the contemporary backlash against the Victorian Gothic, with a return to the classical features owing much to the Beaux Arts style. Its curved walls were a fairly new architectural departure and this U-plan was only made possible by early twentieth century developments in reinforced concrete. The famous dome was designed to reflect the curvature of the walls, not to give a domed interior which would have been disastrous acoustically. The Usher Hall organ was designed to be the focal point of the Hall, not just visually but musically as well. The original organ, installed in late 1913 was of outstanding quality and design, and was constructed on the grandest scale with a Spanish mahogany case. Recent refurbishment works are intended after several years of disrepair. In 2002, plans for the essential second phase of refurbishment came together and are currently in development, aiming to turn the Usher Hall into a venue fit for the twenty-first century and beyond.

Lothian Road
Edinburgh EH1 2EA
United Kingdom
Tel: +44 (0)131 228 11 55
www.usherhall.co.uk

TICKETING

Advance Sales: Tickets are released three months in advance.

Price Range: Tickets generally range from £3.00 to £40.00.

Concessions: Students and the unemployed are entitled to a 25% discount on full price tickets. Senior citizens are eligible for 75% discount on the full price.

Box Office

The Box Office is open Monday to Saturday, 10.00 a.m.–5.30 p.m. Tickets are usually mailed within three days of booking. If the booking is made within seven days of the concert, tickets will be available for collection only.
Tel: +44 (0)131 228 11 55
www.usherhall.co.uk

PERFORMANCES

Events occur all year round.

Times: 7.30 p.m. evenings; 1.00 p.m. for lunchtime concerts.

Resident Groups: The Royal National Scottish Orchestra

Annual Festivals/Special Events: The Edinburgh Festival takes place each August.

SEATING

Capacity: 2,900

Organization: The auditorium is arranged into stalls, a grand circle and an upper circle.

Best Seats: The best seats can be found in the stalls.

Good Seats on a Budget: grand circle

Seats to Avoid: Some upper circle seats have restricted views.

FACILITIES

Dining

CHAT is a café/bar which opens from noon, serving a variety of snacks and refreshments.

Services

Guide dogs welcome.

There are ten designated wheelchair spaces in the Hall.

HOW TO GET THERE

Bus: 10, 11, 15, 15A, 16, 17 and 24 to Lothian Road. Adult single, £1.00; Child, £0.60.

Overground: Edinburgh has two railway stations, Waverley and Haymarket, both within a 15 minute walk from the Usher Hall.

Car Parking: There is a NCP car park located on Castle Terrace behind Usher Hall with 750 spaces available for guests, and the car park is open 24 hours. The top area of the car park may be reserved for guests. The hourly rate is £1.20 and the daily rate is £9.50 (24 hours). Nighttime discounts are available.

> Edinburgh has a rich literary history and it would be a shame to visit this great city without enjoying one of its many themed tours. The Edinburgh Literary Tour Trust offer many such experiences. Find out more at www.edinburghliterarypubtour.co.uk

GLASGOW

Royal Concert Hall

The Glasgow Royal Concert Hall rose from the ashes of the St Andrew's Halls when Glasgow was awarded the title European City of Culture in 1990. Part of the demands of the title was the construction of architectural works of great interest for the city, with the new Concert Hall taking its place as the cultural flagship for Glasgow. The incredibly tight building schedule allowed only fifteen months for design and twenty-seven for construction. In reality construction overran by eight weeks but still met its target to be opened on 5 October 1990 by Her Royal Highness, The Princess Royal at a final cost of £29 million. During the building phase the Concert Hall attracted much criticism from the press owing to its huge cost, and the management of its construction, its over-imposing façade, and even the acoustics of the main

> 2 Sauchiehall Street
> Glasgow G2 3NY
> United Kingdom
> Tel: +44 (0)141 353 80 00
> Fax: +44 (0)141 353 80 06.
> www.grch.com

Auditorium. Despite these problems, the issues raised have now largely been forgotten, with the Concert Hall now taking its place as one of Scotland's most prestigious musical venues, and a much-accepted landmark in the city centre.

TICKETING

Advance Sales: Tickets are released up to nine months in advance.

Price Range: Tickets generally range from £5.00 to £30.00.

Concessions: £2.00 off on each ticket for senior citizens, students and the unwaged (when offered).

Box Office

The Box Office is open Monday to Saturday, 10.00 a.m.–5.00 p.m. Opening hours vary on Sundays and public holidays. For remote bookings there is a transaction charge of £1.50 per ticket.
Tel: +44 (0)141 353 80 00
Fax: +44 (0)141 353 80 06
www.grch.com

PERFORMANCES

Events occur all year round.

Times: Usually 7.45 p.m. although this can vary.

Annual Festivals/Special Events: Twice yearly, in Spring and Autumn, The Glasgow

Royal Concert Hall presents its ever popular series of talks by well-known speakers including politicians, journalists, entertainers and sports personalities.

SEATING

Capacity: 2,500

Organization: The auditorium is organized into five price bands. 11 blocks and the upper circle are accompanied by three terraces in the upper floor and the arena stalls in the lower floor.

FACILITIES

Dining

The Glasgow Royal Concert Hall has a total of seven bars located throughout the Hall so visitors can enjoy a pre-concert or interval drink. The Green Room is renowned for its superb food and its exceptional views looking down the length of Buchanan Street and across to the hills to the south of the city.

Services

There is an induction loop system in the main auditorium to assist patrons who have hearing difficulties.

HOW TO GET THERE

Bus: Buchanan Street Bus Station is directly across the road from the Killermont Street entrance to the Concert Hall. Single journey costs £1.00 onwards (£0.50 child). One day Discovery Ticket (unlimited travel) costs £1.90.

Overground: The nearest railway station is Queen Street Station which is a three minutes walk from the Hall. From the station turn right onto Buchanan Street.

Theatre Royal

The Theatre Royal first opened in 1867 and, following two tragic fires reopened in September 1895. After an unfortunate start, this new beginning was the start of a long and successful association of the Theatre Royal with the best in the world of entertainment. The Theatre Royal presents a wide variety of drama, dance, comedy, opera,

282 Hope Street
Glasgow G2 3QA
United Kingdom
Tel: +44 (0)870 060 66 47
www.theambassadors.com

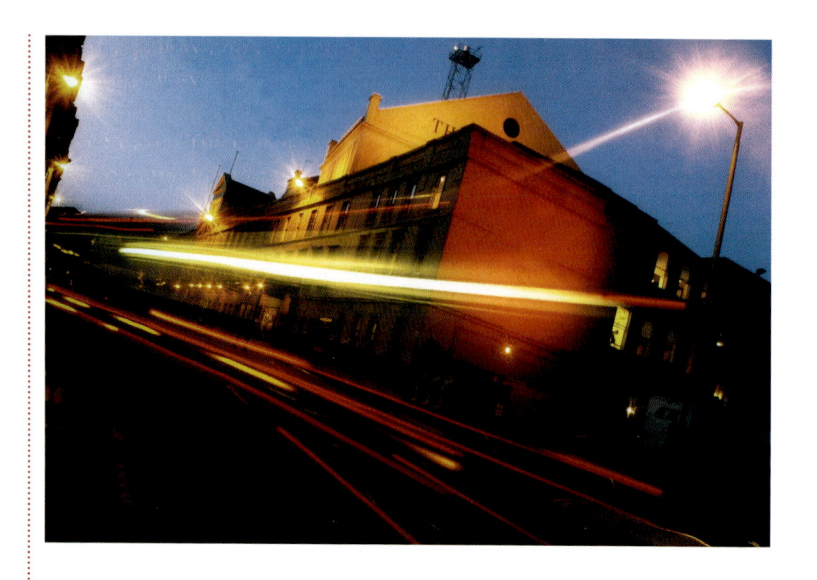

musical and children's theatre. Home to Scotland's resident companies, the Scottish Opera and Scottish Ballet, the venue has also proven to be a unique city centre venue for conferences, meetings and seminars. The Victorian auditorium and stylish contemporary corporate areas provide privacy and flexibility for many occasions. On March 2005, the Ambassador Theatre Group took over the management of the Theatre, and it continues to present first class entertainment, providing a wide array of programmes and events including family fun days and educational shows.

TICKETING

Advance Sales: Tickets are released six months in advance.

Price Range: Tickets generally range from £9.00 to £170.00.

Concessions: Children and other concessions are entitled to discounts on the top three price bands for Monday to Thursday evening performances, some matinees and some one-night events. Full-time students, the unwaged, the over-60s and people with disabilities get £3.00 off; and under-16s get £5.00 off. Concessions may vary. Wheelchair bookings give approximately 25% off on the maximum ticket price where offered.

Box Office

The Box Office is open Monday to Saturday, 10.00 a.m.–8.00 p.m.
Tel: +44 (0)141 240 11 33
www.theambassadors.com/theatreroyalglasgow

PERFORMANCES

Events occur all year round.

Times: Generally 7.45 p.m.

Resident Groups: Scottish National Opera

SEATING

Capacity: 1,541

Organization: The auditorium is divided into a balcony, upper circle, dress circle and stalls.

FACILITIES

Dining

Café Royal is open on performance days, serving pre and post-performance meals. To reserve a table Tel: +44 (0)141 332 13 70. In addition, the Circle Café, situated in the Hemmings Foyer on the dress circle level provides a range of light meals and snacks and is open 75 minutes before the commencement of each show. Reservations are not required. In addition, there are fully licensed bars on all levels of the auditorium, open before performances and during intervals.

Services

Guide dogs welcome.

Wheelchair spaces are available in the stalls for all performances.

The Theatre Royal has an infra-red system to aid people with hearing difficulties; headsets are available from the main foyer.

HOW TO GET THERE

Bus: Buchanan Street Bus Station is located on the same road as the venue. Single journey costs £1.00 onwards (£0.50 child). One day Discovery Ticket (unlimited travel) £1.90.

Overground: Queen Street Station is a five minutes walk from the Theatre.

Car Parking: Glasgow city council operates a supervised 24 hour multi-storey car park one block from the Theatre in Cambridge Street. Parking after 6.00 p.m. costs £1.00 and this charge entitles visitors to park until 9.00 a.m. the following day.

GLYNDEBOURNE

Glyndebourne Opera

One of the most exclusive opera houses in the UK, the Glyndebourne Opera in Lewes is the home of the famous, and ever exclusive Glyndebourne Opera Festival. Tickets are offered for sale first of all by postal ballot to Members of the Festival Society, Associate Members, the Festival Mailing List and subsequently to the general public. It originated under John Christie at his private Glyndebourne House in 1934 and was soon enlarged and improved after the initial production of 'The Marriage of Figaro'. Christie announced in 1990 that a new theatre, capable of seating 1,200 people, would be constructed in 1992. The old theatre hosted its last festival in 1992, and construction of a brand-new theatre was underway. It was completed at a cost of some £34 million, 90% of which was raised through donations, giving the donors control over 28% of the seats. The inaugural performance in the new theatre on 28 May 1994 was 'The Marriage of Figaro', performed sixty years after its first performance at the old theatre. During the Touring Opera season patrons are invited to look at the gardens from 5.00 p.m. (2.00 p.m. on Saturdays) to enjoy the beautiful surroundings of this elite and wonderful venue.

Glyndebourne
Lewes
East Sussex BN8 5UU
United Kingdom
Tel: +44 (0)127 381 23 21
Fax: +44 (0)127 381 27 83
www.glyndebourne.com

TICKETING

Advance Sales: One month for public booking from 10 April (member's have priority).

Price Range: Tickets generally range from £10.00 to £190.00.

Concessions: Prices for disabled visitors and their carers are inclusive of the wheelchair user and carer. There are two spaces at £135 each at the foyer circle level and four spaces in the side boxes at £60.

Box Office

The Box Office is open Monday to Friday, 10.00 a.m.–7.00 p.m. Weekends, 10.00 a.m.– 5.00 p.m.
Tel: +44 (0)127 381 38 13
Fax: +44 (0)127 381 46 86
www.glyndebourne.com – online booking form.

PERFORMANCES

Events take place from May to August.

Resident Groups:
Glyndebourne Opera

Annual Festivals/Special Events: The Glyndebourne Festival takes place from May to August annually.

SEATING

Capacity: 1,200

Organization: The auditorium is arranged into stalls, a foyer circle and upper circle. Some seats are not available during member's priority booking, i.e. the foyer circle sides, circle sides, slips and standing room areas.

Best Seats: The best seats are located in the stalls.

Good Seats on a Budget: The upper circle is good value for money in terms of views.

Seats to Avoid: Some seats have restricted views owing to the horseshoe shape of auditorium. For acoustic reasons visitors should try to avoid seats located in the slips, standing room, foyer circle, circle sides, centre box C and side boxes.

EDUCATION

Guided Tours

Guided Tours take place in the middle of November and during the first week of February. For further information, email: info@glyndebourne.com.

FACILITIES

Dining

The tearooms are open two hours before the start of each performance and operate on a first come first served basis. Tea, coffee, cakes, scones, sandwiches and soup are all available. Early arrival is recommended to avoid disappointment and queues. The Long Bar is open two hours before the performance commences. In addition, there is a coffee and tea service available on the circle balcony during the interval.

Services

The auditorium is equipped with a Sennheiser infra-red sound enhancement system. Receivers can be borrowed from the House Manager's office.

HOW TO GET THERE

Overground: There are train services from London (Victoria) to Lewes with coach connections to and from Glyndebourne.

Car Parking: Parking in the main audience car park is free for patrons.

LIVERPOOL

Liverpool Philharmonic Hall

Once described by the famous British conductor Thomas Beecham as, 'the best in Europe', the Philharmonic Hall in Liverpool has delighted audiences since 1849, and has established itself as an acclaimed and integral part of the artistic life of Liverpool. The original building burnt down in 1933, and was replaced by the present hall, designed by Herbert Rowse and serving the dual purpose of being both a cinema and concert hall. An additional refurbishment was completed in 1995, with parts of the foyer redecorated with influences which some say are based on decoration of the tomb of Tutankhamun. The Royal Liverpool Philharmonic Orchestra is the venue's resident ensemble, and is one of Britain's longest established orchestras, giving over 60 concerts a year, and featuring world-class artists at its home venue. Over the years it has also had many famous principal conductors, including Sir Henry Wood, Sir Malcolm Sargent, Max Bruch and Sir John Pritchard.

TICKETING

Advance Sales: Tickets are released nine months in advance.

Price Range: Tickets generally range from £5.00 (concessions) to £31.00.

Concessions: Children, students and the unemployed can purchase tickets from as little as £5.00. In addition, disabled patrons are entitled to 50% off on the ticket price.

Hope Street
Liverpool L1 9BP
United Kingdom
Tel: +44 (0)151 210 28 95
Fax: +44 (0)151 210 2902
www.liverpoolphil.com

Box Office

The Box Office is open Monday to Saturday, 10.00 a.m.–5.30 p.m.; Sunday, noon–5.00 p.m. There is a £1.00 per ticket for telephone credit card bookings only. Debit card transactions incur no charge. Online bookings incur a £3.00 transaction fee. Tel: +44 (0)151 709 37 89 http://purchase.tickets.com or follow the links on the official website.

PERFORMANCES

Events occur all year round.

Times: 1.00 p.m. and 7.30 p.m.

Resident Groups: Liverpool Philharmonic

SEATING

Capacity: 1,708

Organization: The auditorium is arranged into stalls, boxes, a grand circle, middle case and upper area circle.

Best Seats: The best seats are in the boxes and centre of the grand circle.

Good Seats on a Budget: The middle circle provides good value for money.

Seats to Avoid: All seats provide unrestricted view of the stage.

The online booking service at www.liverpoolphil.com allows you to see the view from different seats before buying your tickets.

FACILITIES

Dining

The Lower Place Restaurant serves a refreshing range of contemporary food and wines, and is located inside the Philharmonic Hall. In addition, on selected concert nights, themed food and drink is offered in the Grand Foyer Bar. Pre-concert and interval drinks are offered in the grand foyer, open from 5.00 p.m.–11.00 p.m. (10.30 p.m. on Sundays).

Services

Guide dogs welcome.

In addition to level access, which is available in many parts of the building, spaces for wheelchairs plus companions are available in boxes 7 and 16, and in the front and rear stalls.

An infra-red hearing system is available. Visitors are advised to contact a steward on arrival to obtain one.

Large print and audio versions of brochures are available from the marketing department by calling: +44 (0)151 210 28 95 or emailing: marketing@liverpoolphil.com.

HOW TO GET THERE

Bus: Merseyside's SMART Bus nos. 1 and 4 link Hope Street with Liverpool city centre, Lime Street Station and Central Station. Adult single, £2.40; Child, £1.80.

Car Parking: Philharmonic Hall car park, situated on Caledonia Street, is open from 8.30 a.m. until 15 minutes after the end of concerts. Blackburne House car park, situated on Falkner Street, is open on concert nights from 5.30 p.m. until 20 minutes after the end of the concert. The Philharmonic Hall car park costs £4.00 after 5.30 p.m. and £5.00 before. Blackburne House car park costs £4.00.

Olympia

Originally intended as an indoor circus and variety theatre, the Liverpool Olympia has evolved into a multi-purpose venue, hosting events from boxing matches to a variety of classical music concerts. Reminders of the building's former purpose are evident throughout, with the ornate interior still reflecting the Olympia's past with images of elephants and lions set into Indian panelling. Built in 1905 by the architect Frank Matcham, in its prime it could accommodate 3,750 people in the stalls and three balconies. The theatre was purchased by the ABC Theatre Company and converted into a cinema in 1930, later being used as a Naval Depot during World War II. The 1960s saw it transformed into a Bingo Hall, which became its main purpose for the next twenty years. The Olympia reopened in the 1990s, after a short spell of closure, and today it continues to present the variety of events which has led to its colourful history and reputation as a diverse and versatile venue.

West Derby Road
Liverpool L6 9BY
United Kingdom
Tel: +44 (0)151 263 66 33
Fax: +44 (0)151 263 49 85
www.liverpoololympia.com

TICKETING

Box Office

The Box Office is open Monday to Friday, 10.00 a.m.–6.00 p.m.
Tel: +44 (0)151 263 66 33
www.ticketline.co.uk

SEATING

Capacity: 1,200 seated, 1,500 standing.

Seats to Avoid: All seats provide unrestricted views of the stage.

FACILITIES

Dining

The Stage Door Bar and Grill provide visitors with a fine dining environment, serving a range of hot meals to be enjoyed before or after the event. To book a table, contact the restaurant directly at +44 (0)151 263 66 33 or download a dining booking form from the website.

Services

HOW TO GET THERE

Bus: 12, 13, 15, 18A, 212, 218 and 274. Adult single, £2.40; Child, £1.80.

Car Parking: 300 parking spaces are available on-site.

LONDON

Barbican Centre

On first glance, the Barbican Centre has no obvious external presence, being embedded in an arts centre within a huge residential development whose decks and elevated walkways bear little visible relationship with the pre-existing geography. The vast, bomb-flattened area on the northern edge of the city was developed in two stages: Golden Lane from 1953–63 and Barbican from 1962–82, both of them designed by Chamberlin, Powell & Bon, and both marked significant developments in architectural, town planning and social terms. The team of Chamberlin Powell & Bon (John Honer and John Connaughton), first with Richard Southern as theatre consultant and later with Peter Hall, John Bury and other advisors, produced a remarkable result. No theatre design has ever pleased every critic. Some actors and theatregoers have certainly found this one, in some ways, less than perfect, but the Barbican is something of a rarity in having attracted consistent praise from both architectural commentators and theatre experts. Victor Glasstone described it in 1982 as, 'the finest medium-sized house to be built in Britain since the war and, by international standards, one of the greats'.

Silk Street
City of London
London
EC2Y 8BQ
United Kingdom
Tel: +44 (0)207 638 41 41
www.barbican.org.uk

TICKETING

Advance Sales: Tickets are released six months in advance.

Price Range: Tickets generally range from £6.00 to £60.00.

Concessions: Concessions for selected groups can be gained by joining the access list online at www.barbican.org.uk.

Box Office

The Box Office is open Monday to Saturday, 9.00 a.m.–11.00 p.m.; Sundays and public holidays, noon–11.00 p.m. Some tickets are also cheaper online according to offers.
Tel: +44 (0)207 638 88 91
Lines are open daily, 9.00 a.m.–8.00 p.m.
www.barbican.org.uk

PERFORMANCES

Events occur all year round.

Resident Groups: The London Symphony Orchestra and the BBC Symphony Orchestra.

Annual Festivals/Special Events: The Mostly Mozart Festival takes place every summer. The London Jazz Festival is held every November.

SEATING

Capacity: 1,162

Organization: Three shallow Balconies and raking side slips over steeply raked stalls make up the arrangement in the Barbican Centre.

FACILITIES

Dining

Several food outlets are located on-site, including Searcy's, providing visitors with spectacular views of the city skyline across the Barbican lakeside; balcony Bistro, which offers modern European cooking in a chic and relaxed setting, and the Waterside Café, for guests who prefer a less formal setting in a self-service dining area. Full details can be found on the website.

Services

Guide dogs welcome.

16 spaces for wheelchairs are located at the back of the stalls.

An induction loop system is available.

Large print programmes are available for selected performances.

HOW TO GET THERE

Bus: 8, 11, 23, 26, 35, 42, 43, 47, 48, 55, 56, 76, 78, 100, 133, 141, 149, 153, 172, 214, 242, 243, 271 and 344. Single journey costs £1.00 (with Oyster, £2.00 without). One day bus pass costs £3.50.

Underground: Circle, Metropolitan and Hammersmith & City Lines to Barbican; Northern Line (Bank Branch) to Moorgate. Single journey costs from £1.50 (with Oyster, £4.00 without). One day off-peak travelcard zones 1–2 (journeys after 9.30 a.m.) costs £5.10, £2.00 child.

Car Parking: The Barbican is clearly sign-posted and has four car parks. Parking up to one hour costs £2.20; up to two hours, £4.20; up to three hours, £6.00; up to four hours, £8.50 and up to five hours, £10.50. Alternatively, save by pre-booking a car parking voucher online for £5.00. The voucher is valid for entry after 5.00 p.m. on weekdays and all day weekends and bank holidays. Disabled patrons can obtain a voucher allowing free parking by presenting their Blue Badge at the Box Office/Ticket Desks.

Book the same number of tickets for three or more selected performances and receive up to 25% discount. Seasonal conditions apply. See the venue website for more details.

231

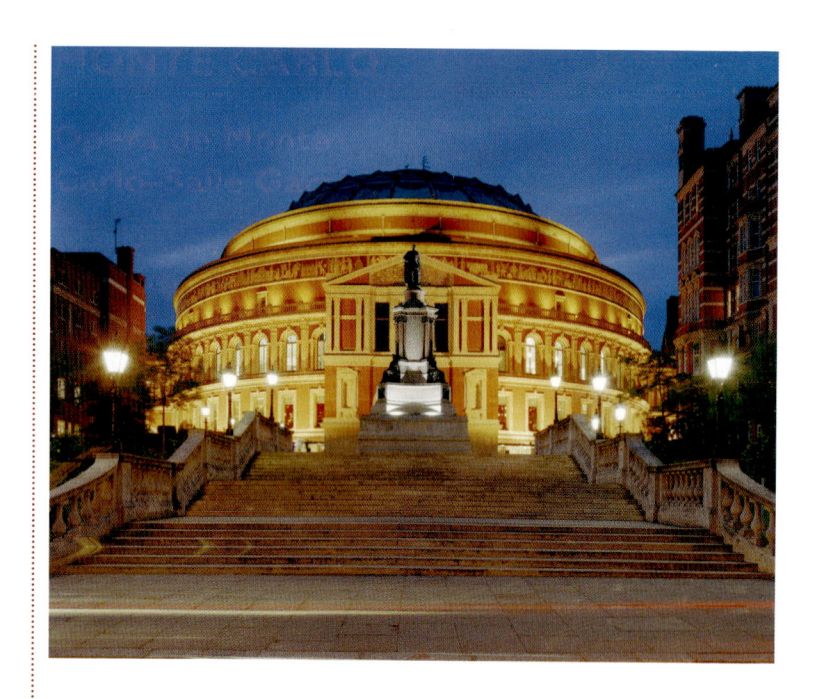

Royal Albert Hall

The legendary Royal Albert Hall is one of London's most famous and iconic concert venues. Playing host to the world's biggest stars and offering a wide range of entertainment from music to sport, the venue has also hosted the world famous Annual BBC Promenade Concerts, better known as the Proms, every summer since they were bombed out of the Queen's Hall in 1941. Surrounding the outside of the Hall is a great terracotta frieze, depicting 'The Triumph of Arts and Sciences', in reference to the Hall's dedication to the two fields which had been exhibited so successfully at the 1851 Great Exhibition at Crystal Palace. In this way, the venue provides a lasting memorial to Prince Albert, the Prince Consort, a man determined to continue the success of the Great Exhibition through a permanent set of facilities for

Kensington Gore
London SW7 2AP
United Kingdom
Tel: +44 (0)207 838 31 10
Fax: +44 (0)207 584 14 06
www.royalalberthall.com

the enlightenment of the general public. Today, the Royal Albert Hall does just that. Its grand design and prime location makes it a must-visit for all classical music lovers, whether with an exclusive ticket in-hand for the Last Night of the Proms, or simply to enjoy the unique atmosphere of this Central London venue.

TICKETING

Price Range: Tickets generally range from £5.00 to £55.00.

Concessions: Two tickets for the price of one are available for disabled people and carers. Other concessions are not generally available.

Box Office

The Box Office is open daily, 9.00 a.m.–9.00 p.m. There is a £3.50 transaction charge for all remote bookings.
Tel: +44 (0)207 838 31 10
www.royalalberthall.com

PERFORMANCES

Events occur all year round.

Annual Festivals/Special Events: The Annual BBC Proms held in August and September have become one of the venue's most famous concert series and are always a crowd puller.

SEATING

Capacity: 7,000 (although for safety reasons, the maximum capacity is now 5,544 including standing space.)

Organization: The circular auditorium is arranged into stalls, a circle, boxes, as well as a gallery where visitors are able to purchase standing tickets.

Seats to Avoid: There are no seats with restricted views.

EDUCATION

Guided Tours

Visitors are invited to join a special 45 minute tour where they can witness some of the unseen workings and preparations as the venue prepares for its next show. There are six tours a day, which run from Friday to Tuesday. Highlights of the tour include exclusive access to the Royal Retiring Room, a look inside the Queen's Box and an insight into the daily goings-on for staff at the Hall. The Hall is open in daytime for tours. Contact,
Tel: +44 (0)207 589 32 03 or

+44 (0)207 838 31 05 for further enquiries or to book a ticket. There is a £0.25 booking fee for all tour tickets purchased online or via telephone.

Cost: £7.50

Concessions: £6.50. Under-5s are free. A family ticket for up to two adults and three children costs £25.00.

FACILITIES

Dining

Bars are located in the West Arena Foyer and on the ground floor, while a Starbucks Café can be found at the entrance to the South Porch in Café Consort, which also offers wireless internet access.

Services

Guide dogs welcome.

There are 12 wheelchair spaces located in the stalls, six spaces in the circle and four wheelchairs available for customer use.

There is an infra-red system in the auditorium. Induction loop at Box Office counter.

HOW TO GET THERE

Bus: 9, 10, 52, 70. Single journey costs £1.00 (with Oyster, £2.00 without). One day bus pass £3.50.

Underground: District, Circle and Piccadilly Lines to South Kensington. Single journey costs from £1.50 (with Oyster, £4.00 without). One day off-peak travelcard zones 1–2 (journeys after 9.30 a.m.) costs £5.10, £2.00 child.

Royal Opera House

The Royal Opera House's illustrious history began in 1728 when John Rich, actor and manager at Lincoln's Inn Fields, commissioned 'The Beggar's Opera' from John Gay. The success of the venture provided

Bow Street
Covent Garden
London WC2E 9DD
United Kingdom
Tel: +44 (0)207 240 12 00
www.royalopera.org

the capital with the first Theatre Royal at Covent Garden, designed by Edward Shepherd. The first serious musical works to be heard at Covent Garden were the operas of Handel. From 1735 until his death in 1759 Handel gave regular performances in Covent Garden, and many of his operas and oratorios premiered at the Royal Opera House. On 5 March 1856 disaster struck. For the second time the theatre was completely destroyed by fire. Although rebuilding was felt to be imperative, financial considerations delayed matters. Work on the third and present theatre eventually started in 1857 and the new building opened on 15 May 1858 with a performance of Meyerbeer's 'Les Huguenots'. The present incarnation of the Royal Opera House opened on 4 December 1999. Its reconstruction actually began on-site in 1996 with the last performance in the 'old' house in July 1997. In three years the most inadequate of the great opera houses of the world was transformed, not only for audiences, but equally for performers and the hundreds of other people who work there. Situated on its historic site, the Royal Opera

House has enriched Covent Garden and reinforced its status as part of London's cultural heartland.

TICKETING

Advance Sales: Depending on when one of the four booking season opens, tickets are sold up to six months in advance.

Price Range: Tickets generally range from £3.00 to £190.00.

Concessions: The Royal Opera House offers special £10.00 student standby tickets on any unsold tickets for performances by the Royal Ballet and the Royal Opera which are made available to students over the internet a minimum of 24 hours in advance. Children, seniors, disabled visitors and the unemployed also qualify for up to 50% discount on the ticket price. Disabled carers are often given free entry with a wheelchair user.

Box Office

The Box Office is open Monday to Saturday, 10.00 a.m.–8.00 p.m.
Tel: +44 (0)207 304 40 00
Fax: +44 (0)207 212 94 60
www.royalopera.org

Please note that the site is unavailable to take bookings between 4.00 a.m.–7.00 a.m., all tickets in the house including restricted view seating and standing places are available to book online, except box seating in the grand tier and balcony.

PERFORMANCES

The Royal Opera House season runs from September to July.

Times: Concerts generally take place at 7.30 p.m., with some free concerts held at 1.00 p.m. in the Crush Room.

Resident Groups: The Orchestra of the Royal Opera House, the Royal Opera and Royal Ballet

SEATING

Capacity: 2,262

Organization: 12 ticket price bands separate the main auditorium, with upper slips, lower slips, amphitheatre seats, balcony, balcony seats, the Donald Gordon Grand Tier, grand tier boxes, stall circles and orchestra stalls.

Seats to Avoid: Some seats may have restricted views in all tiers apart from the orchestra stalls and the grand tier.

EDUCATION

Guided Tours

The Royal Opera House's Backstage Tours include an introduction to the colourful history of the theatre, an insight into the redevelopment of the Royal Opera House and a look at aspects of current productions. See www.royalopera.org for the latest special programmes and prices.

FACILITIES

Dining

The Amphitheatre Restaurant and Café Bar are both open from Monday to Saturday, noon – 3.00 p.m. and on Sundays when there is a performance or when a special event is held. Please note that there is a £19.00 minimum food spend per person. For those wishing to enjoy an evening meal, the Floral Hall Balconies Restaurant opens with the House an hour and a half before the curtain rises. Afternoon tea is available in the Pit Lobby when there is a matinee at £17.00 a person. Further details and booking arrangements can be found on the website.

Services

At least one wheelchair space and companion seat will be made available for sale from 10.00 a.m. on the day of the performance. Wheelchair access is available in the stalls circle, grand tier, balcony and upper amphitheatre, and Linbury Studio Theatre. A lay-by allows vehicles to pull off Bow Street immediately outside the Floral Hall to drop off disabled passengers.

There is an assisted hearing facility for people with impaired hearing in both auditoriums and the Vilar Floral Hall.

HOW TO GET THERE

Bus: 1, 4, 6, 9, 11, 13, 15, 23, 26, 68, 76, 77a, 91, 168, 171, 176, 188 and 501 (southbound only), 505, 521, X68 all go to the Aldwych, which is close to the Theatre. Single journey £1.00 (with Oyster, £2.00 without). One day bus pass £3.50.

Underground: Piccadilly Line to Covent Garden or Leicester Square; Northern Line (Charing Cross Branch) to Leicester Square. A single journey costs from £1.50 (with Oyster, £4.00 without). One day off-peak travelcard zones 1–2 (journeys after 9.30 a.m.) costs £5.10, £2.00 child.

Car Parking: There is no designated parking at the Royal Opera House for ticket holders. The nearest NCP car parks are five minutes walk from the Hall at Drury Lane and Shelton Street.

In addition to offering world-class opera, the Royal Opera House has a programme of changing exhibitions of material from the Royal Opera House, collections and touring exhibitions from other organizations. The exhibitions are throughout the House and can be seen, free of charge, Monday to Saturday, 10.00 a.m.–3.30 p.m.

St John's, Smith Square

Valued for its superb acoustics, St John's presents an extremely varied programme of classical music throughout the concert season, ranging from choirs and symphony orchestras to solo instrumental recitals. Built in 1728, and restored after damage in World War II, St John's is one of the finest examples of English Baroque architecture and is considered a masterpiece of this style. The Hall has been dubbed 'Queen Anne's Footstool', due to a legend that the architect, Thomas Archer, consulted Queen Anne on the design of the new church. In reply, the Monarch petulantly kicked over her footstool and snapped 'like that!', thus the four towers are said to give the building the semblance of an upturned footstool, and today, the superb, atmospheric restaurant in the

Smith Square
London SW1P 3HA
United Kingdom
Tel: +44 (0)207 222 10 61
Fax: +44 (0)207 233 16 18.
www.sjss.org.uk

crypt is aptly named after this legend. St John's, Smith Square is a short walk from Westminster Underground Station, with the stroll taking visitors through one of the most historical parts of London, past Big Ben, the Houses of Parliament and Westminster Abbey.

TICKETING

Advance Sales: Tickets are released six months in advance.

Price Range: Tickets generally range from £6.00 to £26.00.

Concessions: Various concessions are available for selected performances.

Box Office

The Box Office is open Monday to Friday, 10.00 a.m.–5.00 p.m., or until 6.00 p.m. on concert days. After 6.00 p.m., the Box Office is open for personal callers for that evening's concert only.
Tel: +44 (0)207 222 10 61
Fax: +44 (0)207 233 16 18

PERFORMANCES

The website's diary features dates up to a year in advance, although generally most tickets are released from three months before the performance, with new events being added all the time.

Times: Most evening performances start at 7.30 p.m., but this can vary. Lunchtime concerts are generally at 1.00 p.m., although this can also vary.

SEATING

Capacity: 600

Organization: Three price structures are in place according to the event, with some events having four, three and two prices depending on their nature.

Best Seats: The best seats are located in the centre.

Seats to Avoid: The lowest priced tickets are for unnumbered, unreserved side seats, most of which have restricted or very poor views. This also applies to gallery seats, when available, which are also unnumbered and have restricted or no view.

FACILITIES

Dining

The atmospheric, brick-vaulted, Footstool restaurant in the crypt provides a wonderful environment to enjoy a meal or a glass of wine before or after the concert. The restaurant is open on concert evenings only, from 5.30 p.m. on weekdays and from 90 minutes before the start of a concert on weekends and public holidays. On weekdays the restaurant is also open for lunch from 11.30 a.m.–2.45 p.m. For further information and booking, Tel: +44 (0)207 222 27 79.

Services

Guide dogs welcome.

Wheelchair access may be difficult in certain areas as it is an old building. Contact Box Office for further assistance.

The hall is equipped with an induction loop system. Visitors are advised to ask the Box Office when booking.

A taped transcription of the venue brochure together with information about concerts at other main London venues is available six weeks in advance of concerts. For more information, please call the Disability Resources Team on +44 (0)208 943 0022.

HOW TO GET THERE

Bus: 3, 87, 88, C10, 507. Single journey costs £1.00 (with Oyster, £2.00 without). One day bus pass £3.50.

Underground: District and Circle Lines to St James's Park; Victoria Line to Victoria. Single journey costs from £1.50 (with Oyster, £4.00 without). One day off-peak travelcard zones 1–2 (journeys after 9.30 a.m.) costs £5.10, £2.00 child.

The Coliseum

Boasting the widest proscenium arch in London, and home to the English National Opera, the Coliseum has become a famous feature of the West End with its distinctive façade and high tower topped with a globe. Designed by Frank Matcham in 1904, the venue is a Grade II listed Italian Renaissance-style building and was one of the first of its kind to install electrical lighting. The Coliseum became home of Sadlers Wells Opera Company (now ENO) in 1968, and in 1992 the ENO acquired the freehold to the Coliseum. Located footsteps from the boutiques of Covent Garden, and the dazzling West End shows of Theatreland, it is the ideal point from which to explore other theatres of London, the National Gallery and Portrait Gallery and the many shops and restaurants of Central London.

TICKETING

Advance Sales: Tickets are released six months in advance.

Price Range: Tickets generally range from £16.00 to £83.00.

Concessions: Each adult buying a full price ticket can purchase a seat for a child aged 5–16 years at half price. Other

St Martin's Lane
London WC2N 4ES
United Kingdom
Tel: +44 (0)207 845 95 00
Fax: +44 (0)207 379 12 64
www.eno.org

concessions are also available. Contact the Box Office for details.

Box Office

The Box Office is open Monday to Saturday, 10.00 a.m.–8.00 p.m.
Tel:+44 (0)870 160 5055
Fax: +44 (0)207 379 12 64
www.eno.org

PERFORMANCES

Events take place from 1 September to 2 February; March to 3 May and from May to July.

Resident Groups: English National Opera

SEATING

Capacity: 2,358

Organization: The auditorium is arranged into a balcony, upper circle, dress circle, stalls, with eight price bands.

Seats to Avoid: From row H backwards in the dress circle, and row K backwards in the upper circle, visitors will be unable to see the surtitles.

EDUCATION

Guided Tours

Pre-performance talks on the ENO's current programme are conducted in the Coliseum's

Clore Education Room. The talks, lasting approximately 45 minutes, are given by a variety of expert speakers, from academics to those who have worked closely on a particular production, offering audiences the chance to explore the operas in the ENO's repertory. Current dates and themes can be found on the website under, 'Talks and Study Events'. Tel: +44 (0)870 160 5055 or email: box.office@eno.org for further information.

Cost: £4.00

FACILITIES

Dining

The Coliseum has several bars located throughout the building, serving a range of snacks and refreshments, and even champagne for those wishing to treat themselves. These are available before performances and during intervals, with orders able to be placed in advance or on the evening. Tables are also available in the Dutch and Skybars. For those seated in a box, a service is available where food can be hand-delivered, so guests can enjoy food and refreshments without leaving the comfort of their seats.

Services

Four wheelchair spaces are located in the stalls, two new wheelchair spaces in the dress circle and existing wheelchair space in the stall's boxes. Transfer seats are also available for those who prefer to transfer out of their wheelchairs, four in the dress circle and six in the balcony.

Audio cassettes of the season brochure and an audio map detailing the route to the theatre and layout of London as well as an audio-introduction, are available at every performance. Talking Notes gives a brief synopsis and vivid description of the sets, costumes and characterizations. These audio cassettes are available on request from the Box Office.

HOW TO GET THERE

Bus: 3, 6, 9, 11, 12, 13, 15, 23, 24, 29, 53, 77a, 88, 91, 139, 159 and 176. Single journey costs £1.00 (with Oyster, £2.00 without). One day bus pass £3.50.

Underground: Northern Line (Charing Cross Branch) to Charing Cross or Leicester Square; Bakerloo Line to Charing Cross. Single journey costs from £1.50 (with Oyster, £4.00 without). One day off-peak travelcard zones 1–2 (journeys after 9.30 a.m.) costs £5.10, £2.00 child.

Car Parking: English National Opera (ENO) patrons receive a 50% discount at the following Masterpark car parks: Cavendish Square, Chinatown (Newport Place), Marble Arch and Park Lane, Poland Street, Rochester Row, Spring Gardens and Whitcomb Street. To qualify, ask the Box Office to validate the car park Ticket and present it at the barrier when leaving.

The Royal Festival Hall

Situated in the cultural heart of London, the South Bank Centre, the Royal Festival Hall (RFH) occupies a spectacular position overlooking the Thames. The RFH was opened in 1951 as part of the Festival of Britain, a post-war initiative intended to act as a 'tonic to the nation' following the devastation of World War II. London's only major concert hall, the Queen's Hall, had been destroyed in 1941, and the city's cultural life had suffered greatly as a result. In 1949, the Prime Minister Clement Attlee laid the first foundation stone, and only two years later, in 1951, the RFH was inaugurated with a ceremonial concert attended by King George VI and Queen Elizabeth. Since its opening, the RFH has gone from strength to strength, consistently stimulating Londoners with an ever-changing range of artists and events, from cutting-edge contemporary dance to the revival of forgotten classical works. As host to

Belvedere Road
London SE1 8XX
United Kingdom
Tel: +44 (0)870 380 43 00
Fax:+44 (0)870 163 38 98
www.rfh.org.uk

performers from all over the globe, the RFH represents the diverse and cosmopolitan population of Britain's capital city, reaching out to all through a series of free events and interactive workshops in addition to its formal performance programme. The recent renovation of the riverside complex in which the RFH is situated has injected new life into the area, which is now more popular than ever as a venue for concerts, exhibitions, dining and socializing.

TICKETING

Advance Sales: Tickets go on sale up to a year in advance.

Price Range: Tickets generally range from £6.00 to £35.00.

Concessions: Half-price tickets are available for children, students, senior citizens and the unemployed. Disabled concessions are available only if the patron is registered with the RFH's Access List. The form for this can be downloaded from the access section of the venue's website, with further information also available from accesslist@rfh.org. Registered carers accompanying a disabled person are entitled to a free ticket.

Box Office

The Box Office is located in the Riverside Foyer, and is open from noon to 8.00 p.m. daily. Telephone and online bookings are also welcome. For remote bookings, a £1.50 transaction charge applies. Tickets can be collected from the Box Office up to the beginning of the performance.
Tel: +44 (0)870 380 0400
Open daily, 9.30 a.m. to 8.00 p.m.
Fax: +44 (0)207 921 08 21
www.rfh.org.uk

PERFORMANCES

Events occur all year round. Up-to-date information is available on the website www.rfh.org.uk. Programmes of upcoming performances can be obtained from most tourist information offices and various tourist destinations throughout the city, as well as from the foyer of the RFH itself.

Times: Times vary, as the RFH hosts a wide range of concerts and events. Lunchtime concerts typically begin at 1.00 p.m., with evening performances commencing at 7.30 p.m.

Programmes: Programmes can be obtained from the Box Office and from the ushers prior to the performance. Programmes typically range from £2.00–£6.00.

Resident Groups: The London Philharmonic and Philharmonia, and the South Bank Gamelan Players.

Annual Festivals/Special Events: The London Jazz Festival takes place each November.

SEATING

Capacity: The Royal Festival Hall consists of three main performance venues: The RFH itself, the Queen Elizabeth Hall and the Purcell Room. The RFH has a 2,900 seat capacity, while the Queen Elizabeth Hall and Purcell Room contain 917 and 370 seats respectively.

Organization: Seating in the Queen Elizabeth Hall and Purcell Room consists of stalls only. In the RFH, seating is organized into choir stalls, stalls, and a balcony.

Best Seats: In all three venues, the centre of the stalls provide an excellent view. When not in use, the choir stalls are a good vantage point from which to watch the orchestra. The online booking service at www.rfh.org.uk allows visitors to see the view from different seats before buying tickets. Those with long legs would benefit from the extra leg room in rows A and D of the Purcell Room, and rows A of both the front and rear stalls in the Queen Elizabeth Hall.

Good Seats on a budget:
The choir stalls in the RFH cost only £6.00, and provide an excellent view of the conductor and orchestra. If these are not available, the middle seats in the rear stalls are good value.

Seats to Avoid: All seats have a reasonable view, without any major obstructions.

FACILITIES

Dining

The newly-refurbished riverside complex provides a wide range of options for dining, including a Wagamama Noodle Bar, Strada for Italian cuisine, the family-friendly Giraffe Café and an EAT Sandwich Bar. On the south side of the RFH is the ever-popular Festival Square Café Bar. Drinks and light snacks are also available in the Queen Elizabeth Hall Foyer.

Services

Gifts available.

There are nine wheelchair spaces available in the main Festival Hall, and four in the Queen Elizabeth Hall and the Purcell Room.

Sign-interpreted performances are a frequent occurrence at the RFH. Check with the Box Office for specific performances. The RFH auditorium is equipped with an infra-red hearing facility, for which receivers are available from the Box Office.

HOW TO GET THERE

Bus: RF1, X68, 1, 26, 59, 68, 76, 77, 139, 168, 171, 172, 176, 188, 211, 243, 341, 381, 507 and 521

Overground: Trains stop at Waterloo, Waterloo East and Charing Cross.

Underground: Jubilee Line to Waterloo; or District and Circle Lines to Embankment. A single journey costs from £1.50 (with Oyster, £4.00 without). A one day off-peak travelcard zones 1–2 (journeys after 9.30 a.m.) costs £5.10, £2.00 child.

Car Parking: Parking is available at the Hungerford Bridge, beneath the Hayward Gallery, and beneath the Royal National Theatre. The car park is open 7.00 a.m.–1.00 a.m. daily, £6.00 daily with a ticket validated at the RFH Box Office.

Before or after a performance, take a walk along the riverside, which offers spectacular views of London and the Thames. A trip to the Royal Festival Hall could be combined with a visit to the Tate Modern, the Hayward Gallery, the National Film Theatre, the Globe, the Royal National Theatre, the London Aquarium or the London Eye. The South Bank is also host to the only outdoor second-hand bookmarket in London, which is open daily.

MANCHESTER

Bridgewater Hall

Described as 'a magnificent statement on the role of music in the cultural life of Manchester, the prestigious Bridgewater Hall opened in September 1996 and has since continued to receive plaudits from artists and audiences alike for its stunning design and marvellous acoustics. The visual impact of the auditorium culminates in the spectacular façade of the organ, an instrument more completely integrated into the architectural and spatial composition of the space than in any other Hall yet built. This remarkable £1.2 million pipe organ was designed and built by Marcussen, a Danish family-owned company whose traditional working methods have scarcely changed since they were established in 1806. Every joint in the massive wooden carcass was cut by hammer and chisel, and the

Lower Mosley Street
Manchester M2 3WS
United Kingdom
Tel: +44 (0)161 907 90 00
Fax: +44 (0)161 907 90 01
www.bridgewater-hall.co.uk

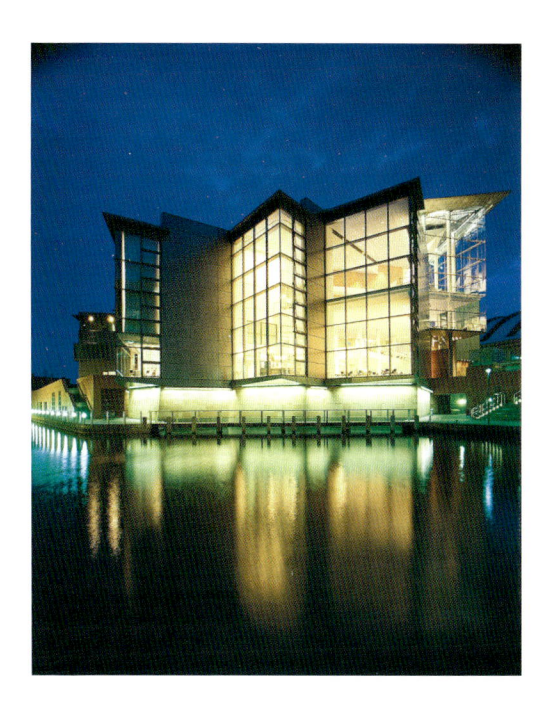

swell boxes and casework are as beautifully crafted as hand-made furniture. Today, this magnificent centrepiece sits on a foundation of earthquake-proof isolation bearings that insulates it from noise and vibrations outside. Showcasing approximately 250 performances a year, audiences at the Bridgewater can benefit from a series of wondrous performances throughout the year, truly encapsulated in a musical world free from external disturbances.

TICKETING

Advance Sales: Tickets are released nine months in advance.

Price Range: Tickets generally range from £8.00 to £35.00.

Concessions: Students are entitled to 20% off on the full ticket price, seniors 30% and disabled visitors 50%.

Box Office

The Bridgewater Hall is open to patrons Monday to Friday, 11.00 a.m.–2.30 p.m., and from 5.00 p.m. on concert days. Closing times vary depending on the duration of the evening event.
Tel: +44 (0)161 907 90 00
Fax: +44 (0)161 907 90 01
www.bridgewater-hall.co.uk

PERFORMANCES

Events occur all year round.

Times: Many evening performances commence at 7.30 p.m., although this can vary. Lunchtime performances generally start at 1.10 p.m.

SEATING

Capacity: 2,341

Organization: The auditorium has four levels: stalls – 704 seats; the choir circle – 160 seats; choir seats – 276 seats; the circle – 597 seats and the gallery – 604 seats.

FACILITIES

Dining

On concert evenings, bars are open on all four levels, serving both before the concert and during the interval. Coffee is served in the stalls and circle-bars and interval drinks can be pre-ordered on all four levels. A stalls Café Bar dining menu is offered from 5.30 p.m.–6.45 p.m. on concert nights; seats can be reserved at the Box Office. In addition, the Charles Hallé Restaurant offers an award winning menu for pre-concert diners. Visitors can reserve their table when booking tickets.

Services

Guide dogs welcome.

There are 16 spaces for wheelchair users in the auditorium, spread across all four levels. For further assistance and more information on disabled access, please contact the Box Office or visit the venue's website.

All auditorium levels have a Sennheiser infra-red hearing system. There are three types of receivers – the stethoscope receivers (for patrons with impaired hearing), the necklet induction couplers (for use with switchable hearing aids) and the earpiece receiver (for use with digital in-ear hearing aids). Any of these aids may be borrowed from the cloakroom on the ground floor foyer and the Box Office can advise on the most suitable seating areas.

HOW TO GET THERE

Bus: 2, 255 and 256

Underground: All Bridgewater Hall concert patrons can take advantage of special discounted return fares of £3.00 per adult and £1.50 per child from any station on the Metrolink system. In order to obtain the discount, visitors must purchase their Metrolink voucher when making a concert booking. Please note that vouchers are only valid after 5.00 p.m.

Car Parking: Car park vouchers for evening events are available to all Bridgewater Hall patrons for the NCP Central car park beneath GMEX which is linked directly to the Hall by a well-lit undercover walkway.

Free lunchtime concerts regularly take place in the stall's foyer of the Bridgewater Hall from May to September, allowing anyone who is passing by the opportunity to take time out for a few well-deserved minutes to soak up the atmosphere of the Hall and treat themselves to a 'little bit of music'. These concerts encompass a variety of different styles and have made the series an important part of the musical life of the Hall since it opened in 1996.

SOUTHAMPTON

Mayflower Theatre

1 February 1928 saw the Managing Director of Moss Empires R H Gillespie lay the foundation stone of the Mayflower Theatre. Built on shallow foundations because the land was barely above water level, the building was and still is the largest theatre in the south of England. The stalls were built on the natural slope of the land

and its massive auditorium covered nearly all the available land, leaving little room at the front for a foyer and bars. The design was described as Neo-Grecian though the influence of the popular art deco of the time was evident. Hard edges and angles were eschewed in favour of curves. The dominant colours were cream and gold, with touches of blue and strawberry. A dome in the ceiling of the auditorium opened to allow heat and cigarette smoke to escape. A permanent 26 member orchestra provided the music. This was particularly important in the days before amplification and pre-recording allowed much smaller bands to produce big sound. Originally the 'Gaumont', on Tuesday 24 February 1987, 'The Mayflower' opened officially with a production of Peter Pan.

Commercial Road
Southampton
Hampshire SO15 1GE
United Kingdom
Tel: +44 (0)238 071 18 00
Fax: +44 (0)238 071 18 13.
www.mayflower.org.uk

TICKETING

Price Range: Tickets generally range from £17.00 to £33.00.

Concessions: Children are entitled to 50% off on the full ticket price. Students, senior citizens, disabled visitors and the unemployed are eligible for £5.00 off each full price ticket. Discounts do not apply on Friday and Saturday performances.

Box Office

The Box Office is open Monday to Saturday, 9.30 a.m.–8.00 p.m. When there is no performance, the Box Office closes at 6.00 p.m. on weekdays and at 5.30 p.m. on Saturdays.
Tel: +44 (0)238 071 18 11
Fax: +44 (0)238 071 18 13
www.the-mayflower.com

SEATING

Capacity: 2,200

Organization: The Mayflower Theatre is arranged into a balcony, rear circle, dress circle, boxes, standing boxes and stalls.

FACILITIES

Dining

The Mayflower's luxurious Wessex Suite provides a range of dining options for visitors, including the opportunity to book a two or three-course meal as part of a pre-show dinner. For further information and booking, contact the restaurant on +44 (0)238 071 18 33.

Services

Guide dogs welcome.

The site has been made as wheelchair-friendly as possible, with excellent facilities ensuring all visitors gain the most from their visit. With 16 designate spaces for wheelchairs, the auditorium is fully flexible and can be adapted to suit individual needs. For extensive information on all the facilities available, see the website under 'Accessibility'.

The Box Office is equipped with an induction loop system. In addition, the auditorium is fitted with an infra-red amplification system for which an amplification aid can be obtained from the Box Office. Signed and captioned performances are a regular feature of the Mayflower, and lists of current performances can be found on the website.

The Mayflower provides a wide range of facilities for visually impaired guests. Two pairs of seats are held at the front of the stalls (B1 & 2, B24 & 25) until one week before the performance for a blind person who has a registered assistance dog and a companion, if required. Visitors can also reserve these seats if partially sighted and require closer proximity to the stage. In addition, visitors can request the Mayflower's Events Diary in large print, Braille version and on an audio cassette at no extra charge via the website.

HOW TO GET THERE

Car Parking: Car parking facilities are available in nearby Grosvenor Square and West Park.

YORK

National Centre for Early Music

1997 saw a breakthrough by the York Early Music Foundation. Initially established to support the York Early Music Festival, the Foundation secured a grant of £1.5 million from the Arts Council National Lottery Fund plus partnership monies from a variety of sources including English Heritage, the Garfield Weston Foundation and the Foundation for Sport and the Arts. The money was used to create the award winning National Centre for Early Music, providing a base for the festival

St Margaret's Church
Walmgate
York
Yorkshire YO1 9TL
United Kingdom
Tel: +44 (0)190 463 22 20
Fax: +44 (0)190 461 26 31
www.ncem.co.uk

and a year-round series of complementary activities, concerts and educational workshops. Today the site offers concerts from string quartets to jazz, and an eclectic mix of world music. The National Centre for Early Music is created from the medieval church of St Margaret's, an important historic church which lies within the city walls and had stood empty since the 1960s. Used as a theatrical store by the York Theatre Royal up until 1996, St Margaret's was one of the last two churches in the city of York that remained unrestored. The church is of considerable architectural significance as its most distinguishing features are an ornate Romanesque porch from the twelfth century, with carvings of mythological beasts, and an unusual brick bell tower, serving today to bring rich history together with modern innovation at the National Centre for Early Music.

TICKETING

Price Range: Tickets generally range from £3.50 to £15.00.

Concessions: Children qualify for a discount of 30% on ticket prices. Students qualify for as much as 75% off, with seniors, disabled visitors and the unemployed qualifying for a 50% discount.

Box Office

The Box Office is open Monday to Friday, 9.00 a.m.–5.00 p.m., and one hour before performance commences.
Tel: +44 (0)190 465 83 38
www.ncem.co.uk

PERFORMANCES

Annual Festivals/Special Events: Chinese New Year Festival, York Early Music Festival

SEATING

Capacity: 1,300

FACILITIES

Services

Guide dogs welcome.

The National Centre for Early Music is completely flat-floored throughout, making it an accessible building for wheelchair users with or without an accompanied helper.

The Centre's auditorium is fitted with a state-of-the-art induction loop ensuring good sound quality for all.

Although there are no specific facilities for the visually impaired on-site, the Centre has a copy of a Braille map of York city centre, produced by the Royal Institute for the Blind, which visitors are welcome to study.

HOW TO GET THERE

Bus: There is an excellent Park and Ride Service that alights just after Walmgate Bar and is a two minutes walk from the National Centre for Early Music. Adult single, £1.70.

GREECE

ATHENS

Megaron

A modern landmark in an ancient city, the Megaron Concert Hall is a bold demonstration of cutting edge design. Now a huge complex with state-of-the art facilities, its past was not always as smooth as its designers would have intended. The conception of the Megaron began when a small group of internationally renowned Greek musicians, including the conductor Dimitris Mitropoulos and the soprano Alexandra Triandi, formed the Friends of Music Society in response to the lack of facilities for classical music in the cradle of classical civilization. Despite financial support from these artists and a donation of land by the Greek government in 1956, the Concert Hall was not completed until 1991. Now a state-of-the art extension has

---

Megaron Mousikis (Great Hall Mousikis)
Vas. Sofias & Kokkali
Athens
11521
Greece
Tel: +30 (0)172 82333
Fax: +30 (0)210 728 2300
www.megaron.gr

been completed, the Megaron has finally become everything those eminent musicians had dreamt of 50 years earlier. The dull concrete exterior betrays its 1970's design, but the interior is well ornamented and the acoustics of both halls are excellent. The Friends of Music Hall also boasts a magnificent modern organ, together with many modern facilities, including moving panels that can be used to modify acoustics as well as the layout of the hall itself. The Megaron also houses one of the best music and arts libraries in South Eastern Europe, holding over 80,000 titles, as well as providing archives and teaching areas for researchers from all around the world.

TICKETING

Advance Sales: Tickets are generally released three weeks in advance of performance. Online booking opens the day after booking opens at the Box Office.

Price Range: Tickets generally range from €5.00 to €100.00.

Concessions: There are discounts available for children and students on all concerts. For senior citizens all tickets are sold at youth prices after 6.00 p.m. on day of concert.

Box Office

The Box Office is open Monday to Friday, 10.00 a.m.–6.00 p.m.; Saturday, 10.00 a.m.–2.00 p.m. On performance days: Monday to Friday, 10.00 a.m.–8.30 p.m.; Saturday, 10.00 a.m.–2.00 p.m. and 6.00 p.m.–8.30 p.m.; Sunday, 6.00 p.m.–8.30 p.m. Tel: +30 (0)210 7282333 www.megaron.gr

PERFORMANCES

Events occur all year round except for the summer break in July/August. Full performance details can be obtained by emailing at tickets@megaron.gr to join the mailing list.

Times: Evening performances typically start at 8.30 p.m., although start times vary. Sunday morning concerts for the young start at 11.30 a.m.

Resident Groups: Kamerata – The Friends of Music Orchestra

SEATING

Capacity: The Megaron consists of the Dimitris Mitropoulos Hall, with 450 seats.

The Friends of Music Hall holds 1,961 seats. The newly built extension also holds the Nikos Skalkottas Hall, which is used for concerts and lectures and holds 400 seats, and the brand new Alexandra Trianti Hall which is used for symphony concerts and opera and holds 1,750 seats.

Organization: The Friends of Music Hall has sloped stalls, seating on the floor and a large balcony containing the grand tier seating. The Dimitris Mitropoulos Hall has sloped floor seats only, all with good views of the stage.

Best Seats: www.megaron.gr has virtual guided tours of the Hall. The grand tier seats have the best view of the stage.

Good Seats on a Budget: The cheapest seats are at the back of the stalls. They provide a good view and the acoustics are good.

Seats to Avoid: All seats have a reasonable view, without any major obstructions.

FACILITIES

Dining

Megaron's Allegro Restaurant provides an in-house place to dine, offering a buffet service in the evenings. There is also C@feNet, a cáfe providing internet access while visitors enjoy their refreshments.

Services

There are 20 spaces for disabled visitors in the Friends of Music Hall and four in the Dimitris Mitropoulos. Wheelchair access is located at the main entrance with toilets for the disabled located on all floors.

HOW TO GET THERE

Bus: 3, 7, 8, 13, 408, 419, 601, 603, E6, E7, A5, G5, X14 and X95. An adult single costs €0.45 when purchased in advance.

Underground: Line 3, Megaron Mousikis. €0.80 (single).

> The Megaron complex is close to downtown, and Vassilissis Sophias Avenue hosts no less than five museums which trace the magnificent history of Greece from pre-history to modern times, including many archaeological artefacts and art.

HUNGARY

BUDAPEST

Magyar Állami Operaház

The Hungarian State Opera House is one of the most splendid examples of Neo-Renaissance architecture. Built by Miklós Ybl from 1875 to 1884, it is a richly-decorated building and is considered one of his masterpieces. In front of the building are statues of Ferenc Erkel, the composer of the Hungarian national anthem, and Franz Liszt, both pieces by Alajos Stróbl. The Austrian composer Gustav Mahler was director in Budapest from 1888 to 1891. The statues on the corner projections, between the Corinthian half columns, represent Terpsichore, Erato, Thalia and Melpomene, the Muses of dance, love-poetry, comedy and tragedy. The statues of great composers on the façade were renovated in 1966. These represent from left to right: Monteverdi, Scarlatti, Gluck, Mozart, Beethoven, Rossini, Donizetti, Glinka, Wagner, Verdi, Gounod, Bizet, Moussorgsky, Tchaikovsky, Moniuszko and Smetana. Renovations of the building have

Hungarian State Opera House
22 Andrássy út VI
Budapest
Hungary
Tel: +36 (0)332 7914
Fax: +36 (0)311 9017
www.jegymester.hu

meant that the 43 metre deep stage can be lifted or lowered by 4 metres by means of a hydraulic mechanism, adding yet another dimension to this magnificent venue.

TICKETING

Price Range: Tickets generally range from HUF 300.00 to HUF 10,900.00.

Box Office

The Box Office is open Monday to Saturday, 11.00 a.m. until the beginning of performances (until 5.00 p.m. on days when there is no performance); on Sunday and holidays, 11.00 a.m. to 1.00 p.m., and 4.00 p.m. to the beginning of performances.
Tel: +36 (0)135 30170
www.jegymester.hu

PERFORMANCES

The season runs from mid-September to mid-June.

Resident Groups: The Hungarian State Opera

Annual Festivals/Special Events: The Summer Operafest takes place annually between July and August.

SEATING

Capacity: 1,300

Organization: The auditorium is arranged into stalls and three balcony circles.

Best Seats: The dress circle provides the best seats.

Good Seats on a Budget: Seats located on the balcony side provide good value for money and good views.

Seats to Avoid: There are several seats on the balcony (third floor) and in the back rows of the upper circle (second floor) from where the stage is completely or partly obscured.

EDUCATION

Guided Tours

Tours of the venue can be arranged from Monday to Friday, allowing visitors an insight into the opera house and its workings.

Times: Tours are conducted at 3.00 p.m. and 4.00 p.m.

Cost: HUF 900.00.

FACILITIES

Dining

There is a restaurant/bar located on-site.

Services

Disabled access.

HOW TO GET THERE

Underground: Opera Metro Station is a short walk away. Take MetroLine 1.

Car Parking: Tour guides recommend visitors not to drive in Budapest unless they are familiar with the area.

Pátria Hall

The Budapest Congress & World Trade Centre, adjoining the Novotel Budapest Congress Hotel, is the largest and oldest convention venue in Hungary.

H 1123
Jagello ut 1–3
Budapest
Hungary
Tel: +36 (0)137 25400
Fax: Tel: +36 (0)137 25735
www.bcc.hu

The Pátria Hall which was completely renewed at the end of September 2005, accommodates up to 1,788 people in a theatre-style venue designed for conferences, opening ceremonies, product launches, concerts, gala dinners and exhibitions. Eighteen medium-sized and smaller meeting rooms accommodate between 8 to 300 people and are ideal places for breakout meeting rooms, seminars and other meeting requirements. With the Aula, Gallery and Mirror corridor, there is more than 900m² of space on two floors, ideal for exhibitions and a great place to enjoy music at this multi-purpose venue.

TICKETING

Price Range: Ticket prices and concessions depend on the promoter and event.

SEATING

Capacity: 1,788

Organization: The Pátria Hall is divided into stalls and an upper circle balcony area.

Best Seats: The best seats can be found in the balcony.

Seats to Avoid: All seats have unobstructed views.

EDUCATION

Guided Tours

Guided tours can be organized for free when arranged in advance. Tel: + 36 (0)137 25400 to organize a tour.

FACILITIES

Dining

The Pátria Hall provides a range of dining facilities where guests can relax and enjoy a variety of refreshments. Côté Jardin Restaurant provides an a la carte menu based on fresh, seasonal ingredients where visitors can enjoy their meal on the Centre's terrace. In addition, the lobby bar is open from 7.00 a.m.–1.00 a.m.

Services

HOW TO GET THERE

Bus: 8, 112 from Deli train station. Adult single, HUF 185.00 in advance, HUF 210.00 on board.

Car Parking: 250 parking spaces are located at the Centre.

ICELAND

REJKJAVIK

Salurinn

Salurinn's Kopavogur Concert Hall, the first specially designed concert hall in Iceland, was opened on 2 January 1999. Particular emphasis was placed on making the acoustics as good as possible and Salurinn has been highly praised by performers and guests alike for its exceptional sounds. The size and shape of the hall, its sloping floor and comfortable seats, make for a special intimacy between artist and audience. The hall seats 290 and is equipped with good facilities for the disabled. Salurinn is available for all kinds of musical events or recording sessions and also has good facilities for meetings, lectures and small conferences. The building's modern design and the use of Icelandic building materials make Kopavogur Concert Hall a place worth visiting. A variety of concerts are given at Salurinn each year, covering all kinds of music from Renaissance to modern, in the form of solo concerts, recitals and groups performing jazz, chamber and electronic music to name a few, with celebrated Icelandic performers as well as visiting international musicians providing what can only be described as a diverse and varied programme.

Hamraborg 6
200 Kopavogur
Iceland
Tel: +354 (0)5 700 400
Fax: +354 (0)5 700 401
www.salurinn.is

TICKETING

Price Range: Tickets generally range from ISK 1,500.00 to ISK 2,300.00 (The average price for a ticket is usually ISK 2,000.00).

Concessions: Under-12s can purchase tickets at a reduced rate of ISK 800.00. Students, senior citizens and disabled patrons can purchase tickets for around ISK 1,600.00.

Box Office

The Box Office is open Monday to Friday, 10.00 a.m.–4.00 p.m. and one hour before concerts.
Tel: +354 (0)5 700 400
Fax: +354 (0)5 700 401

PERFORMANCES

Events take place all year round, although the venue is closed in July.

Annual Festivals/Special Events: The TIBRA concert series takes place from September to May (other musicians hire the Hall all year round).

SEATING

Capacity: 290

Organization: The auditorium is arranged into stalls and balcony with a uniform price for all seats.

Good Seats on a Budget: All the seats are of same price.

Seats to Avoid: There are no restricted seats, Salurinn only seats 290 and is a modern facility.

FACILITIES

Services

There are eight designated spaces for wheelchair users during every performance.

HOW TO GET THERE

Bus: S1, S2 to Salurinn. Adult single, ISK 250.00.

The Icelandic Opera

The roots of the Icelandic Opera date back to the end of the 1970s, making it a relatively young venue in comparison with the long-standing opera houses of Europe that have traditions reaching back centuries. Despite this, the site has never lacked ambition and energy, and now, as it leaves its youth and enters adulthood, it intends to go on playing an established and important role in the future. From the outset, one of the main aims of the Icelandic Opera has been to build up and strengthen a professional basis for Icelandic singers. An agreement concluded with the Ministry of Education and Culture in 2001, which ran to the end of 2005, has enabled the venue to pursue its aims with greater force. Continuing its endeavour to create a continuous, varied and ambitious programme over the winter months, so opera lovers are able to

Ingólfsstræti
P.O. Box 1416
121
Reykjavik
Iceland
Tel: +354 (0)511 6400
Fax: +354 (0)552 7384
www.opera.is

rely on a consistent and varied programme at the Icelandic Opera at all times, the choice of repertoire in the coming years continues to maintain its broad theme. Most of the larger works are still well-known operas, but lesser-known works, old and new, are also featured. In addition, the Icelandic Opera continues to contribute to the creation of new operatic works, in which it remains committed to collaborating with both domestic and foreign parties.

TICKETING

Advance Sales: Tickets are released nine months in advance.

Price Range: Tickets generally range between ISK 2,700.00 and ISK 6,900.00.

Box Office

The Box Office is open Tuesday to Sunday, 10.00 a.m.–6.00 p.m. (and up to performances). Tel: +354 (0)511 4200
www.opera.is

PERFORMANCES

Events take place from October to May.

SEATING

Capacity: 473

FACILITIES

Dining

There is a bar/restaurant next door to the opera house which serves a range of meals and refreshments.

Services

Disabled access.

HOW TO GET THERE

Bus: 12. Adult single, ISK 250.00.

IRELAND

CORK

Cork Opera House

The pride of the Cork middle classes since 1855, the Cork Opera House started life as the Athenium, a venue for intellectual pursuits that played host to figures like Dickens and Parnell. The foundation stone of the present theatre was laid in 1963 after a fire destroyed the old venue. Fortunately, all people were evacuated when what began as an electrical fault blazed into an inferno within minutes. On 23 February 1963, the tender of Messrs O'Shea, South Mall was accepted for the rebuilding of the Opera House. A month later the work began, the foundation stone being laid by Lord Mayor Casey on 21 June 1963. When the building was finally unveiled, much criticism was levelled at the lack of architectural or artistic decoration on the exterior of the new building, and the square, squat tower on top of the roof designed to ease set changing, came in for a lot of unfavourable comment and criticism. However, the venue has recently undergone another extensive refit that has kept the theatre up to date. Only occasionally a venue for opera, it also puts on musicals, theatre and traditional music concerts, ensuring the continuation of the original intentions of architect Sir John Benson, for the 'promotion of science, literature and the fine arts, and the diffusion of architectural knowledge'. Part of the pattern of the cultural and social life of the city for well over a century, today its grand façade stands proudly in the wake of an historic past and in the expectancy of a vibrant and enriching future.

TICKETING

Price Range: Tickets vary according to the performance.

Concessions: Discounts are generally available for children, students, senior citizens and the unemployed.

Emmet Place
Cork
Ireland
Tel: +353 (0)21 427 4308
Fax: +353 (0)21 427 6357
www.corkoperahouse.ie

Box Office

The Box Office is open Monday to Saturday, 9.00 a.m.–5.30 p.m. Remote bookings generally incur a transaction charge which varies according to the performance.
Tel: +353 (0)21 427 0022
Fax: +353 (0)21 427 6357
www.corkoperahouse.ie

PERFORMANCES

Events take place all year round. Information is available from the website, as well as from hotels and tourist information points in the city.

Times: Performance times vary. Check with the Box Office for individual performances.

SEATING

Capacity: 1,000

Organization: There are stalls on the ground floor and two balconies.

Best Seats: The best seats are located in the centre of the auditorium in the stalls.

FACILITIES

Services

Disabled access.

HOW TO GET THERE

Car Parking: There is public car parking at Paul Street.

DUBLIN

Gaiety Theatre

The Gaiety Theatre is the oldest theatre in Dublin, boasting a repertoire which includes opera, theatre, pantomime and even a night club. The inspiration behind the Gaiety came from the energetic Gunn brothers, John and Michael, whose background was a family music business in Grafton Street. Together with the architect C J Phipps, they constructed a building in just 25 weeks from laying the first brick to the

South King Street
Dublin 2
Ireland
Tel: +353 (0)1 679 5622
Fax: +353 (0)1 677 1921
www.gaietytheatre.ie

opening night, equipped with a handsome Venetian façade, and twelve years later, an interior filled with charming Baroque adornments, thanks to renowned architect Frank Matcham. 2003 saw an additional investment of over €2 million in the biggest restoration programme the Gaiety Theatre has seen in over 50 years. Despite this, the theatre has had its critics, with some suggesting the facilities are not ideal for an opera venue, with a suggestion that the orchestra pit is too small and the seating still cramped despite the improved legroom adjustments by the renovation. Nevertheless, the Gaiety Theatre is an innovative and enthusiastic venue which has proven successful despite many constraints. Playing host to opera greats including Salvini, Pavarotti, Joan Sutherland, Veronica Dunne and Bernadette Greevy; Maureen Potter, who was the smiling face of the Gaiety to thousands of Dubliners, summed it up best: 'The Gaiety is the most aptly named place I know'.

TICKETING

Price Range: Tickets generally range from €20.00 to €60.00.

Box Office

The Box Office is open Monday to Saturday, 10.00 a.m.– 7.00 p.m. Transaction charges vary according to the price of the tickets, check the website for details.
Tel: +353 (0)1 677 1717
www.gaietytheatre.ie

PERFORMANCES

Opera Ireland presents two short seasons a year in November and April. Information is available from the website, as well as hotels and tourist information points in the city.

Times: Performance times vary. Check with the Box Office for individual performances.

Resident Groups: Opera Ireland

SEATING

Capacity: 1,200

Organization: There is a parterre section on the ground floor and two balconies.

Best Seats: The best seats are at the front of the first balcony.

FACILITIES

Services

Wheelchair access is available on the ground level. Contact the Gaiety Box Office to purchase tickets for this area.
Tel: +353 (0)1 677 1717.

HOW TO GET THERE

Bus: 11, 15A, 15B, 25X, 32X, 39X, 40A, 46N, 46X, 58X, 67X, 70X and 84X. A single journey costs between €0.95 and €1.90 depending on distance.

Underground: St Stephen's Green (Luas Green Line). A single journey costs €1.25.

Car Parking: There is a public car park in the nearby St Stephen's Green Centre.

> The Gaiety Theatre is situated at the top of Grafton Street, an important shopping street in Dublin full of bars and restaurants. Nearby Museums include the National Gallery and the Chester Beatty Library in Dublin Castle.

National Concert Hall

'Good music will never be as popular as it could and deserves to be until a proper Concert Hall is built in Dublin.' The words of the famous conductor Sir John Barbaroli, and a wish finally granted after forty years of delay when President Patrick Hillery opened the National Concert Hall on the 9 September 1981. This followed sixty years after independence when Ireland was without a single adequate musical venue. When University College Dublin moved from its grand nineteenth century premises in the city centre to a new campus, music lovers seized the opportunity to create a venue, and the Aula Max became the new auditorium of the National Concert Hall. Now the hall offers a full programme of visiting orchestras and soloists in addition to the National Symphony Orchestra's regular Friday night concerts.

> Earlsfort Terrace
> Dublin 2
> Ireland
> Tel: +353 (0)1 417 0077
> Fax: +353 (0)1 417 0078
> www.nch.ie

TICKETING

Advance Sales: Tickets can be purchased for all confirmed concerts.

Price Range: Tickets generally range from €9.00 to €90.00.

Concessions: Concessions available for many groups. Call the Box Office for details.

Box Office

The Box Office is open Monday to Saturday, 10.00 a.m.–7.00 p.m.
Tel: +353 (0)1 417 0000
Fax: +353 (0)1 475 1507
www.nch.ie

PERFORMANCES

Events take place throughout the year.

Times: A typical concert starts at 8.00 p.m., although performance times vary.

Resident Groups: The National Symphony Orchestra of Ireland

SEATING

Capacity: The main auditorium holds 1,200. The John Field Room is actually the bar, and not a completely satisfactory venue for a concert.

Organization: There is a large section of stalls on the ground floor, an upper balcony, side and choir balconies.

Best Seats: The best seats are located in the centre of the auditorium in the stalls.

Good Seats on a Budget: If available, the choir balcony seats are inexpensive with a good view of the conductor.

Seats to Avoid: All seats are comfortable with decent views.

EDUCATION

Guided Tours

For all visitors, both young and old, a trip round the beautiful Iveagh Gardens, just behind the National Concert Hall, one of Dublin's best kept secrets, followed by a tour of the National Concert Hall itself, learning about the history of this building that was built in 1865 for the Dublin Exhibition can be arranged for interested visitors. Contact for further details and booking information.
Tel: +353 (0)1 417 0077 or email: marketing@nch.ie

FACILITIES

Dining

The Terrace Café serves a range of food and refreshments, with special post-concert suppers available for visitors to enjoy after the performance, as well as a range of alcoholic and non-alcoholic beverages.
Tel: +353 (0)1 478 5005 for reservations.

Services

Some performances are sign-interpreted. Check with the Box Office.

Limited wheel chair spaces are available at the rear of the stalls in the main auditorium. Please contact the Box Office directly to reserve one of these seats.

HOW TO GET THERE

Bus: 10, 11, 13, 14, 14A, 15, 15A, 15B, 15C, 27C, 44, 46A, 46B, 48A and 86. A single journey costs between €0.95 and €1.90 depending on distance.

Underground: Harcourt (Luas Green Line). A single journey costs €1.25.

Car Parking: There is public car parking in the nearby St Stephen's Green centre. There is a small car park at the venue.

> The National Concert Hall is a short walk from St Stephen's Green, a beautiful park in the centre of Dublin.

WEXFORD

Theatre Royal

The Theatre Royal in Wexford became a major social and cultural focus during the nineteenth century with frequent performances and visits from touring companies from England. A regular feature was the Wexford Amateur Light Opera Society, which performed annually in the house. By 1942, the final private owner sold the building to a consortium, which converted it to a cinema. Despite numerous alterations, the stage was retained and the building continued to be used by amateur societies. The theatre was acquired by the local city council in the 1950s and gradual restoration began to take place with an appeal being launched and help provided by the Irish Tourist Board. A new foyer provided a more attractive entrance, extra rows of seats were cantilevered out over the back of the balcony, and many backstage improvements were undertaken. The next few years will see the building regenerated yet again, this time from scratch. Scheduled for completion in 2008, on its reopening it will resume its role as the home of Wexford Festival, which specializes in obscure and forgotten operas. With extra seating and brand new facilities, it is hoped that the theatre will be able to operate as a year round arts venue for additional Wexford Festival productions as well as visiting productions, building the foundations for what is hoped to be a solid future for opera and the arts in Wexford.

> Wexford Festival Opera
> 49 North Main Street
> Wexford
> Ireland
> Tel: +353 53 912 2400
> Fax: +353 (0)53 91 24289
> www.wexfordopera.com

TICKETING

Advance Sales: Tickets for the festival go on general sale in June.

Price Range: Tickets generally range from €15.00 to €75.00.

Concessions: There are generally no concessions available.

Box Office

> The Box Office is open Monday to Friday, 10.00 a.m.–5.00 p.m. All tickets are mailed in September.
> Tel: +353 (0)5391 22144
> Fax: +353 (0)5391 47438

PERFORMANCES

Events take place from October to November. The brochure is available from the festival website.

Times: Performance times vary, check with the Box Office for individual performances.

Resident Groups: Wexford Festival Opera

HOW TO GET THERE

Overground: Wexford Main Station is located 10 minutes from the venue.

ITALY

BOLOGNA

Teatro Comunale di Bologna

The Opera Temple hosts eighty shows per year, more than seventy concerts during the season and many international touring operatic performances, providing an unrivalled temple of high quality opera and dance. Located on the left-hand side of Piazza Verdi (the centre of the University campus), the Teatro Communale adjoins the magnificent Bentivoglio Palace. The list of famous artists who have graced the theatre includes composer Gioacchino Rossini and performers like Beniamino Gigli, Luciano Pavarotti, Renata Tebaldi and Mirella Freni.

TICKETING

Advance Sales: Tickets generally go on sale for the new season from November.

Largo Respighi 1
Bologna
I-40126
Italy
Tel: +39 (0)516 17 42 99
Fax: +39 (0)515 29 995
www.tcbo.it

Price Range: Tickets generally range from €5.00 to €120.00.

Concessions: The under-18s receive a two for one offer in 'Kids in the Opera' programme (selected concerts). People under 30 receive reductions on particular performances, usually matinees and Sundays. Also, senior citizens receive reductions on particular performances, usually matinees and Sundays.

Box Office

The Box Office is open Tuesday to Saturday, 11.00 a.m.– 6.30 p.m. and two hours prior to performances.
Tel: +39 (0)199 10 70 70
Fax: +39 (0)51 52 99 95
www.communalebologna.it

PERFORMANCES

Events take place from November to April.

Times: 9.00 p.m.

SEATING

Capacity: 900

Organization: The auditorium is arranged into stalls, boxes and a circle.

Best Seats: The best seats can be found in the platea stalls.

FACILITIES

Dining

The Teatro Comunale's Bar serves a variety of food and refreshments.

Services

Disabled access.

HOW TO GET THERE

Bus: 51

Underground: Bologna Station is 20 minutes away from the venue. A connecting bus line is recommended. Adult single, €1.00; day pass, €3.00; 'City Pass', valid for 8 journeys, €6.50.

FLORENCE

Teatro Comunale

Music has always had a fundamental role in the artistic life of Florence, where, at the end of the sixteenth century, the very first operas were performed, following the theory and practice of the Camerata dei Bardi. Today the Maggio Musicale Fiorentino, the centre of musical life in Florence, is based at Teatro Comunale, and produces the Maggio Musicale Festival – together with Bayreuth and Salzburg, the oldest, most important European music festival – as well as its annual concert, opera and ballet seasons. The Teatro Comunale originated in the Florentine Politeama, which was designed in 1862 by Telemaco Bonaiuti, an open arena over which the present structure was built. It seats 2,003 people and is made up of a large stall section, and two wide semi-circular galleries giving the impression of an amphitheatre. Near the main auditorium is the Piccolo Teatro, a small, modern

Corso Italia, 16
Florence
Italy
Tel: +39 (0)552 779 350
www.maggiofiorentino.com

theatre seating approximately 600 spectators. Partially destroyed twice, in the bombing of 1944 and in the flood of 1966, the Comunale was quickly rebuilt, symbolizing the determination of the citizens to re-emerge and demonstrate their loyalty to the city.

TICKETING

Price Range: Tickets generally range from €5.00 to €150.00.

Box Office

Tuesday to Friday, 10.00 a.m.–4.30 p.m. On Saturdays, 10.00 a.m.–1.00 p.m.
Tel: +39 (0)55 213 535
Fax: +39 (0)55 287 222
www.maggiofiorentino.com

PERFORMANCES

Times: 8.30 p.m.

Annual Festivals/Special Events: The Maggio Musicale Festival

SEATING

Capacity: 2,000

FACILITIES

Dining

Although there are no restaurants or specific dining areas on-site, the area has ample restaurants where visitors can dine at their leisure.

Services

Disabled access.

MILAN

La Scala

Italy's greatest opera house, Milan's Il Teatro alla Scala (or simply La Scala) reopened on 7 December 2004 and is once again the cultural highlight of Milan. It now boasts a fully-restored, dazzling auditorium and a brand new technologically advanced stage to match its enchanting atmosphere. Designed by Piermarini, the theatre was built between 1776 and 1778 under the patronage of Maria Theresa, Empress of Austria when much of the northern Italy was ruled by the Habsburg dynasty. During the course of the nineteenth century, however, La Scala became a symbol of the Risorgimento, the struggle for Italian unification, largely through its link with the life of the great composer Giuseppe Verdi. His stirring arias, often not-so-veiled references to yearnings of the oppressed, became patriotic calls-to-arms. The theatre's civic significance was crowned in 1872, when it became the property of the City of Milan. La Scala is one of the meeting points for Milan's elite. Seats are coveted internationally; obtaining them is not always easy, and certainly never cheap, but for those who can afford it, are worth every penny.

> Piazza del Duomo
> Galleria del Sagrato
> Milan
> MM1 Duomo
> Italy
> Tel: +39 (0)288 791
> Fax: +39 (0)288 794 24 or
> +39 (0)288 793 31
> www.teatroallascala.org

TICKETING

Advance Sales: Tickets can be purchased up to three months in advance, but this varies according to the performance.

Price Range: Tickets generally range from €40.00 to €500.00.

Concessions: There is a 5% discount available for under-18s and senior citizens. New to this season is the 'Domenica alla Scala' (Sunday at La Scala) initiative, a series of four concerts on Sunday afternoons, with free admission for any child accompanied by an adult.

Box Office

The Box Office is open daily, noon–6.00 p.m. Also open two hours before and until 15 minutes after the start of the performance. Closed for the Summer Holiday between 29 July to 28 August and on the following days: New Year's Day, 1 November, 8 December, Christmas Eve, Christmas Day and Boxing Day.
Tel: +39 (0)272 003 744
Lines are open daily, 9.00 a.m.–6.00 p.m. (8.00 p.m. with evening performances).

PERFORMANCES

Times: All performances must finish before midnight, therefore long operas start accordingly in the afternoon. See the website for specific times.

Resident Groups: La Scala Philharmonic

Annual Festivals/Special Events: La Scala Philharmonic Season.

SEATING

Capacity: 2,800

Organization: The auditorium is arranged into the main floor, four levels of boxes and two galleries above this.

Seats to Avoid: The cheap seats in the galleries often have poor sightlines to the stage.

FACILITIES

Dining

There is a restaurant located on-site which serves a variety of food, refreshments and light snacks.

Services

Disabled access.

HOW TO GET THERE

Underground: Metro lines 1 and 3 to Duomo. More transportation info. can be found on the website; overground, car parking, and buses included at http://www.teatroallascala.org/en/comeraggiungerci/teatroscala.html

NAPLES

Teatro di San Carlo

Built to replace the dilapidated Teatro San Bartolomeo, Teatro di San Carlo stands today as the oldest active opera house in Europe and is recognized as a UNESCO World Heritage site. To endow Naples with a new and larger theatre, Carlo III of Naples decided to build a new venue for patrons to enjoy. The venue was inaugurated on 4 November 1737 with a performance of Domenico Sarro's 'Achille in Sciro', a grand show in what was then the largest theatre in Europe. As was the misfortune of many theatres of the time, the building was largely destroyed by a fire in 1816, but was regenerated within ten months on the order of King Ferdinand IV. 1845 saw an additional refurbishment, with the sumptuous blue and gold Bourbon interior replaced by now-traditional red and gold

Via San Carlo
98/F
Napoli
I–80132
Italy
Tel: +39 (0)817 972 331
Fax: +39 (0)81 40 09 02
www.teatrosancarlo.it

designs. An orchestra pit designed by Verdi was accompanied by the installation of electricity in 1890. The theatre has remained largely unchanged since this time, as even World War II was unable to stop its activities. Damaged by bombing, the venue was quickly repaired, reopening within six months of the damage, ready to continue the traditions which have made this venue a permanent and enduring source of culture and refinement in Naples.

TICKETING

Advance Sales: Tickets are released three months in advance.

Price Range: Tickets generally range from €40.00 to €180.00.

Concessions: A young person's (under 30) complete season subscription costs €80.00. In addition, last minute tickets are available to the under-30s for prices as low as €15.00, available from an hour before performance.

Box Office

The Box Office is open Tuesday to Saturday, 10.00 a.m.– 6.30 p.m. and one hour before every performance.
Tel: + 39 (0)817 972 331 or +39 (0)817 972 412
Fax: +39 (0)814 009 02
http://sell.charta.it It is also possible to book by emailing at biglietteria@teatrosancarlo.it with credit card details.

PERFORMANCES

Times: 5.00 p.m., 6.00 p.m. and 8.30 p.m.

Resident Groups: The Orchestra of the San Carlo Theatre

EDUCATION

Guided Tours

Guided tours of the venue are conducted daily at 9.00 a.m. and 7.00 p.m. in various languages. Tel: +39 (0)816 645 45 or email: teatrosancarlo@itineranapoli.com for further information.

PALERMO

Teatro Massimo

In 1864, an international competition for construction of the opera house was announced by the Palermo Council, primarily at the initiative of Mayor, Antonio Starrabba di Rudinì. For many years there had been plans to build a big new theatre in Palermo, worthy of the second biggest city in southern Italy after Naples, that would be designed to promote the image of the city following the recent national unity. The Teatro Massimo is the largest theatre in Italy (and the third largest opera house in Europe). Its architect, Giovanni Battista Filippo Basile, was inspired by ancient and classical Sicilian architecture and, thus designed, the exterior in the high Neo-Classical style incorporating elements of the Greek temples at Selinute and Agrigento. Realized in the late-Renaissance style, the auditorium

Piazza G. Verdi
Palermo
I–90138
Italy
Tel: +39 (0)916 053 111
www.teatromassimo.it

was planned for 3,000 people, but, in its current format, it seats 1,350, with seven tiers of boxes rising up around an inclined stage. The foyer presents a majestic frieze over the entrance, enormous candelabra, elegant decorative pillar strips, and a commemorative bust of Giovanni Battista Filippo Basile, a work by Antonio Ugo. Above the foyer, on the piano nobile, vestibules and corridors open on to the Royal Box. The auditorium measures 19.75 metres by 26.50 metres and is horse shoe-shaped, like the operas in Paris, the operas in Vienna, and the Carlo Felice Opera House in Genoa.

TICKETING

Price Range: Tickets generally range from €10.00 to €100.00.

Concessions: Concessions are available for young people up to 28 years. All concessions are restricted to audiences attending performances B, C, D, E and F. Disabled visitors qualify for tickets priced at Section 4 (roughly 50% of max price).

Box Office

The Box Office is open Tuesday to Sunday, 10.00 a.m.–3.00 p.m. On performance days, the Box Office opens at 7.00 p.m. (two hours before the performance commences).
Tel: +39 (0)648 078 400
Lines are open Monday to Sunday, 10.00 a.m.–5.00 p.m.
Fax: +39 (0)913 229 49
www.leonidaniele.it
Full price tickets only.

PERFORMANCES

Performances take place all year round, with a break in August.

Times: 9.00 p.m.

SEATING

Capacity: 1,350

Organization: The auditorium is arranged into stalls and surrounding balcony circles. There are ten price bands, not all of which are used for each show.

EDUCATION

Guided Tours

Guided tours of the venue take place from Tuesday to Sunday. The tour lasts about 25 minutes and is available in different languages. Tel: +39 (0)916 090 831 or see the website, www.teatromassimo.it/servizi for further information.

Times: 10.00 a.m.–3.00 p.m. (the last tour leaves at 2.30 p.m.). Tours last approximately 25 minutes.

Cost: €5.00

Concessions: €3.00 (under 18, and over 65, groups of at least 25 persons) Free admission for children under the age of 6.

FACILITIES

Dining

There is a cafeteria located inside the bookshop, opening hours of which are: Tuesday to Sunday, 10.00 a.m.–3.00 p.m. During performances the cafeteria service operates in the space on the ground floor under the foyer, and there is also a buffet service in the corridors of the fourth level.

Services

Guide dogs welcome.

There are eight seats in Section 1 reserved to wheelchair users at the price of Section 4. Tickets must be purchased at least five days before the performance.

HOW TO GET THERE

Bus: 101, 106, 107, 614, 615, 645 and 837. Single ticket €1.00. Day ticket €3.50.

Car Parking: Car parking is available at Piazza G Verdi, Piazza Spinuzza and Piazzale Ungheria.

PARMA

Teatro Regio

The Teatro Regio has become one of the most famous opera theatres in the world. Built between 1821 and 1929 for

Via Garibaldi
16/A
Parma
I–43100
Italy
Tel: +39 (0) 521 039 399
Fax: +39 (0) 521 504 224
www.teatroregioparma.org

Maria Luigia, the second wife of Napoleon Bonaparte and later, Duchess of Parma, it was inaugurated on 16 May 1829 with a performance of 'Zaira', by Vincenzo Bellini. The building encompasses a splendid Neo-Classical façade with a portico and a double row of windows, with the Neo-Classical atrium leading into the elliptic stalls surrounded by four orders of stages and by the gallery. Today, the theatre maintains a close affinity to the conductor Arturo Toscanini, who was born in Parma and in particular Giuseppe Verdi, who was also born in Parma, and lived nearby the venue. Its annual 'Festival Verdi' celebrates the famous Italian Romantic composer through a series of concerts, tours, conventions and readings of the works which have inspired artists and composers worldwide.

TICKETING

Advance Sales: Tickets for the current season generally go on sale from late November. Online sales generally commence the day after tickets are released for sale at the Box Office.

Price Range: Tickets generally range from €8.00 to €100.00.

Concessions: Concessions are available, but vary according to the performance. Ask at the Box Office for further details.

Box Office

The Box Office is open Tuesday to Friday, 10.00 a.m.–2.00 p.m. and 5.00 p.m.–7.00 p.m.; Saturday, 10.00 a.m.–1.00 p.m. and 4.00 p.m. 7.00 p.m. The theatre is normally closed on Sundays and Mondays. However, on days where there are performances falling on these dates, opening hours are as follows: Sunday, 10.00 a.m.–noon and 2.00 p.m.–6.00 p.m.; Monday, 10.00 a.m.–noon and 5.00 p.m.–8.30 p.m. For online bookings, the ticket price includes a 12% commission charge.
www.leonidaniele.it

PERFORMANCES

Events take place from December to April.

Annual Festivals/Special Events: Festival Verdi takes place each October, celebrating the life and works of the composer.

FACILITIES

Services

There is space in row P of the stalls for two wheelchairs and accompanying companions.

ROME

Auditorio dell'Accademia di Santa Cecilia

Regarded historically as the one of the most ancient and significant musical conservatories in the world, the Academy of Santa Cecilia has transformed itself from a local society of musicians to an internationally renowned centre for musical excellence, with an impressive amphitheatre to match. Founded in 1585 by Sisto V, it was originally a centre for ecclesiastical music, subsequently forming an important site for the working composers of Papal Rome. The centre developed into a conservatory for students of music and still has links to schools and educational agencies all over Rome. Since the 1990s, the academy has established an official academic body constituting of 100 members, seventy of whom actively form the Sinfonici Orchestra and chorus, which has achieved global fame,

Luciano Berio n. 3
Rome
I–00196
Italy
Tel: +39 (0)680 242 501
www.santacecilia.it

with over 100 concerts performed worldwide. The academy now plans to further expand its didactic potential by transforming one section into an instrument museum.

TICKETING

Advance Sales: Tickets for the entire season are generally released each January.

Price Range: Ticket price ranges depend on individual performances.

Box Office

The Box Office is open daily, 11.00 a.m.–8.00 p.m. For remote bookings, 10% of the ticket price is added to the purchase as a service charge. Tel: +39 (0)637 001 06
http://biglietteria.listicket.it
Users are required to register on the website to purchase tickets.

PERFORMANCES

Times: Evening performances generally start either at 6.00 p.m., 7.30 p.m. or 9.00 p.m. Matinee performances generally commence at noon.

SEATING

Capacity: 2,800

Organization: The Santa Cecilia Hall is arranged into terraces, which surround the stage.

Auditorium Parco della Musica

The new home of the Orchestra di Santa Cecilia, the Auditorium Parco della Musica is the biggest concert facility in Europe, hosting regular classical, pop, world music and a variety of exhibitions. Designed by the famous Renzo Piano, the Auditorium's construction began in September 1995, with each of the three different halls constructed with the aim of satisfying the needs of any music genre. The Santa Cecilia Hall can be used for large orchestral and choral symphonic concerts. The Sinopoli Hall, because of its greater acoustic flexibility, is more apt for a great variety of musical genres. This is also because its orchestra position can be modified with respect to the audience. Finally, the Petrassi Hall has been assigned to contemporary musical genres, theatre performances and cinema, equipped with an inbuilt system which allows both the musical source and the audience to be shifted and the sound reverberation tuned. This eclectic range of flexible facilities, added to the diverse range of performances on offer, all contribute to the many reasons why Auditorium Parco della Musica is a popular choice for visitors and opera-lovers alike.

TICKETING

Advance Sales: Tickets are released three months in advance.

Price Range: Tickets generally range from €10.00 to €35.00.

Concessions: Some concerts give 20% off for under-16s and over-60s. However, these special rates are not available for online purchase.

Viale Pietro de Coubertin 30
Rome
I–00196
Italy
Tel: +39 (0)680 241 1
Fax: +39 (0)680 241 211
www.auditorium.com

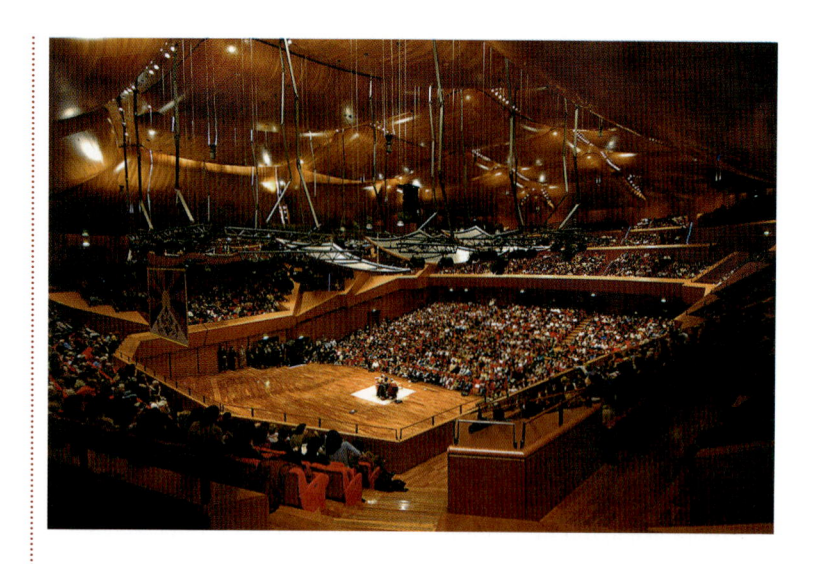

Box Office

The Box Office is open daily, except Wednesday, 11.00 a.m.–6.00 p.m. On concert nights, the Box Office opens from 8.00 p.m. and when there is a Sunday morning concert, the Box Office opens one hour prior to performance start time. Tel: +39 (0)199 109 783. Those wishing to book tickets from abroad should call the overseas booking line on +39 (0)637 001 06
www.auditorium.com

PERFORMANCES

Times: 9.00 p.m.

Resident Groups: Orchestra of the Academy Santa Cecilia

Annual Festivals/Special Events: Symphonic Season, Chamber Season, and Summer Season

SEATING

Capacity: The auditorium Parco della Musica has three halls, The Santa Cecilia Hall, the Sinopoli Hall and the Petrassi Hall, seating 2,742, 1,133 and 673 people respectively.

EDUCATION

Guided Tours

The Auditorium Parco della Musica provides its visitors with

a guided tour of many aspects of the venue, providing them with a full understanding of the history, the architecture, the cultural and urban value of Renzo Piano's great auditorium. Visitors are led through a fascinating itinerary explaining the architectural, structural and acoustical characteristics of the premises. All regular tours are in Italian. Tours in other languages (English, German, French and Spanish) should be arranged with the venue in advance. Regular tours take place during weekends and holidays every hour from 10.30 a.m.–4.30 p.m. Tours during the week should be booked in advance (minimum ten people required).
Tel: +39 (0)680 241 281 or email: visiteguidate@musicaperroma.it for further information or to book a tour.

Cost: €9.00

Concessions: Over-65s and groups, €7.00; Under 26, students and organized school parties, €5.00.

FACILITIES

Dining

ReD is an original restaurant with an exclusive design where visitors can enjoy a mix of traditional and contemporary dishes. The restaurant is open every day from noon until late, serving apertifs daily from 6.30 p.m.–9.00 p.m. and brunch on Sundays from 12.45 p.m.–3.00 p.m. Tel: +39 (0)6 8069 1630 for further information and reservations. In addition BArt is open daily and offers a range of cocktails, infusions and various types of tea in a modern and plain ambience.

HOW TO GET THERE

Bus: 53, 217, 231 and 910

Underground: Metro line A to Flaminio; then connect with a tram or train to Piazza Euclide. Single biglietto semplice (B.I.T.) costs €1.00. Day ticket (B.I.G.) costs €4.00.

Car Parking: There are large car parking facilities, 700 spaces, by the auditorium Parco della Musica with designated areas for disabled visitors.

Teatro dell'Opera

Since its foundation in the nineteenth century, Teatro dell'Opera has continued to stage magnificent productions, many of which have been truly historical. In fact, the first performance of Puccini's 'Tosca' took place as part of Teatro dell'Opera's 1899–1900 season. As the primary venue for opera, ballet and symphonic music seasons, Teatro dell'Opera attracts some of the most renowned musical talent in the world. The venue was originally known as the Teatro Costanzi after the contractor who built it, Domenico Costanzi, who in turn commissioned the Milanese architect Achille Sfondrini, a specialist in the building and renovation of theatres to construct the site. Designing the theatre, Sfondrini paid particular attention to the acoustics, conceiving the interior structure as a 'resonance chamber', as is evident from the horseshoe shape in particular. In November 1926 the Costanzi was bought by Rome city council and its name was changed to Teatro Reale dell'Opera. Following the end of the monarchy, the name of the opera house was changed again to Teatro dell'Opera, and in 1958, the building was remodeled and modernized by the Rome city council. The theatre's legendary acoustics can still bear comparison with any other auditorium in the world and has hosted through its long history stunning performances such as Giacomo Puccini's 'Turandot', Mozart's 'Le Nozze di Figaro' and Verdi's 'Don Carlos'.

TICKETING

Advance Sales: Tickets are released three months in advance.

Price Range: Tickets generally range from €20.00 to €130.00.

Concessions: During the Winter Season, under-25s and senior citizens are entitled to a 50% discount. During the Summer Season this is 20%.

Piazza Beniamino Gigli 1
Rome
I–00184
Italy
www.operaroma.it

Box Office

The Box Office is open
Monday, 9.00 a.m.–1.00 p.m.;
Tuesday to Saturday,
10.00 a.m.–4.00 p.m.
Tel: +39 (0)648 160 255
Fax: +39 (0)648 817 55
www.helloticket.it;
www.vivaticket.it and
www.charta.it

PERFORMANCES

Times: Weekend performances generally commence earlier, at 5.00 p.m. or 6.00 p.m., otherwise 9.00 p.m.

SEATING

Capacity: 1,600

Organization: The auditorium is arranged into stalls, private boxes, a balcony and gallery.

Best Seats: The best seats are located in the stalls.

Good Seats on a Budget: Top level gallery and balcony.

Seats to Avoid: Seats in the boxes are unnumbered, therefore late arrivals cannot be guaranteed a good seat. Some box seats may only have a three-fourth view of the stage.

FACILITIES

Dining

There are several theatre bars located on-site, serving a range of snacks and refreshments to be enjoyed before the performance or during he interval.

Services

The stalls of the Teatro dell'Opera are equipped with an Oticon system to enhance listening for people wearing hearing aids.

HOW TO GET THERE

Bus: 60, 64, 70, 71, 170, 116T, 16, 75, 84, 150, 360, 590, 649 and 714

Underground: Line M-A, Republic Teatro Opera. Single biglietto semplice (B.I.T.) €1.00. Day ticket (B.I.G.) €4.00.

Villa Medici

The Villa Medici is the home of the French Academy in Rome, an educational organization run for the winners of an arts scholarship. A villa in the Borghese gardens in Rome, it was founded by Ferdinando I de' Medici, Grand Duke of Tuscany in the sixteenth century. When the Medici name became extinct in 1737, the villa passed to the house of Lorraine and, briefly in Napoleonic times, to the Kingdom of Etruria. During this time, Napoleon Bonaparte came into possession of the Villa Medici, which he subsequently transferred to the French Academy at Rome. Since then it has housed the winners of the prestigious Prix de Rome, under distinguished directors like Ingres and Balthus. The building itself has a somewhat austere façade contrasting with elaborate rococo decoration inside, modelled on La Scala including many antique sculptures. The beautiful gardens are an attraction in themselves but unfortunately public access is limited and the Villa Medici is largely open only to theatre patrons.

Viale Trinità dei Monti 1
Rome
I–00187
Italy
Tel: +39 (0)667 61 1
Fax: +39 (0)667 61 278
www.villamedici.it

TICKETING

Concessions: Discounts are available for children, students and senior citizens and is generally 30% off the ticket price.

SEATING

Organization: There is only one type of seat in the auditorium.

EDUCATION

Guided Tours

Tours of the venue are provided on Saturdays and Sundays.

Times: 10.00 a.m. and 11.15 a.m.

Cost: €7.00

Concessions: €5.00

FACILITIES

Dining

There is a café located on the main floor.

Services

Guide dogs welcome.

TURIN

Teatro Regio

The idea to build the Teatro Regio of Torino was first conceived in 1713. Many years passed before a plan for a new theatre came to fruition. On 26 December 1749, the theatre officially opened with the premier of Francesco Feo's 'Arcase'. Teatro Regio boasts the premieres of hundreds of important works, including Giacomo Puccini's 'La Boheme' and Richard Strauss' 'Salome'. Although it is widely thought that the ballet 'Giselle' was first danced on the La Scala stage, it actually premiered at Teatro Regio in 1842. The flourishing theatre became a mecca for works composed by Wagner and Strauss and showed its progressive attitude by being one of the first theatres to perform new French Opera. In February 1939 a devastating fire consumed the theatre's stage and hall and later, World War II

Piazza Castello 215
Torino
I–10124
Italy
Tel: +39 (0)118 815 557
Fax: +39 (0)118 815 214
www.teatroregio.torino.it

bombings claimed the remainder of the building. The Teatro Regio that currently stands was rebuilt on the same ground and opened in 1973. Today, a quarter of a millennium from its foundation, the Teatro Regio continues to be a witness to the rich history and musical excellence of Turin and Italy.

TICKETING

Price Range: Tickets generally range from €20.00 to €170.00.

Concessions: Visitors up to 25 years old receive a 30% reduction on the ticket price. Families with children under 16 receive 10% off adult ticket. In addition, senior citizens and disabled visitors also qualify for a 10% reduction. Disabled carers receive a free ticket when accompanying a wheelchair user.

Box Office

The Box Office is open Tuesday to Friday, 10.30 a.m.–6.00 p.m.; Saturday, 10.30 a.m.–4.00 p.m., and an hour before performances.
Tel: +39 (0)118 815 241/242
Fax: +39 (0)118 815 601

PERFORMANCES

Events take place from October to July.

Times: 9.00 p.m.

SEATING

Capacity: 1,592

FACILITIES

Dining

There are a number of restaurant and café facilities in close proximity to the theatre.

Services

Guide dogs welcome.

There are four special spaces designed to accommodate wheelchairs.

Turin's tourist attractions include the Mole Antonelliana, a strange, spire-topped building which features on the Italian 2 euro-cent coin. Within the building is an excellent museum of cinema. Other Turin museums include the wondrous Egyptian Museum.

VENICE

Gran Teatro La Fenice

With an aim to be the 'most satisfying to the eye and ear of the audience', the Gran Teatro La Fenice was to be the brainchild of the winner of a 1789 competition to design a new theatre in the heart of Venice. It was a typically Italian choice, with winner Gian Antonio Selva recreating within the building the conditions of an Italian piazza, a natural amphitheatre where people could be both at home and in the open. The closed-box system had its disadvantages, but was justified by the fact that the public of the day would never have agreed to forego the comforts of the separate loggias, which made each box a miniature home. Sadly, in 1996 the building was destroyed in a malicious fire. It was rebuilt and reopened in 2003 to a week

Fondazione Teatro La Fenice di Venezia
1965
Venice
I–30124
Italy
Tel: +39 (0)41 24 24
www.teatrolafenice.it

of musical events in the new Fenice including Richard Wagner's 'Three Symphonic Marches', securing the Fenice's return to the heart of Venetian culture.

TICKETING

Price Range: Tickets generally range from €10.00 to €180.00.

Box Office

> The Box Office is open daily, 10.00 a.m.–6.00 p.m., and from an hour before performances. Transaction charges for remote bookings vary.
> Tel: +39 (0)41 24 24
> Fax: +39 (0)41 24 18 028

SEATING

Organization: The auditorium is arranged into stalls, central boxes, side boxes, circle and the section known as 'the Gods'.

Best Seats: Orchestra stall seats, and front-of-the-box seats.

Good Seats on a Budget: Midweek tickets are considerably cheaper than weekend tickets.

Seats to Avoid: Seats are marked and priced according to quality of view, so visitors can buy specific 'listening only' seats or 'restricted view' seats.

EDUCATION

Guided Tours

The Gran Teatro La Fenice invites its visitors to explore the theatre in a variety of ways. Visitors can pick up an audio-guide, which takes them among the plasters and the golds of the prestigious halls, allowing them to discover the grounds and the unknown secrets of the Theatre. Tours last 45 minutes, and are available in Italian, English, German, French and Spanish. The audio-guides can be rented from the Ticket Office. In addition, the venue offers tours for larger groups or small parties, providing a more personal experience, and can even be accompanied with a cocktail.
Tel: +39 (0)41 24 24 or:
+39 (0)41 528 37 80 or
email: marketing@velaspa.com or info@festfenice.com for the 'Promenade in the Theatre' cocktail tour.

Cost: Prices are available on request, and depend on tour requirements.

FACILITIES

Dining

Visitors are invited to cocktails and a buffet in the theatre's Apollinee Rooms during the interval or after performances, where they can obtain a variety of food and refreshments. For further information and packages available go to www.festfenice.com.

HOW TO GET THERE

Bus: Waterbus Line 1, Main train station and Piazzale Roma. A single day Vaporetto (water bus) ticket costs €5.00. Day tickets can also be bought for €12.00. Land bus single tickets cost €1.00.

Car Parking: Garage San Marco S.p.A. Piazzale Roma costs €17.00 for a maximum stay of 12 hours. Upon reservation and if spaces remain, a discount can be requested by telephoning: +39 (0)41 52 32 21.

> Apart from the famous canals, Venice is one of the world's greatest cities to wander around, allowing yourself to become lost in the labyrinthine walkways. Many walking and canal tours are available, ranging in price from €20–€50, most of which depart from St. Mark's Square.

VERONA

Arena di Verona

The famous outdoor Arena in Verona was originally built around 30 BC, at the time accommodating up to 30,000 people. However, it was not until the summer of 1913 that the Arena di Verona was conceived, helped by great natural acoustics. To celebrate the centenary of the birth of Giuseppe Verdi, a magnificent lyrical festival was planned in his honour, led by the tenor Giovanni Zenatello and the theatre impresario Ottone Rovato. With the staging of Aida, the Arena di Verona became the biggest open-air lyrical theatre in the world, a supremacy that it still holds today. Since then, the seventy-nine seasons that can be counted from the summer of 1913, has seen the venue undergo numerous transformations. Today, the venue attracts a diverse range of visitors, from the most passionate lovers of lyrical music to curious tourists looking to explore, the Arena creates a unique meeting point for these two types of visitors, combining the quality of the music and vocal interpretation with the magnificence and splendour of such a historic site.

Fondazione Arena di Verona
Piazza Bra 28
Verona
I–37121
Italy
Tel: +39 (0)45 800 51 51
www.arena.it

TICKETING

Price Range: Tickets generally range from €20.00 to €160.00.

Concessions: Under-26s, over-60s, disabled visitors and carers qualify for reduced prices.

Box Office

The Box Office is open Monday to Friday, 9.00 a.m.–noon, and 3.15 p.m.–5.45 p.m.; Saturday, 9.00 a.m.–noon. On performance days, (including Sundays) 10.00 a.m.–9.00 p.m. Please note that reduced tickets and Theatre Philharmonic tickets cannot be bought online.
Tel: +39 (0)45 800 51 51
www.arena.it

PERFORMANCES

Events take place from June to September.

SEATING

Organization: The auditorium is arranged into stalls, together with special reserved and unreserved seats on the stone steps.

Best Seats: The first sector in the stalls provides the best seating for visitors.

Good Seats on a Budget: The unreserved steps, 'Gradiata' provide good value for money, particularly on a Sunday.

Seats to Avoid: All have good views.

FACILITIES

Dining

Various restaurants remain open around Pizza Bra and in the streets around the ampitheatre and in the surrounding area of Piazza delle Erbe, until the early hours of the morning.

Services

Wheelchair accessible seats are located in the stalls. Companions may be seated next to wheelchair.

HOW TO GET THERE

Bus: 11, 12, 13, 14, 72 and 73. Single ticket from €1.00. Day ticket from €3.50 for AMT services.

Overground: The main railway station is Verona Porta Nuova, which is the crossroads of both the Milan-Venice line and the Brennero-Rome line. From here take the bus routes to Piazza Bra.

LATVIA

RIGA

Great Guild Hall

'Do not say what people like to hear, But that, which expresses goodness.' A translation of the Latin inscription which can be found above a sculpture in the Fireplace Hall of Riga's Great Guild Hall, which stands today as one of the oldest and most unique buildings in the Latvian capital. Located adjacent to what used to be a Franciscan monastery in the thirteenth century, the Great Guild Hall is seeped in rich history with the Münster Hall, built in 1330 and still located in the building even today holding the title of being the oldest section of a public building in the Baltic States. Despite numerous reconstructions of the building, the Hall has been well preserved, with its Gothic cross arches, central stone pillars, and musicians' balcony surviving the centuries largely intact. During the nineteenth century, plans were introduced to build a new hall above the old halls, which would occupy the entire top floor. In 1936 the Great Hall with its splendid woodwork interior was adapted for the needs of a Congress Hall. Unfortunately it was ruined by fire in 1963. It was rebuilt soon after as a concert hall in accordance with the project by architect M Gelzis. Today, this purpose continues, elevating the Great Guild as the primary venue for the Latvian National Symphony Orchestra, which gives regular performances both at the Guild and at various venues around Europe.

Livu Square
5 Amatu Street
Old Riga
Riga
Latvia
Tel: +371 (0)721 3643

TICKETING

Price Range: Tickets generally range from LVL 3.00 to LVL 15.00.

Box Office

The Box Office is open daily, noon–7.00 p.m.
Tel: +371 (0) 721 3643

PERFORMANCES

Times: Evening performances take place at 7.00 p.m. Matinee performances are at noon and 3.00 p.m.

Resident Groups: The Latvian National Symphony Orchestra

SEATING

Organization: The Hall is arranged into stalls and has an upstairs gallery.

Seats to Avoid: All seats have good views of the stage.

FACILTIES

Dining

There is a café in the Guild Hall, serving a selection of food and light refreshments.

> Another noteworthy stained glass composition is in the annexed entrance hall on the second floor, which is called the Stained Glass Hall. In 1936 Ansis Cirulis created four scenes in these stained glass windows that depict important activities in Riga.

Opera House

Centrally located and culturally significant, the Latvian National Opera House was built as part of the city centre's reconstruction programme. Space was created for the venues by the architects Otto Dietze and Johann Daniel Felsko, with the 1860 design by architecture professor Ludwig Bohnstedt gaining universal approval for the venue's execution. The House was built on the former bastion of the city's fortifications and opened in 1863. Unfortunately, Riga's Great Fire of 1882 destroyed much of the theatre building, which was left badly in need of major reconstruction. This was completed in 1887, with additional refurbishments conducted throughout the next century. The latest major change was completed in 1995, which saw the venue reopen after five years of closure. Equipped with new facilities, a modernized stage and a restored interior, today the venue hosts a wide range of performances, including the debut

> Aspazijas Bulvaris 3
> Riga
> LV-1050
> Latvia
> Tel: +371 (0)707 3777
> Fax: +371 (0)722 8930
> www.opera.lv

of approximately six new productions of opera and ballet every year. In addition, since 2005, the LNO has featured a series of special summer performances so visitors to Riga can share the experiences that the inhabitants have grown accustomed to throughout the year.

TICKETING

Price Range: Tickets generally range from LVL 3.00 to LVL 30.00.

Concessions: Children of pre-school age may attend matinees for free and evening performances provided they do not need a seat. Variable discounts are available to disabled visitors.

Box Office

> The Box Office is open daily, 10.00 a.m.–7.00 p.m.
> Tel: +371 (0)70 73745 or +371 (0)70 73776
> Fax: +371 (0)70 73782
> www.bilesuparadize.lv

PERFORMANCES

Events take place from September to May.

Times: Evening performances generally commence at 7.00 p.m., Sunday matiness generally begin at 3.00 p.m., although this can vary.

Programmes: Detailed information in English is available on the website for many of the venue's performances.

Annual Festivals/Special Events: The Riga Opera Festival takes place each June.

SEATING

Capacity: 967

Organization: The auditorium is arranged into stalls, a parterre section, a dress circle, and two balconies.

Good Seats on a Budget: Standing room tickets are the cheapest visitors can buy.

Seats to Avoid: Certain seats in the auditorium have only a partial view of the stage.

EDUCATION

Guided Tours

The LNO invites groups of ten or more to explore the home of the Latvian National Opera and learn many secrets about the building's history and everyday life. Contact the tours department

for further booking information.
Tel: +371 (0)70 73820

Cost: LVL 3.00.

Concessions: LVL 1.50.

FACILITIES

Dining

The Café Opera serves a selection of food, refreshments and a special buffet supper, allowing visitors to sample a range of food before enjoying the performance. Tel: +371 (0)72 11236 for further information and reservations.

Services

Wheelchair access and assistance is available by notifying the venue in advance.

HOW TO GET THERE

Bus: 1, 32, Inzenieru Street; Trolley-bus 3, 15, Inzenieru Street or Central Station. Single journeys cost LVL 0.20 and can be bought on board.

Overground: Trams 5, 7, 9 to National Opera; 6, 11, 14 to the Central Station; 2, 4, 10 to Janvara Street.

Car Parking: The parking lot next to the Opera House, owned by the Municipality of Riga, can be used at the leisure of the venue's guests. On weekdays from 8.00 a.m. until 6.00 p.m. the charge is LVL 1.00 per hour, at other times, on weekends and holidays, it may be used free of charge.

Should visitors wish to give flowers to any of the performers, they are asked to leave them with the ushers on the left-hand side of the stalls, indicating the recipient. At the end of the performance flowers are presented on stage.

Riga Cathedral

A grand design for a modest purpose, the Riga Cathedral in Latvia towers over the Doma Laukums ('Dome Square') in the Old Town, and was consecrated in 1211 by Bishop Albert of Riga who played an important role in the Christianization of Latvia. Initially constructed in the Romanesque style, the Cathedral was modified and expanded over time, incorporating Gothic and Baroque details. The interior was altered in the seventeenth century with the adoption of Lutheran liturgical practices, however the original layout with central nave and side aisles survives. The fourteenth century stone pillars separating the nave and side aisles are decorated with carved coats of arms, with free admission for the public during the day to view the famous architecture. The Riga Doms specializes in performances of sacred choral music, by both Latvian composers and famous European greats, and organ music. The Riga Cathedral organ was installed in 1884, boasting over 6,000 pipes and remaining a wonder in itself, with pianist and composer Franz Liszt writing a dedication to the instrument.

> Riga Doms
> Doma laukums 1
> Riga
> LV-1050
> Latvia
> Tel: +371 (0)721 3498 or:
> +371 (0)722 7573 or:
> +371 (0)721 3213.
> www.doms.lv (no English)

Although the Cathedral may not be the most archetypal classical music venue for visitors, it remains a place where sacred music can be heard amongst traditional ethos, without any of the pretensions associated with some of the more elaborate venues.

TICKETING

Price Range: Tickets generally range from LVL 1.00 to LVL 3.00.

Box Office

The Box Office is open daily, noon–3.00 p.m. and 4.00 p.m.–7.00 p.m., the Riga Dom also opens 30 minutes before concerts.
Tel: +371 (0)72 10817

PERFORMANCES

Times: 7.00 p.m.

Annual Festivals/Special Events: The International Sacred Music Festival takes place each Summer.

HOW TO GET THERE

Bus: Bus lines 21, 22 or 32; Trolley-bus 3, 13, 15 or 18; Tram routes 3, 6, 7, 8, 10 or 13. Single journeys cost LVL 0.20 and can be bought on board.

LIECHTENSTEIN

BALZERS

Operette Balzers

Keeping in line with a long tradition, Operette Balzers, together with its sister venue, Operettenbühne Vaduz, have staged top-quality performances since the 1940s. The venue was established as the home of a singing group in 1913, although the parish concert hall was not built until the 1920s. A new building was erected in 1961, with both venues today attracting over ten thousand visitors every year. Unwilling to restrict itself to opera, the Hall puts on a wide range of performances, hosting concert music and other staged works, creating a diverse atmosphere which provides musical delights not just for opera lovers.

Gatter 12
Balzers
FL-9496
Liechtenstein
Tel: +423 (0)384 38 38
Fax: +423 (0)384 38 39
www.operette-balzers.li

TICKETING

Advance Sales: Tickets can be purchased from two months before the start of the season.

Price Range: Tickets generally range from CHF 45.00 to CHF 60.00.

Box Office

The Box Office is open Monday to Saturday, 9.00 a.m.–11.00 a.m. and 2.00 p.m.–5.30 p.m. Closed Wednesday and Saturday afternoons.
Tel: +423 (0) 384 38 38
Fax: +423 (0) 384 38 39
www.operette-balzers.li offers a service where visitors can reserve their tickets online and pay for them later via an invoice.

PERFORMANCES

Times: Evening performances generally commence at 7.30 p.m. Sunday matinee performance times can vary.

Resident Groups: The Balzers Opera Company

SEATING

Organization: The hall is organized into stalls, a platform, a balcony and a gallery.

Best Seats: The best seats are at the front of each section (but not in the gallery).

Seats to Avoid: All seats provide good views and acoustics.

HOW TO GET THERE

Bus: Bus routes 2, 4, 160 and 182 serve the Balzers Opera. A day pass on the bus costs CHF 7.00.

VADUZ

Operettenbühne Vaduz

With a relatively small programme compared to other opera powerhouses around Europe, Operettenbühne Vaduz is perhaps easily overshadowed by some of its bigger rivals. However, taking centre stage in the Liechtenstein capital, the venue is accompanied by other cultural sites, including the National Museum, which holds some of Liechtenstein's most coveted treasures and the distinctive Kunstmuseum Liechtenstein, which provides an aesthetic experience of its own. Playing host to just one operetta per year, the most is made of this special occasion, with thousands of visitors flocking to the venue to witness the annual musical spectacle.

Bangarten 14
Vaduz
FL-9490
Liechtenstein
Tel: +423 (0)232 56 48
Fax: +423 (0)232 56 42
www.operette-vaduz.li

TICKETING

Advance Sales: Tickets can be purchased from two months before the start of the season.

Price Range: Tickets generally range from CHF 50.00 to CHF 65.00.

PERFORMANCES

Events take place from January to March. Please note that there is only one opera per season; and there is not necessarily a season every year.

Times: There are perfomances at 3.00 p.m., 5.00 p.m. and 7.30 p.m.

Resident Groups: The Vaduz Opera Company

SEATING

Organization: The auditorium is arranged into stalls, raised stalls, a gallery and a seperate front of gallery.

Best Seats: The best seats are located in the front of the gallery.

Seats to Avoid: All seats provide good views of the stage.

HOW TO GET THERE

Bus: 807, 809, 805, 811 all serve the area of the Vaduz Opera. Single fares cost from CHF 2.00/CHF 1.40 for children and concessions. An all zone daily bus pass costs CHF 7.00/CHF 5.00 (concession).

LITHUANIA

VILNIUS

National Philharmonic Hall

The Lithuanian National Philharmonic Hall organizes symphonic and chamber music concerts both at their home in Vilnius and abroad. Performing and organizing concerts dedicated to various composers, the venue offers an exciting programme of solo recitals, and concert series, featuring Lithuanian and international collectives and performers, and devotes major attention to the national repertoire. The most prominent international performers are invited to give concerts in Lithuania including violinists, foreign orchestras and jazz musicians. The resident National Philharmonic Society of Lithuania was established on 4 December 1940. At the beginning, the Society consisted of a symphony orchestra, mixed choir, and folk song and dance ensemble, gradually expanding and refining its repertoire into the successful ensemble it offers today.

National Philharmonic Hall
Ausros Vartu 4
Vilnius
LT-01129
Lithuania
Tel: +370 (0) 52 66 52 10
Fax: +370 (0)52 66 52 66
www.filharmonija.lt

TICKETING

Price Range: Tickets generally range from LTL 20.00 to LTL 50.00.

Concessions: Children, students, senior citizens and the unemployed can purchase tickets at a special rate of LTL 5.00 for selected performances.

Box Office

The Box Office is open Tuesday to Saturday, 10.00 a.m.–7.00 p.m.; Sunday, 10.00 a.m.–noon. Closed Mondays. In addition, the Box Office opens one hour before each performance.
Tel: +370 (0) 5 266 52 33, +370 (0) 5 266 52 16, +370 (0) 6 862 22 10
Fax: +370 (0)52 66 52 66

PERFORMANCES

Resident Groups: The Lithuanian National Philharmonic, Vilnius String Quartet and Lithuanian Chamber Orchestra

Annual Festivals/Special Events: The Vilnius Festival takes place every June.

SEATING

Capacity: 680

Organization: The auditorium is arranged into stalls and a balcony.

Opera & Ballet Theatre

Committed to the creation and production of scenic works for musical theatre, the Lithuanian National Opera and Ballet is a national budgetary institution which regularly performs classical music and opera to its highest artistic level. The history of opera in Lithuania dates back to the seventeenth century, when in 1636, 'Il ratto di Helena', written by an anonymous composer and set to a libretto by the then famous Italian librettist and musician, Virgilio Puccitelli, was first performed in Lithuania. The modern building was opened in 1974, purposely built for the

A Vienuolio 1
Vilnius
LT-01104
Lithuania
Tel: +370 (0)52 62 07 27
Fax: +370 (0)52 62 35 03
www.opera.lt

National Opera and Ballet. It sits in the historic Old Vilnius part of town alongside popular Baroque architecture. Many performances are in Lithuanian, demonstrating how a post-Soviet Lithuania is breaking free from its past.

TICKETING

Advance Sales: Tickets can be reserved up to six months in advance. Individual advance bookings cease a week before the performance.

Price Range: Tickets generally range from LTL 20.00 to LTL 350.00.

Concessions: Children, students, senior citizens and disabled visitors are eligible for discounts of up to 80%. Carers of disabled visitors gain free entry.

Box Office

The Box Office is open Monday to Friday, 10.00 a.m.–7.00 p.m.; Saturday, 10.00 a.m.–6.00 p.m.; Sunday, 10.00 a.m.–3.00 p.m.
Tel: +370 (0) 52 62 07 27
Fax: +370 (0)52 62 35 03
www.opera.lt
Tickets are confirmed by email and bought at least one day before the performance. (Three days for group bookings).

PERFORMANCES

Events take place from September to June.

Times: Evening performances begin at 6.00 p.m. Sunday matinee performances generally start at noon.

Resident Groups: The Lithuanian National Opera

Annual Festivals/Special Events: The Vilnius Festival takes place each June.

SEATING

Capacity: Main Auditorium – 984 seats; Chamber Hall – 250 seats

Organization: The auditorium is arranged into stalls and two balconies.

Best Seats: The front of the first balcony offers the best seats for visitors.

Good Seats on a Budget: The seats close to the front of the stalls provide good value.

EDUCATION

Guided Tours

Tours of the venue take place every Tuesday. Email: edukacija@opera.it for further information or to book a ticket.

Times: Tours are held at 9.30 a.m. and noon.

Cost: LTL 6.00 per person, LTL 80.00 for groups from 15 to 25 people.

Concessions: Concessions for students and seniors: LTL 3.00 per person, LTL 40.00 for groups of at least 10 people.

FACILITIES

Dining

There is a restaurant on the premises where visitors can relax and unwind before or after performances.

Services

Disabled access.

HOW TO GET THERE

Bus: Trolley-buses 2, 3, 5, 6, 12 and 14 serve the area, together with nos. 21, 26, 43 and 53.

A single ride ticket (called a talonas) costs up to LTL 1.40 (LTL 1.10 if bought in newspaper kiosks before boarding). A one day ticket costs LTL 6.00. For visitors wishing to stay longer, a three day ticket costs LTL 14.00.

Car Parking: There is a large adjacent parking space on J Lelevelio Street. The hall is a 15 minute drive from Vilnius International Airport with good bus taxi routes.

MALTA

VALLETTA

Manoel Theatre

In 1731, Grand Master Antonio Manoel de Vilhena, identifying the need for a central building, in his own words, 'for the honest recreation of the people', commissioned and funded the construction of a new public theatre. Completed in ten months, the original interior of the Theatre was modelled around the Palermo Theatre, a semi-circular structure with straight sides projecting to the stage. The Manoel Theatre, reputed to be Europe's third-oldest working theatre, is a small venue with a lavish, oval-shaped auditorium, three tiers of boxes constructed entirely of wood decorated with 22-carat gold leaf and a pale blue trompe l'oeil ceiling that resembles a round cupola. Hidden behind an austere façade that is fully in keeping with Valletta's Mannerist architecture is a richly adorned glorious Rococo interior. Despite numerous alterations over the years, it retains many of its old architectural features such as the white marble staircase, shell-shaped niches, and Viennese chandeliers. Two water reservoirs beneath the floor create an acoustic environment that is so precise that even the hushed page-turnings of an orchestra conductor can be heard clearly throughout the auditorium. Now officially the country's National Theatre, it has hosted countless productions by both local talent and international stars, and continues to be the catalyst for both the growth and appreciation of dramatic art in Malta.

The Manoel Theatre
115 Old Theatre Street
Valletta
Malta
Tel: +356 (0)21 22 26 18
www.teatrumanoel.com.mt

TICKETING

Price Range: Tickets generally range from MTL 2.00 to MTL 12.00.

Box Office

Tel: +356 (0) 21 24 63 89
Fax: +356 (0)21 23 73 40
www.teatrumanoel.com.mt

PERFORMANCES

Events take place all year round.

Times: Evening performances generally begin at 7.30 p.m. or 8.00 p.m. Lunchtime concerts start at 1.00 p.m.

Resident Groups: The Malta National Orchestra

Annual Festivals/Special Events: The Theatre hosts the Valletta Baroque Festival, the Arts Festival and the Opera Festival, also an annual children's pantomime.

SEATING

Capacity: 650.

Organization: The auditorium is arranged into stalls, two tiers and an upper gallery.

Good Seats on a Budget: The box seats in the centre provide good views.

Seats to Avoid: The view from some side tier seats may be partially obscured.

EDUCATION

Guided Tours

The Teatru Manoel Museum provides visitors with a unique insight into the venue's history and formation. A section is also dedicated to the Royal Opera House which was destroyed during a World War II air raid. Tours of both the museum and theatre take place Monday to Friday at 10.30 a.m., 11.30 a.m., and 2.30 p.m.; Saturday, 1.30 p.m. Tickets are available from the Manoel Theatre Bookshop in Palazzo Bonici.

Cost: MTL 1.70

FACILITIES

Dining

De Vilhena Restaurant and café serves a wide range of food and refreshments to visitors.

HOW TO GET THERE

Bus: All bus routes in Valetta serve the Manoel. The cost of a bus route ranges from MTL 0.10 cents–MTL 0.25 cents. A one day ticket costs MTL 1.50.

> Free lunchtime concerts take place at the smaller Sala Isouard. The Manoel has a theatre museum open for visits daily from 9.00 a.m.–1.00 p.m. The cost is MTL 1.

St James Cavalier Centre

Malta's 'Centre for Creativity' first opened its doors to the public on 22 September 2000. As the Maltese government's Millennium Project, it has taken on the role of pushing forward Malta's cultural aspirations welcoming both local and foreign artists, writers, singers and actors, dancers, musicians as well as thinkers, scientists and other creators. It has staged operas and premiered plays, held major exhibitions of contemporary pieces as well as of past masters. The Centre has held a strong historical importance for the island. Built originally as a Cavalier to provide raised gun-platforms in order to counteract land attacks, the building was originally designed to keep people out rather than welcome them

St James Cavalier Centre for Creativity
Valletta
Malta
Tel: +356 (0)21 22 32 00
Fax: +356 (0)21 22 32 18
www.sjcav.org

in, hence in its transformation major structural changes had to take place. Today, the alterations have not removed the building's historic foundations, with both the sixteenth century and the modern sitting side by side. The St James Cavalier Centre is an ongoing project to change the face of Valletta and continues to provide opportunities for creativity in all its aspects.

TICKETING

Box Office

Tel: +356 (0) 21 22 32 00
The online booking site is under construction.
email: boxoffice@sjcav.org/

PERFORMANCES

Events take place all year round.

Times: Performances begin at 12.30 p.m. for lunchtime concerts and 7.30 p.m. during evenings, although there are master classes and lectures in the afternoons.

FACILITIES

Dining

Inspirations!, located at the centre is a pasta house, coffee shop and outside catering facility which provides a variety of food and refreshments. Opening hours are Monday to Saturday, noon–2.00 p.m. and Thursdays, Fridays and Saturdays, 7.00 p.m.–11.00 p.m.

MONACO

MONTE CARLO

Opéra de Monte Carlo–Salle Garnier

An exact replica in miniature of the Palais Garnier in Paris, Monaco's Salle Garnier was constructed at the behest of King Charles III, who commissioned famous architect Charles Garnier to replicate the theatre which had proven so popular in the French capital. After an initial inauguration ceremony, the opera house opened with its first performance of Jean-Robert Planquette's 'Le Chevalier Gaston' on 8 February 1879, which was followed by three additional operas in the first season. Although the 'Golden Age' of the Salle Garnier no longer exists, with smaller companies unable to host productions entailing extravagant costs, the theatre's active programme has seen it host no less than 45 premieres throughout its colourful history. Amongst these, Saint-Saëns' 'Helene' in 1904 and Puccini's 'La Rondine' in 1927 have all seen their debut on the Salle Garnier stage. This range of performances continues, with the theatre still showcasing around five or six operas every season.

TICKETING

Advance Sales: Booking is open one month in advance.

Price Range: Tickets generally range from €15.00 to €70.00.

Concessions: Under-25s receive a discount on all performances, usually 50%.

Box Office

The Box Office is open Tuesday to Sunday, 10.00 a.m.–noon and 2.00 p.m.–5.00 p.m.
Tel: +377 (0) 98 06 2828

PERFORMANCES

Events take place from November to March.

Resident Groups: The Monte Carlo Opera

SEATING

Capacity: 524

Box 139
Monte Carlo
MC-98007
Monaco
Tel: +377 (0)98 06 2828
Fax: +377 (0)98 06 2829
www.opera.mc

Seats to Avoid: All seats have a good view of the stage.

FACILITIES

Dining

There is a drinks bar in the opera house. Restaurants are also located nearby.

Services

HOW TO GET THERE

Car Parking: Parking is available at the Boulingrins Parking Lot.

> There is a strict dress code at the Salle Garnier: jacket and tie for men and appropriate evening wear for women.

THE NETHERLANDS

AMSTERDAM

Het Muziektheater – De Nederlandse Opera Concertgebouw

Renowned for its adventurous and theatrical stagings, its mixed repertoire of modern and established operas, and its strong ensemble orientation, De Nederlandse Opera (DNO), has established itself as the leading venue for opera in the Netherlands. The DNO was established shortly after the end of World War II as a repertory company with a permanent ensemble. In the post-war period it toured extensively in the Netherlands from its home base in the Stadsschouwburg. Renamed in 1964 as 'De Nederlandse Operastichting' (The Dutch Opera Foundation), the company adopted a stagione orientation, inviting different soloists and artistic teams for each new production. In 1986, the company moved to the new Muziektheater building on the bank of Amstel River, where it remains today, sharing the site with the Dutch National Ballet, and thereafter becoming known as De Nederlandse Opera (DNO). Foreign opera houses and festivals regularly express interest in DNO productions, with the company making appearances at the Metropolitan Opera House, the Brooklyn Academy of Music and the Lincoln Center Festival in New York as well as in the Adelaide Festival in Australia.

TICKETING

Advance Sales: Tickets generally go on sale three months in advance. An sms text service is available online to inform visitors of open booking dates.

Price Range: Tickets generally range from €20.00 to €100.00.

Concessions: Under-25s and senior citizens receive a 5%–20% discount depending on the performance and seat.

Waterlooplein 22
Amsterdam
NL-1011 PG
The Netherlands
Tel: +31 (0)20 551 8922
www.dno.nl

Box Office

The Box Office is open Monday to Saturday, 10.00 a.m. until the beginning of the performance; Sunday and public holidays, 11.30 a.m. until the beginning of the performance. Opening hours for days without a performance and days with only a matinee performance: 10.00 a.m.–6.00 p.m.
Tel: +31 (0)20 625 5455
www.dno.nl

PERFORMANCES

Events take place from November to June.

Times: 1.30 p.m. and 7.00 p.m.

Resident Groups: The Dutch National Opera

Annual Festivals/Special Events: The Holland Festival takes place every June.

SEATING

Capacity: 1,600

Organization: The auditorium is arranged into stalls and two balconies.

Best Seats: The best seats are located in the centre of stalls and first balcony.

Good Seats on a Budget: Top balcony

Seats to Avoid: Seats located in the far side of the stalls provide poor value for money. In addition, some seats have restricted view of the surtitles. Enquire at Box Office when booking.

EDUCATION

Guided Tours

A special backstage tour is conducted for visitors every Saturday afternoon at 3.00 p.m. Visitors get the opportunity to visit the massive backstage area and hear explanations of how the stage lifts and the fly tower works, as well as gaining an insight into the costume workshops and rehearsal studios.
Tel: +20 (0) 551 8054 or see the website for further information.

Cost: €5.00

Concessions: Two children between the age of 7 and 12 may enter for free with an adult. Tickets for students, the unemployed and senior citizens cost €4.00.

FACILITIES

Dining

The Opera has several buffet counters where coffee, tea, wine and cold drinks are available. Champagne or delicious pastries are available from the delicatessen bar. Also highly recommended are the sweets that are on offer at several counters. The Opera also offers freshly made French rolls with savoury fillings.

Services

The auditorium has a loop induction system for the hard of hearing.

There are special areas reserved for wheelchair users and companions, although visitors are unable to see the surtitles from these seats.

HOW TO GET THERE

Underground: From Amstel Station: Metro 51, 53 and 54 (Waterlooplein stop). GVB single ticket costs from €3.00/€4.50 return. One day ticket costs €6.30/€4.20 concessions.

Bus: From Central Station in Amsterdam: tram lines 9 (Waterlooplein stop) and 4 (Rembrandtplein stop).

Car Parking: Parking space in the immediate vicinity of Het Muziektheater is limited. Visitors may prefer to park their car in the outskirts of the city and travel to the centre with public transport, parking, for instance, at the Transferium of the Amsterdam Arena. There is an underground car park at the Opera but this is not exclusively for theatre patrons and so is often full.

ROTTERDAM

De Doelen Concertgebouw

Combining typical 1960s architecture with a modern Congress Centre, De Doelen is a site comprising three complexes. Offering its visitors a combination of fantastic facilities and a great location in the heart of Rotterdam, the building was originally constructed in 1934, but was

Schouwburgplein 50
Rotterdam
NL-3012 CT
The Netherlands
www.dedoelen.nl

destroyed in 1940 during bombings in World War II. It was rebuilt in 1966, housing both a concert hall and a Congress Centre. De Doelen's resident orchestra, the Rotterdam Philharmonic, is considered the second most important ensemble in the country after Amsterdam's Concertgebouw Orchestra. It was founded in 1918 by several musicians as a private institution. The first musical director was Willem Felzer, who was the manager of two Rotterdam music schools. In May 1930, Eduard Flipse was appointed conductor, a position he held until 1962. Under his lengthy stewardship, the amateur ensemble evolved into a professional orchestra. Establishing an 'Instrument Fund' to raise funds for new instruments and other necessities, the orchestra became known for its special attention to contemporary music, featuring the work of Dutch composers such as Johan Wagenaar, Willem Pijper and Alphons Diepenbrock. Today, the Orchestra continues its prominent reputation in the world of classical music and, backed by De Doelen, continues to provide audiences with stunning performances in a modern and progressive venue.

TICKETING

Box Office

The Box Office is open daily, 10.00 a.m.–6.00 p.m. Tickets must be picked up at least two weeks after reservation. If the performance is within two weeks tickets must be picked up at least one hour before the event is about to start.
Tel: +31 (0)10 217 1717
www.ticketmaster.nl

PERFORMANCES

Resident Groups: The Rotterdam Philharmonic Orchestra

Annual Festivals/Special Events: The Rotterdam Jazz Festival takes place in late September and the Gergiev Festival in October.

SEATING

Capacity: Jurriaanse Zaal Complex – 600; Grote Zaal Complex – 2,200; Willem Burger Zaal Complex – 700

Organization: The grand hall is organized into the floor, ring, tribune (balcony) and boxes.

FACILITIES

Dining

Various caterers are located on-site.

Services

Disabled access.

HOW TO GET THERE

Underground: Rotterdam Central Station is located two minutes from the venue. Single ticket costs from €1.60 (prices are determined by distance travelled). One day pass for use on all RET public transport costs €6.40 (regular) and €3.20 (concessions).

Bus: 33, 36, 37, 38, 44, 49 and 55. Tram lines 4, 5, 7, 8 and 21.

Car Parking: The hall is 15 minutes from Rotterdam airport by bus or taxi. Next to the Doelen is an underground parking facility (Parking Schouwburgplein), accommodating up to 850 vehicles. By means of a pedestrian tunnel the parking is directly connected to the main entrance of De Doelen.

UTRECHT

Muziekcentrum Vredenburg

What was once a thriving castle during the sixteenth century and the former site of Utrecht's law courts is today a unique musical complex designed to accommodate a whole variety of events throughout the year. The venue has not moved from its original site in Vredenburg Square since it was built 500 years ago and throughout its history has always maintained a cultural connection with the city, regularly hosting both fairs and festivals. In 1808, the venue was given the designation 'royal' by King Louis Napoleon, and was replaced by a new theatre after a fire in 1821. For many years, the venue shared a connection with another concert hall in Utrecht, the Tivoli. In many ways the Vrendenburg is superior, the venue was for decades the dazzling centre of Utrecht's musical and social life, and the home base of the Utrecht City Orchestra founded in 1895. However, after World War II much of the building was left dilapidated, and was finally demolished in 1956. The new millennium saw a unique collaboration between the Tivoli and the Vrendenburg, one which will see the two venues unite and the site transformed into a new musical palace, equipped with new facilities ready for the coming decades. The change is already in progress, and the results will be unveiled during the coming years.

TICKETING

Concessions: Special discounts for senior citizens and younger visitors are available for selected concerts. See the latest concert programme on the website for specific rates.

Box Office

Vredenburgpassage 77
Utrecht
NL-3511
Netherlands
Tel: +31 (0)30 286 2286
Fax: +31 (0)30 231 6522
www.vredenburg.nl

The Box Office is open Monday, noon–7.00 p.m.; Tuesday to Saturday, 10.00 a.m.–5.00 p.m.
Tel: +31 (0)30 231 4544
Lines are open Monday, noon–5.00 p.m.; Tuesday to Saturday, 9.00 a.m.–5.00 p.m.
www.vredenburg.nl (Please note that the booking part of the website is only available in Dutch)

PERFORMANCES

Times: Evening performances generally start at 8.15 p.m. Matinee and lunch performance times vary.

FACILITIES

Dining

The venue's bars provide visitors with a range of light refreshments and snacks.

Services

Disabled access.

HOW TO GET THERE

Overground: Vredenburg is a few minutes walk from the Central Station. Trains from every corner of the country stop at Utrecht Central Station.

Car Parking: Visitors to the Vredenburg qualify for a special car parking rate. Concert-goers can park in the parking garages of Hoog Catharijne, Monday to Saturday after 5.00 p.m., and unrestricted parking on Sundays and public holidays for just €6.20 for the whole evening. The closest parking garages are in Vredenburg and Station Street. On the northern side of the complex (Vredenburg Street) several parking bays are reserved for disabled visitors. The parking places are accessible from the slip road on Catharijnebaan.

NORWAY

BERGEN

Grieghallen

The Grieghallen is Bergen's distinctive concert hall, opened in 1978 and extensively refurbished in 1996. It is a modern building with a monumental structure, clearly visible in Bergen, providing an important landmark for the people of the town. The concert hall was originally built to provide a home for the Bergen Philharmonic Orchestra and is named after the famous Norwegian composer Edvard Grieg. In addition to having a resident symphony orchestra, the Grieghallen is also home to the Bergen International Festival and has hosted a number of events over the years, including the Eurovision Song Contest in 1986. The hall is widely used for guest performances by internationally-acclaimed artists and is also used for opera, ballet and theatre.

Edvard Griegs Plass 1
Bergen
N-5015
Norway
Tel: +47 (0)55 21 61 00
Fax: +47 (0) 55 21 61 99
www.grieghallen.no

TICKETING

Price Range: Ticket prices vary according to the performance and the promoter.

Box Office

Tel: +47 (0)55 21 61 50
www.ticketmaster.no or
www.billettservice.no

PERFORMANCES

The concert season runs from September to May.

Times: Events take place every Thursday and some Fridays and Saturdays, usually at 7.30 p.m.

SEATING

Capacity: 1,509

Organization: The auditorium is arranged into stalls and six other seating blocks.

FACILITIES

Services

Guide dogs welcome.

There are six spaces designated for wheelchair users in the auditorium.

HOW TO GET THERE

Underground: The Grieghallen is five minutes taxi ride from Bergen train station. A taxi ride costs approximately NOK 50.00.

Car Parking: There is a brand new underground car parking facility located underneath the new Edvard Griegs plass, alongside the Grieghallen.

Enjoy the picturesque local area of Bergen, with the famous Fish Market or the charming Main Square Torgalmenningen nearby.

OSLO

Den Norske Opera

The Den Norske Opera or Norwegian National Opera (NNO) was founded in 1957 and was the first fully professional company for opera and ballet in Norway. The Norwegian National Opera is a very young institution by European standards, with the

PO Box 8800
Youngstorget
Oslo
N-0028
Norway
Tel: +47 (0)31 544 488
Fax: +47 (0) 23 31 50 30
www.operaen.no

1931 building, originally a movie theatre, founded as a national institution for opera and ballet in 1958 by the government, carrying with it from the start a wide national responsibility. Today, the NNO is a theatre firmly rooted in the opera literature of the classical and Romantic periods. However, although the main repertoire is traditional, it also contains works by twentieth century and contemporary composers. Although the Norwegian National Opera's main stage is situated in Oslo, the company also tours the nation extensively to produce opera and ballet together with local orchestras and choirs. In 2008, the Norwegian National Opera will move to the new opera house at Bjørvika in the harbour of Oslo.

TICKETING

Price Range: Tickets generally range from NOK 210.00 to NOK 460.00.

Concessions: A 50% youth discount is available for everyone under the age of 25 for all ordinary performances in the main theatre if they buy the ticket one week before the performance. In addition, there is a 25% discount for pensioners.

Box Office

The Box Office is open Monday to Friday, 10.00 a.m.–6.00 p.m.; Saturday, 10.00 a.m.–2.00 p.m. On performance days the Box Office is open until the performance begins.
Tel: +47 (0)81 544 488
www.operaen.no

PERFORMANCES

Events take place from September to June.

Times: 7.30 p.m.

Resident Groups: The Norwegian National Opera

SEATING

Capacity: 1,051

Best Seats: Rows 1–13 in the stalls and rows 1–6 in the balcony provide the best seats.

Good Seats on a Budget: Standing room tickets provide good value for money for those who do not mind standing.

Seats to Avoid: All seats have clear views of the stage.

EDUCATION

Guided Tours

Tours of the venue can be arranged by contacting the hall directly.

Cost: NOK 100.00.

Times: Tours conducted in English take place daily at 11.00 a.m.

FACILITIES

Dining

The bars on the first and second floors offer a variety of refreshments during the intervals, whilst the café on the second floor serves coffee, tea and cakes. Visitors can book a table and refreshments prior to the performance and during the interval. Fax requests to: +47 (0)23 315 213.

Services

Guide dogs welcome.

Two wheelchair spaces are available in the hall. Visitors are advised to contact the hall beforehand.

HOW TO GET THERE

Overground: Oslo Central Railway Station is less than half a mile away. One hour tickets cost NOK 20.00/30.00 NOK (advance/on board). 24 hour ticket costs NOK 60.00. A one day Oslo pass costs NOK 195.00.

> At weekends there is an additional ticket charge of NOK 60.00. Remaining tickets are sold at a 40% discount two hours before the performance commences. There is often a free lecture about performances beforehand.

STAVANGER

Stavanger Concert Hall

The Stavanger Concert Hall was completed in 1982 and holds a central place in the cultural life of the city of Stavanger. It presents performances from the region of Stavanger and Rogaland County as well as by internationally acclaimed artists. The Concert Hall seeks the widest possible performance profile and thus, although concert presentation is its main activity, it also serves

Bjergsted
Stavanger
N-4007
Norway
Tel: +47 (0)51 508 810
www.stavanger-konserthus.no

a number of other purposes. In addition to a wide range of concerts, Stavanger Concert Hall hosts gala performances, shows and musicals as well as classical ballet and modern dance. The foyer is often used for concerts, receptions and conferences.

TICKETING

Advance Sales: The sale of tickets to non-subscription holders for the first concerts of various series commences two days before the first concert begins.

Price Range: Tickets generally range from NOK 120.00 to NOK 220.00.

Concessions: A 50% discount is available to children and students. Senior citizens are eligible for a 10% discount.

Box Office

The Box Office is open Monday, Tuesday, Wednesday and Friday, 10.00 a.m.–4.00 p.m.; Thursday, 10.00 a.m.–7.00 p.m., and 10.00 a.m.–7.30 p.m. on concert days. Saturdays from 31 August onwards, noon–3.00 p.m.
Tel: +47 (0)51 53 7010
Fax: +47 (0)51 53 7001
www.billetluka.no (in Norwegian) www.ticnet.no

PERFORMANCES

Times: 7.30 p.m.

Resident Groups: Stavanger Symphony Orchestra

SEATING

Capacity: 1,078

Best Seats: The best seats are located in the centre of the stalls and the centre of the second tier.

FACILITIES

Services

There are ten designated wheelchair spaces provided.

HOW TO GET THERE

Bus: Lines 8 and 28 serve the Stavanger Concert Hall. A single ticket for an adult costs NOK 22.00 inside one zone.

TRONDHEIM

Olavshallen

Opened in September 1989, the Olavshallen Concert Hall was named after Trondheim's historic 'Olav Tradition', a traditional week-long celebration held in Trondheim to celebrate the life

> Kjøpmannsgata 44
> Trondheim
> N-7410
> Norway
> Tel: +47 (0)73 99 40 00
> Fax: +47 (0)73 99 40 99
> www.olavshallen.no

of St Olav. It is situated on historic ground, believed to be the area where the original Trondheim town, then called Nidaros, was first settled. The Concert Hall is the first in Norway to implement the coordinated accommodation of various services, with the flexible ceiling elements able to be moved up and down to find the most favourable ceiling shape to suit various events. The complex of about 30,000 square metres accommodate the Trondheim Symphony Orchestra, SørTrøndelag College - School of Music, a municipal school of musical education for children, a hotel with cafés and restaurants, together with a large number of shops and services. Olavshallen is Trondheim's largest and most important art centre and seeks to be a central multi-purpose meeting point for the public and cultural life in the region of Trondheim and SørTrøndelag County.

PERFORMANCES

Resident Groups: The Trondheim Symphony Orchestra and Drivhuset

SEATING

Capacity: 1,250

Organization: The Hall is organized into stalls, a balcony and small galleries.

FACILITIES

Dining

A hotel equipped with a restaurant and café forms part of the complex.

Services

There is space available for four wheelchair users.

POLAND

KRAKÓW

Juliusz Slowacki Theatre

Named after the famous Romantic poet of the same name, the Juliusz Slowacki Theatre caused controversy when it was first constructed on top of a former fourteenth-century church and monastery. The decision to demolish the church in 1886 was received badly by many, most notably perhaps with the declaration of Polish painter, Jan Matejko, that he would never exhibit his paintings in Kraków again. However, when the new theatre was unveiled on 21 October 1893, with a programme consisting of excerpts from Aleksander Fredro's 'Zemsta,' Juliusz Słowacki's 'Balladyna' and Adam Mickiewicz's 'Konfederacibarscy', a new era in Polish culture was ushered in, welcomed by many who visited the new and exquisite example of Polish eclectic architecture. The building was originally crowned with the name 'Teatr Miejski', or Municipal Theatre, with its current name being added in 1909. Today, apart from maintaining its primary theatrical function, the venue regularly doubles as a Kraków Opera House. In the early 1990s, for its centennial, the theatre

Sw. Ducha 1 Sq.
Kraków
Poland
Tel: +47 (0)424 4500
Fax: +47 (0)422 40 22
www.slowacki.krakow.pl

underwent a thorough renovation. The huge painted curtain depicting a tragicomic allegory has gained fame as an outstanding work of art, joining an elegant programme of the best in theatre and opera performed at the heart of Kraków city.

TICKETING

Advance Sales: Advance reservations begin two weeks before the performance.

Price Range: Tickets generally range from 25.00 zł to 40.00 zł.

Concessions: Various discounts are available to children, students, senior citizens and the disabled.

Box Office

> The Box Office is open Monday to Saturday, 9.00 a.m.–2.00 p.m. and 2.30 p.m.–7.00 p.m. The Box Office is open on Sundays from four hours prior to performances.
> Tel: +47 (0) 424 4500
> Lines are open Monday to Friday, 8.00 a.m.–5.00 p.m. www.slowacki.krakow.pl. From here an online booking form is sent to the theatre with the requested reservation. This is then confirmed via email and a ticket pick-up/purchase date arranged.

PERFORMANCES

Opera performances are held on Sunday and Monday.

Resident Groups: Kraków Philharmonic Orchestra

SEATING

Capacity: 900

EDUCATION

Guided Tours

Theatre Slowacki runs a special theatre tour where visitors are invited to learn more about the history of the venue and uncover the secrets which have come to shape the theatre through events during the nineteenth and twentieth centuries. Tel: +47 (0) 424 4525 for further information.

Cost: Up to 30 people – 130.00 zł. Over 30 people – 150.00 zł.

FACILITIES

Dining

In the theatre building the Café Pod Chochołami provides visitors with a variety of refreshments to be enjoyed during their visit.

Services

HOW TO GET THERE

Underground: Kraków Glowny Railway Station is two minutes walk from the venue.

Car Parking: There are two parking lots located near the theatre.

WARSAW

Filharmonia Narodowa

Celebrating its centenary in 2001, the Warsaw Philharmonic is one of the oldest musical institutions in Europe. Backed by a group of wealthy financiers and modelled on the Palais Garnier in Paris, the building was designed by architect Karol Kozłowski in the

5 Jasna Street
Warsaw
PL-00950
Poland
Tel: +48 (0)22 551 7128
Fax: +22 (0)55 17 200
www.filharmonia.pl

Viennese Secession style. The first concert was held on 5 November 1901 and presented the music of Polish composers. Destroyed in World War II, it reopened for the 1947–48 season. The building was reconstructed in a totally new style and completed in 1955. Today the theatre's resident orchestra the Warsaw Philharmonic is made up of 112 top-ranking musicians and has completed over 100 tours in five continents.

TICKETING

Advance Sales: Tickets can be purchased from one month in advance.

Price Range: Tickets generally range from 20.00 zł to 55.00 zł for concert for adult; children's concerts start at 5.00 zł.

Concessions: Students and senior citizens are entitled to a 50% discount.

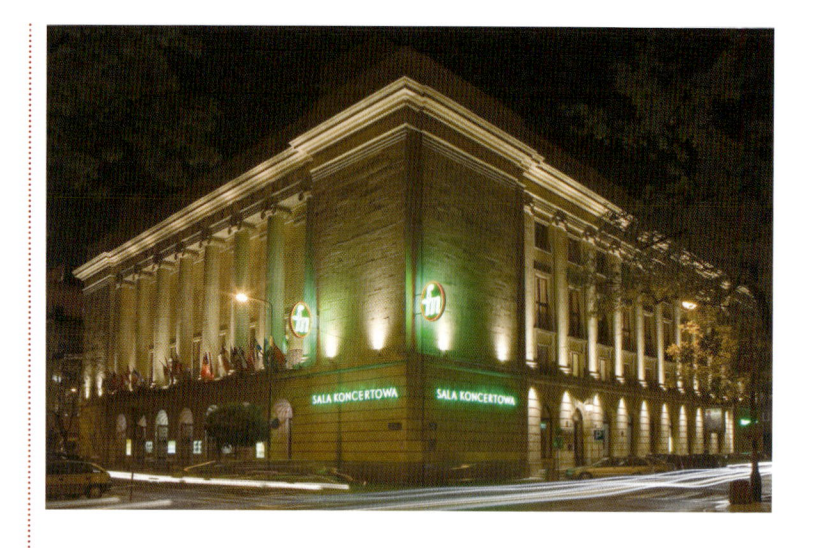

Box Office

The Box Office is open Monday to Saturday, 10.00 a.m.–2.00 p.m. and 3.00 p.m.–7.00 p.m. On the day of the concert, tickets for the day in question can also be bought in a second Booking Office open from 4.00 p.m. until the concert starts. On Sundays, whenever concerts for children are held, the Booking Office opens from 10.00 a.m.–2.00 p.m.
Tel: +48 (0)22 551 7128 for information. Tel: +48 (0)22 551 7130, or +48 (0)22 551 7131 for bookings.
Lines are open daily, 10.00 a.m.–3.00 p.m.
www.bilecik.info
Tickets bought this way can be collected from the Box Office on the day of the performance.

PERFORMANCES

Times: 7.00 p.m.

Resident Groups: The Warsaw Philharmonic Orchestra and National Choir of Poland

Annual Festivals/Special Events: The Warsaw Philharmonic annually hosts the Lutoslawski Forum which features concerts of twentieth century music and a number of exhibitions, lectures and panel discussions. The venue also takes part in the Warsaw Autumn Festival in September.

SEATING

Capacity: 1,072

Best Seats: The best seats are located at the central stalls and front row of the balcony.

FACILITIES

Dining

Refreshment rooms can be found in the foyer on the ground floor and the balcony level bars open 45 minutes before the concert, as well as during the interval.

Services

Guide dogs welcome.

Specially designed hearing aids are available for use at the cloakroom.

There is wheelchair access situated next to the entrance to the Philharmonic from Moniuszki Street. The theatre requests prior contact. Tel: +47 (0)55 17127, 8.00 a.m.–4.00 p.m.

HOW TO GET THERE

Bus: Bus line X08 serves the Filharmonia bus stop and city centre from the airport. A universal public transport ticket costing 2.40 zł can be bought and newspaper kiosks to be validated once on board. A day ticket costs 7.20 zł.

Youth concerts, called 'Thursday Musical Meetings', are regularly organized, as well as special concerts for children on Sundays.

Teatr Wielki

For 170 years Teatr Wielki has been Poland's grandest opera and ballet institution. The building was erected between 1825 and 1833 to designs by the Italian architect Antonio Corazzi of Livorno for the companies of national opera, ballet and drama active at the time in Warsaw, with

Plac Teatralny 1
PO Box 59
Warsaw
PL-00950
Poland
Tel: +48 (0)22 692 0200
Fax: +48 (0)22 836 0423
www.teatrwielki.pl

the first performance in the new building, Rossini's 'Il barbiere di Siviglia', taking place on 24 February 1833. During the Battle of Warsaw in 1939 the Teatr Wielki was bombed and almost completely ruined, with only the Classicist façade surviving the bombing. The restored theatre reopened to the public on 19 November 1965. At that time it was one of the most imposing theatres in Europe, provided with state-of-the-art installations and equipment. The Polish National Opera in the Teatr Wielki continues its 200-year old tradition today and produces works by Polish composers whilst continuing to represent world classics. According to the plans of Antonio Corazzi, which were submitted for execution in 1825, the façade of the Teatr Wielki was supposed to be decorated at the front with a triumphal sculpture of Apollo, patron of the arts, driving a chariot drawn by four horses. The outbreak and ultimate defeat of the November Uprising meant the idea never materialized. The time finally came for the Third Republic of Poland to fill the centuries-old gap in the architectural image of Teatralny Square. At the initiative of the Teatr Wielki, Polish National Opera's then General Director, Waldemar Dabrowski, the sculpture envisaged some 177 years ago finally adorned the Teatr Wielki's façade.

TICKETING

Advance Sales: Tickets can be purchased from one month in advance.

Price Range: Tickets generally range from 15.00 zł to 120.00 zł.

Concessions: There is a 25% discount available for children, students and senior citizens.

Box Office

Two Box Offices, located at the Teatr Wielki and ZASP, al. Jerozolimskie 25 sell tickets for the venue. The Box Offices are open as follows: Teatr Wielki: Monday to Friday, 9.00 a.m.–7.00 p.m.; weekends, 10.00 a.m.–7.00 p.m. ZASP: Monday to Friday, 9.00 a.m.–7.00 p.m.
Tel: Main theatre Box Office: Tel: +47 (0) 226 920 208, +47 (0) 226 920 758 +47 (0) 228 265 019. ZASP Tel: +47 (0)226 219 454
Fax: +48 (0)228 260 268
Tickets can be booked online via several websites listed on the main site.

PERFORMANCES

Events take place from October to June.

Times: performance times vary, with many performances starting at either 7.00 p.m. or 7.15 p.m.

Annual Festivals/Special Events: The theatre takes part in the Annual Warsaw Autumn Festival every September.

SEATING

Capacity: 1,828

Organization: The auditorium is arranged into stalls, a gallery, balcony, upper circle and amphitheatre.

Best Seats: The best seats are located in the front of the balcony and the central stalls.

EDUCATION

Guided Tours

The Theatre Museum is located in the west wing of the Teatr Wielki in the historical Reduta Rooms, and is open Tuesday to Friday, 10.00 a.m.–2.00 p.m. and during intermissions of spectacles at the Teatr Wielki. Tel: +48 (0)226 920 756 or email: muzeum@teatrwielki.pl for further information.

FACILITIES

Services

There are specially designed hearing aids available for visitors to use.

HOW TO GET THERE

Bus: 175 and 188 serve the area. A universal public transport ticket costing 2.40 zł can be bought and newspaper kiosks can validated once on board. A day ticket costs 7.20 zł.

PORTUGAL

LISBON

Calouste Gulbenkian Foundation Auditorium

Located in the picturesque setting of Gulbenkian Park, the Calouste Gulbenkian Foundation was established in 1956 as a private institution of public utility upon the wishes of the man himself, a wealthy Armenian businessman who had an equally keen interest in both the arts and sciences. The venue opened in 1969 and in addition to a large auditorium, the new complex included a space for temporary exhibitions, a congress area, as well as a large section of the building devoted to the Calouste Gulbenkian Museum, which includes a magnificent collection of glass and jewels by the renowned French artist René Lalique. Today, the choir and orchestra, which have been named after Gulbenkian, regularly perform in the auditorium he hoped would continue his passion for the arts, putting on frequent performances within

Avenua Berna 45A
Lisbon
P-1067-001
Portugal
Tel: +351 (0)21 782 3000
Fax: +351 (0)21 782 3041
www.musica.gulbenkian.pt

this unique cultural location in Lisbon's heart.

TICKETING

Price Range: Ticket prices vary according to performances, and can range from €5.00 for a balcony seat to €300.00 for the best seat in a premiere.

Concessions: Various discounts are available for performances, with some groups receiving up to 30% discount on the ticket price. See individual performances or contact the Box Office for details.

Box Office

> The Box Office is open daily, Monday to Friday, 10.00 a.m.–7.00 p.m.; Saturday, 10.00 a.m.–5.30 p.m. or until 7.00 p.m. during concert days. Sunday, 1.00 p.m.–7.00 p.m. during concert days. The Box Office also opens one hour before concerts.
> Tel: +351 (0)21 782 3030
> Fax: +351 (0)21 782 3614
> www.bilheteira.gulbenkian.pt

PERFORMANCES

The resident choir and orchestra's concert season runs from October to May. Concerts are held on a Thursdays, Fridays and Saturdays.

Times: Performance times vary, and although many take place at 7.00 p.m., evening performances sometimes start as late as 10.00 p.m.

Resident Groups: The Gulbenkian Choir and Gulbenkian Orchestra

Annual Festivals/Special Events: The Jaxx Festival is held every August.

SEATING

Capacity: 1,300

HOW TO GET THERE

Underground: Metro to S Sebastião or Praça de Espanha Station. Single journey costs from €0.70. Combined ticket with Carris (bus/streetcar) services cost from €1.10. Day ticket for all public transport costs €3.30.

Bus: 16, 26, 31, 46 and 56

Car Parking: Car parks are located at Avenida de Berna and Avenida Visconde de Valbom.

Teatro Nacional de Sao Carlos

The San Carlo National Theatre stands today as one of the oldest theatres in Europe not to have been destroyed and rebuilt. Unfortunately, the venue's predecessor, the Teatro do Paços da Ribeira did not share San Carlo's good fortune. In March 1755, the King of Portugal built the Ribeira, at the time considered the best opera house in Europe.

Largo de São Carlos
Lisbon
P-1200-442
Portugal
Tel: +351 (0)213 253 045/6
Fax: +351 (0)213 253 047
www.saocarlos.pt

However, its life was short-lived, and the building was destroyed in the disastrous earthquake of November 1755. Seeking a new permanent opera house, a group of merchants and government officials began construction of a new theatre as part of the celebrations of the birth of the first son of Prince João and Princess Carlota Joaquina. The building, designed by José da Costa e Silva, was inspired by named after the Teatro San Carlo of Naples. The theatre is located in the historical centre of Lisbon, with the main façade possessing a decorated clock, the Portuguese coats-of-arms and a grand portico. A Latin commemorative inscription dedicates the theatre to Princess Charlotte of Spain, who arrived in Portugal in 1790 to marry the future king, Prince John. The luxurious Royal Box was lavishly decorated by the Italian Giovanni Appianni, adding to a grand ceiling painted by Manuel da Costa and a stage by Cirilo Wolkmar Machado.

TICKETING

Price Range: Tickets generally range from €10.00 to €70.00.

Concessions: Young persons under the age of 30 and senior citizens over 65 are eligible for a 30% discount. Last minute tickets are also available from two hours before the start of the performance at a heavily discounted rate for all visitors.

Box Office

The Box Office is open daily, 1.00 p.m.–7.00 p.m. On performance days the Box Office opens up until the performance begins. Visitors should note that from two hours before the beginning of the performance, only tickets for that day/evening's performance are sold.
Tel: +351 (0)213 253 045/6
Fax: +351 (0)213 253 047

PERFORMANCES

The opera season runs from September to June.

Resident Groups: The Portuguese National Symphonic Orchestra

SEATING

Capacity: 1,148

Organization: The auditorium is arranged into five tiers of boxes and seats in the stalls.

HOW TO GET THERE

Underground: The closest stop on the Lisbon Metro is Baixa-Chiado. Single journey costs from €0.70. Combined ticket with Carris (bus/streetcar) services cost from €1.10. Day ticket for all public transport costs €3.30.

Bus: 58, 100 and 204

PORTO

Casa da Música

An architectural triumph, acclaimed by critics around the world for its unique and exuberant design, the Casa da Música in Porto represents a prime location for the best in cultural activities and classical music. The building was completed in 2005 as part of Porto's project to become European Capital City of Culture in 2001. It hosts a wide range of concerts, with a classical agenda including chamber music, symphonic works and operas. It also encourages contemporary composers and has a resident classical/jazz/ crossover ensemble 'Remix', which plays the works of different modern composers. The theatre also hosts a number of free concerts, often accompanied by a lecture or workshop with an orchestra.

Av da Boavista
604-610
Porto
P-4149-071
Portugal
Tel: +351 (0)220 120 220
Fax: +351 (0)220 190 298
www.casadamusica.com

TICKETING

Price Range: Tickets generally range from €5.00 to €50.00.

Concessions: There is a 20% discount for the under-25s and over-65s. Carers of disabled visitors are admitted at a reduced price.

Box Office

The Box Office is open daily, 10.00 a.m.–8.00 p.m. All tickets will be held for collection at the Box Office.
Tel: +351 (0) 220 120 220
Fax: +351 (0) 220 190 298
www.casadamusica.com

PERFORMANCES

Times: Performances take place at various times between 6.00 p.m. and 9.00 p.m.

Programmes: Programmes are distributed free of charge from the Box Office with the purchase of a ticket. Programmes are generally in Portuguese with selected programmes available in English.

Resident Groups: The Remix Ensemble and National Orchestra of Porto

SEATING

Capacity: 1,300

Seats to Avoid: There are no seats with restricted views.

EDUCATION

Guided Tours

Tours generally take place daily at hourly intervals. Contact the venue directly for further information.

Cost: Cost of a tour is €2.00.

Concessions: Children under 12 are admitted free.

FACILITIES

Dining

There is a large restaurant located at the top of the complex with room for 250 people and an open terrace.

Services

HOW TO GET THERE

Underground: Casa da Música Metro Station is 2 minutes walk from the Casa da Música. A single journey ticket costs €1.35.

Bus: 78, 82 and 84 to the Cada da Música.

Car Parking: There is a car park at the Rotunda Boavista with 644 places. It costs €0.90 per hour before midnight and €0.70 per hour after until 8.00 a.m.

ROMANIA

BUCHAREST

Ateneul Român

Gorgeous inside and out, this nineteenth-century concert hall, home of the George Enescu Philharmonic Orchestra, is a contender for being possibly the finest building in the city. The Romanian Atheneum, with its sublime Baroque cupola, stands proudly at the flux of the city's busiest public square, competing with the Athenee Palace Hilton hotel, the Royal Palace and the old National Library for attention. The work of French architect Albert Galleron, who was also responsible for designing the National Bank of Romania, the building was inaugurated on 26 February 1888, and was built almost entirely with money donated by ordinary citizens of the capital. Today, the auditorium seats 1,000 spectators comfortably, and is renowned worldwide for its outstanding acoustics. The lobby has a beautifully painted ceiling decorated in gold leaf and curved balconies cascading in ringlets of spiral staircase. A ring of pink marble columns is linked by flowing arches, where elaborate brass lanterns hang like gems from a necklace, making the interior of the building as sumptuous as the acoustics are brilliant.

Str. Franklin nr.1
Bucharest
Romania
Tel: +21 (0)31 56875
Fax +40 (0)21 312 2983
www.fge.org.ro

TICKETING

Box Office

The Box Office is open daily, 1.30 p.m.–6.00 p.m.

PERFORMANCES

Resident Groups: The George Enescu Philharmonic Orchestra

Opera Nationala Bucuresti

Under the patronage of Queen Maria, Romanian Opera became a state institution in 1921. The Romanian Opera's inaugural performance was a very lush 'Lohengrin' staged by Adalbert Markowski and conducted by George Enescu. In 1953 a new base for the Romanian Opera was built, primarily for the World Youth and Student Festival to take place, and later opening to

Bd. Mihail Kogalniceanu 70-72
Bucharest
Romania
Tel: +40 (0) 21 314 6980
Fax: +40 (0)21 315 7849
www.operanb.ro

its first opera, Tchaikovsky's 'Queen of Spades' on 9 January 1954. These luxurious surroundings of the Opera Nationala Bucuresti were in stark contrast to the social condition of the rest of the country. The Opera was often used to project a particular Soviet Communist vision but this ended with the collapse of communism. Today, the Opera shows modern versions of classic operas and ballet together with several new works.

TICKETING

Advance Sales: Tickets can be booked from three months in advance.

Price Range: Tickets generally range from €4.20 to €25.20.

Concessions: Children and students are admitted at the price of €4.20.

Box Office

The Box Office is open daily, 10.00 a.m.–1.00 p.m. and 2.00 p.m.–7.00 p.m. There is no transaction charge, tickets can only be bought with cash at the Box Office.
Tel: +40 (0)21 313 1857

PERFORMANCES

Events take place from October to June.

Resident Groups: The Romanian Opera

SEATING

Capacity: 900

Organization: The hall is organized into stalls, boxes, a balcony and family circle.

Best Seats: The best seats are located in the front of the central balconies.

Good Seats on a Budget: Good value seats can be found in the side boxes.

Seats to Avoid: All seats have unrestricted views.

FACILITIES

Services

HOW TO GET THERE

Underground: Bucharest Central Station is located opposite the Opera.

Bus: 85 runs to the Opera. A single ticket costs €1.00.

RUSSIA

MOSCOW

Moscow P 1 Tchaikovsky Conservatory

For more than 100 years, the concert halls of the Moscow Conservatory have been ranked amongst the top concert halls in Europe and worldwide. The Great Hall of the Moscow Conservatory in particular has been praised as being worthy of international respect, thanks to its wonderful decoration, comfortable location and magnificent acoustics. The Great Hall opened in April 1901 and was the project of architect Vasily Zagorsky. The Hall's famous façade remained a strong feature of the new building, which was formerly a house of Russian Princess Ekaterina Dashkova built at the end of the eighteenth century. In fact, the Great Hall of Moscow Conservatory is much bigger than a concert hall, serving a variety of purposes throughout its lifespan. During World War I it formed the base of a hospital, and during the period between 1924–33, the Hall was used as a popular movie theatre. Since 1940, the Conservatory has been named after Pyotr Tchaikovsky, and in 1954 a monument to the famous composer was unveiled in front of the Great Hall, leaving an indelible footprint of the great Russian artist on this memorable venue.

Bolshaya Nikitskaya street 13/6
Moscow
125009
Russia
Tel: +7 (0)495 629 2060
www.mosconsv.ru

TICKETING

Price Range: Concert ticket prices vary according to events. Subscription tickets are also available for various concert series.

Box Office

Tel: +7 (0)495 629 9401 or +7 (0)495 629 8183 for the general booking office.

PERFORMANCES

Resident Groups: The Moscow State Philharmonic

SEATING

Capacity: The Great Hall seats 1,737, the Small Hall seats 436. The Rachmaninov Hall seats 252.

Organization: The Great Hall is arranged into stalls and two amphitheatre style balconies.

HOW TO GET THERE

Underground: Biblioteka Imeni Lenina, Arbatskaya, Alexandrovsky Sad and Borovitskaya subway stations.

Bus: Trolley-bus nos. 1, 2, 15 and 31 to Nikitskiye Vorota; or nos. 12 and 20 to Ploshchad Mossoveta.

Tchaikovsky Concert Hall

One of the most peculiar structures built during the twentieth century, the Tchaikovsky Concert Hall of the Moscow Philharmonic was completed the year prior to the Nazi invasion of the Soviet Union. The crowning of the new venue in 1940 was celebrated with a gala of performances, including Tchaikovsky's 'Sixth Symphony: "Francesca da Rimini"' and airs from various operas and romances by the State Symphony Orchestra of the USSR. Nowadays, various performances of leading soloists, symphony orchestras, choruses, and choreographic ensembles take place regularly at the Tchaikovsky Concert Hall with opera productions, concert performances and musical dramatic plays all featuring at the venue. In addition, with a repertoire of approximately 300 concerts a year, the Moscow Philharmonic continues to lead the way in Russian classical music, taking the lead from the heart of the Russian capital.

Triumfalnaya Ploshchad 4/31
Moscow
Russia
Tel: +7 (0)95 232 5353

TICKETING

Box Office

Tel: +7 (0) 495 299 0658

PERFORMANCES

Resident Groups: The Moscow State Philharmonic and Tchaikovsky Symphony Orchestra. Several other orchestras play frequently at the venue. For a comprehensive list of these, please consult the local listings guide.

Annual Festivals/Special Events: The Virtuosos of Guitar in March, the Organ Music Festival and the Diaghilev International Festival.

SEATING

Capacity: 1,499

Organization: The Hall is arranged into a small stalls section, three amphitheatre style rings of seats, and a curved balcony at the top of the auditorium.

FACILITIES

Dining

The foyer of the concert hall offers various food stores.

ST PETERSBURG

Glinka Maly Zal

What translates into English as 'small hall' has gained a reputation in St Petersburg as possessing better acoustics than such venues as the vast Bolshoi Zal. Today, the Glinka Maly Zal presents to its visitors a wide range of classical and modern chamber music concerts. The venue was initially established in 1949 in the house of V Engelhard which in turn had stood since the eighteenth century. Throughout its performance history, the venue had played host to a range of well known Russian and international artists including Lizst, Schumann, Viardo, as well as modern composers like Shnitke, Prigozhin, and Banshchikov; a trend it continues, holding its own amongst the bigger classical venues in St Petersburg.

TICKETING

Box Office

The Box Office is open Monday to Friday, 11.00 a.m.–3.00 p.m. and 4.00 p.m.–8.00 p.m.

PERFORMANCES

Times: Performances take place at 3.00 p.m. and 7.00 p.m.

HOW TO GET THERE

Underground: The nearest Metro stations are the Nevsky Prospekt and the Gostiny Dvor. Single ticket (zheton/token) costs RUB 12.00 per journey.

Nevsky Prospekt 30
St Petersburg
Russia
Tel: +7 (0)812 312 4585

Mariinsky Theatre

The Mariinsky Theatre in St Petersburg was known until 1935 as the National Academy of Opera and Ballet and until 1992 as the Kirov Opera and Ballet Theatre. In 1783 Catherine the Great decreed that St Petersburg should produce opera, and a new Imperial Opera and Ballet Company was formed. They performed in various other concert halls until the architect Albert Cavos rebuilt his burnt-down wooden equestrian arena in 1859 as an opera and ballet house with the largest stage in the world in a U-shaped Italian-style auditorium which opened on October 1860 with a performance of 'A Life for the Tsar'. The new theatre was named Mariinsky after its royal patroness, Empress Maria Alexandrovna. The Mariinsky hosts performances by its world famous resident companies and touring groups, of Russian and world classics. The Theatre has a particular affinity with Wagner, the composer having conducted there on numerous occasions.

Teatralnaya Square 1
St Petersburg
190000
Russia
Tel: +7 (0)812 326 4141
Fax: +7 (0)812 314 1744
www.mariinsky.ru

TICKETING

Price Range: Tickets generally range from RUB 325.00 to RUB 3,250.00.

Concessions: There are no standard discounts at the Mariinsky. However, leftover tickets are offered at a discount from one hour before some performances.

Box Office

The Box Office is open daily, 11.00 a.m.–7.00 p.m.
Tel: +7 (0)812 326 4141
Fax: +7 (0)812 314 1744
www.mariinsky.ru

PERFORMANCES

Events take place from October to August.

Times: Matinee performances begin at 11.00 a.m. and evening performances at 6.30 p.m.

Resident Groups: The Mariinsky Orchestra (sometimes known as the Kirov), the Academy of Young Singers and the Mariinsky Opera Company.

SEATING

Capacity: 1,625

Organization: The auditorium is arranged into stalls, a circle, upper circle and boxes.

Best Seats: The middle stalls provide the best seats in rows 5–8, seats 6–25.

Good Seats on a Budget: Central boxes.

Seats to Avoid: The side boxes 1–5 and 20–24 may have limited views of the stage.

EDUCATION

Guided Tours

Tours must be requested one month in advance with confirmation received one week before the proposed date. Contact the general number for further details.

Cost: For groups of ten or more people, the cost is RUB 10.00 per person. For groups smaller than this, the price for ten people must be paid.

FACILITIES

Dining

The 'Backstage' Restaurant, located only a few steps from the Mariinsky Opera House attempts to recreate the post-performance atmosphere of the backstage area of the theatre. Menus are available online at www.mariinsky.ru/en/backstage.

Services

♿ Wheelchair access is available in the stalls.

HOW TO GET THERE

Underground: Metro Station Sadavaya is five minutes walk from the Theatre. Single ticket (zheton/token) costs RUB 12.00 per journey.

Bus: 15, 22 and 27 serve the Mariinsky from the Netsky area.

Mussorgsky Opera & Ballet Theatre

A concert hall 'Born by Revolution' – an epithet which was to become almost synonymous with the Mussorgsky Theatre as the October Revolution gripped the country. About a century earlier, the original theatre was born, and on 8 November 1833 the first performance took place on the stage of what was then known as the Imperial Mikhailovsky Theatre. However, unlike the already established Mariinsky and Alexandrinsky theatres, there was neither a fixed company nor a definite sense of repertoire and genre purpose at the Mikhailovsky. At first the theatre building was mainly used as a concert hall. During the initial years, besides the dramatic plays performed by the Alexandrinsky Theatre Company or by French and German touring actors, many opera performances occurred here. After the

Ploschad Iskusstv 1
St Petersburg
Russia
Tel: +7 (0)812 219 1949; or
+7 (0)812 318 1978
www.mikhailovsky.ru

Bolshevik Revolution had passed, the second birth of the Mikhailovsky Theatre took place on 6 March 1918 with the theatre opening its doors once again to showcase Rossini's 'Barber of Seville'. Having collaborated for many years with the Mariinsky Theatre, the Mussorgsky Theatre was given its current name in 1989 when the company finally became independent. Today, the Theatre's resident opera company has toured the world, continuing to mix pioneering opera with the classical performances which have seen the Mussorgsky flourish in its independence, becoming an intrinsic part of the culture and heritage of St Petersburg.

TICKETING

Price Range: Tickets generally range from RUB 175.00 to RUB 2250.00.

Concessions: There is a standard discount for students if the appropriate ID is presented.

Box Office

The Box Office is open Monday to Friday, 11.00 a.m.–3.00 p.m. and 4.00 p.m.–7.15 p.m. There is no charge if tickets are collected. Tickets can be delivered at a cost of RUB 200.00.
Tel: +7 (0)812 219 1949; or +7 (0)812 318 1978

PERFORMANCES

Times: Evening performances generally start at 7.00 p.m.

Resident Groups:
Mussorgsky Opera

SEATING

Capacity: 1,151

Organization: The Theatre is organized into three galleries, a dress circle, boxes and stalls.

Best Seats: The best seats are located in rows 1–4 of the stalls.

Seats to Avoid: Some of the side boxes may have slightly restricted views.

HOW TO GET THERE

Underground: The nearest Metro stations are the Nevsky Prospekt and the Gostiny Dvor. Single ticket (zheton/token) costs RUB 12.00 per journey.

Shostakovich Philharmonia

Constructed in 1839 by the architects P Jacot and C Rossi for the St Petersburg Assembly of the Noble, the Shostakovich Philharmonia combines wonderful acoustics with a central location which has placed it at the centre of the city's musical life since end of the 1840s. Numerous renowned musicians of the nineteenth century have performed here, including Lizst, Berlioz, Wagner, Mahler and Schumann. Exponents of Russian classical tradition like Borodin, Mussorgsky, and Tchaikovsky have premiered many of their works at the venue. An international roll-call

Mikhailovskaya Ulitsa 2
St Petersburg
Russia
Tel: +7 (0)812 312 9871 or
+7 (0)812 710 4085
www.philharmonia.spb.ru

of orchestras, the Philadelphia, Cleveland, Chicago Orchestras, the Berlin, Vienna and New York Philharmonic Orchestras, and the Konzertgebau of Amsterdam have all heard their musical melodies reverberate through the Shostakovich Philharmonia's walls. Dmitri Shostakovich, after whom the Hall is now named, was a famous Russian composer whose first symphony was premiered at the Philharmonia in 12 May 1926. He continued to showcase successful performances at the venue for many years, and in homage to this great artist, the St Petersburg Philharmonia now bears his name.

TICKETING

Box Office

The Box Office is open Monday to Friday, 11.00 a.m.–3.00 p.m. and 4.00 p.m.–7.30 p.m.

PERFORMANCES

Times: Performances take place at 4.00 p.m. and 7.00 p.m.

Resident Groups: The St Petersburg Academic Symphony Orchestra and St Petersburg Philharmonic Orchestra.

SEATING

Capacity: 1,318

HOW TO GET THERE

Underground: The nearest Metro stations are the Nevsky Prospekt and the Gostiny Dvor. Single ticket (zheton/token) costs RUB 12.00 per journey.

St Petersburg State Capella

One of St Petersburg's best kept secrets, the St Petersburg State Capella stands today as the oldest concert hall in the city. It was founded as the residence of the Emperor Court Choir Capella, the oldest professional choir in St Petersburg, which was established in Moscow in 1479 and transferred to St Petersburg in 1703 by order of Peter the Great. Famous for its choral works, today the venue has broadened its horizons to include symphonic, instrumental, and vocal concerts. The first building of the Capella was constructed during the 1770s. Between 1886–89, the building was completely redesigned by architect Louis N Benois in the French classical style and enclosed within a courtyard off the Moika River. Many famous musicians, including Glinka and Rimsky-Korsakov, have performed in this elegant space. In recent years, the main entrance and the surrounding courtyards have been beautifully restored to offer visitors a classical venue situated right at the cultural heart of St Petersburg amongst such sites as the Alexander Pushkin Museum and the magnificent Winter Palace.

TICKETING

Box Office

The Box Office is open Monday to Friday, noon–3.00 p.m. and 4.00 p.m.–7.00 p.m.

PERFORMANCES

Times: Evening performances generally start at 7.00 p.m.

Resident Groups: St Petersburg State Academic Capella Symphony Orchestra

Naberezhnaya Reki Moika 20
St Petersburg
Russia
Tel: +7 (0)812 314 1153

SEATING

Organization: The auditorium is arranged into stalls, a balcony and a gallery.

HOW TO GET THERE

Underground: The nearest Metro stations are the Nevsky Prospekt and the Gostiny Dvor. Single ticket (zheton/token) costs RUB 12.00 per journey.

SERBIA

BELGRADE

Belgrade Cultural Centre

Diverse in its repertoire and keen to promote young talent, the Belgrade Cultural Centre is a truly multidisciplinary centre founded in 1957 to harness several aspects of visual art and culture under one roof. Much of the Centre's activities revolve around providing a platform for talented young writers, musicians and painters within the repetitive artistic scene, initiating new programmes such as the Culture Periodicals Fair and the Child and Culture Project. Established values and research projects are equally present in the programmes that the Centre organizes today. Besides its traditional programmes and city events, including the October Salon and BELEF (Belgrade Summer Festival), the Centre also supports alternative urban projects and organizes musical festivals such as the Guitar Art Festival, the Flute Festival – Always and Everywhere, and the Organ days, as well as a multimedia project called 'The Festival of a Writer'. Continuing to play

Knez Mihailova 6/I
Belgrade
11000
Serbia
Tel: +381 (0)11 621 469
Fax: +381 (0)11 623 853
www.kcb.org.yu

an active role in Belgrade culture, the framework of the Belgrade Cultural Centre music programme maintains its focus on elevating musical talent, allowing both established and new artists an equal footing on its diverse and multifarious stage.

TICKETING

Price Range: Ticket prices vary according to performances.

Box Office

The Box Office is open Monday to Friday, 9.00 a.m.–8.00 p.m.; Saturday, 9.00 a.m.–3.00 p.m. Tel: +381 (0)11 628 342

PERFORMANCES

Events take place all year round.

Annual Festivals/Special Events: The Guitar Art Festival takes place annually in April.

FACILITIES

Dining

Two cafés, Palette and the Film Workers' Club are a part of the Belgrade Cultural Centre, where visitors can find various refreshments and relax in the pleasant atmosphere.

HOW TO GET THERE

Bus: 24, 26, 34, 36 and 37 stop near the Centre. Bus and tram tickets cost YUM 20.00 on board and YUM 12.00 if bought in kiosks to be validated on board.

Ilije M Kolarca Foundation

In his last will and testament, philanthropist Ilija M Kolarac bequeathed all his property to the Serbian people with the aim to first establish a literary fund dedicated to Belgrade culture, and subsequently to find a site for erecting a Serbian university. Kolarac lived to see his Foundation established, although the opening of the Foundation building was to surpass him. The first concert in his name was held on 4 February 1932, with the Foundation building officially opening on 19 October 1932. Today, the Foundation plays an active part in Belgrade culture, and is dedicated to the learning of others, hosting approximately 200 lectures and over 250 concerts and other events every year. Amongst the musicians who have performed here over the years the list has included Britten, Prokofiev, Arthur

Rubinstein, Evgeny Kissin and Segovia, a list which continues to grow through its regular concert programmes, many festivals and special events which take place throughout the year.

Zadužbina Ilije M Kolarca
Studentski trg 5
Belgrade
11000
Serbia
Tel: +381 (0)11 263 5073
Fax: +381 (0)32 263 6319
www.kolarac.co.yu

TICKETING

Price Range: Ticket prices vary according to performances.

Concessions: There is a discount for children which varies on performances. There is also a 50% discount available for students.

Box Office

The Box Office is open Monday to Friday, 10.00 a.m.–2.00 p.m. and 2.30 p.m.–8.00 p.m.; Saturday, 10.00 a.m.–2.00 p.m. and 6.00 p.m.–8.00 p.m; Sunday, 6.00 p.m.–8.00 p.m. Tickets must be collected from the Ilije M Kolarca Foundation Box Office.

Tel: +381 (0)11 630 550
Fax: +381 (0) 32 82 467

PERFORMANCES

Events take place from September to June.

Programmes: Programmes are available free from the Box Office with the purchase of a ticket. Available in Serbian only.

Annual Festivals/Special Events: The Belgrade Guitar Art Festival, the Belgrade International Cello Festival, the Belgrade Music Festival and the International Review of Composers all take place at the venue.

SEATING

Capacity: Large Hall – 883; Small Hall – 200.

Best Seats: The best seats are located in row 9 in the middle.

Seats to Avoid: There are no seats with restricted views.

FACILITIES

Dining

Situated in the cellar, the venue is equipped with an Italian restaurant which serves a range of meals and drinks to keep visitors' appetite filled.

HOW TO GET THERE

Bus: Trolley-bus 21, 22, 28, 29 and 41 and bus 31. Bus and tram tickets cost YUM 20.00 on board and YUM 12.00 if bought in kiosks to be validated on board.

Narodno Pozorište

Standing proudly as one of Serbia's largest and most luxurious buildings, the Narodno Pozorište or National Belgrade Theatre is reminiscent in its architecture of La Scala in Milan, possessing a similar façade and division of spaces as the Italian venue. The venue opened officially in 1919, after many years of trying to become a professional opera ensemble, and staged its first performance, under the conductorship of Stanislav Binicki, of Giacomo Puccini's 'Madam Butterfly'.

Pozorisni trg 1
Francuska 3
Belgrade
11000
Serbia
Tel: +381 (0)11 620 946
Fax: +381 (0)11 262 2560
www.narodnopozoriste.co.yu

The opera house continued to grow from strength to strength, with performances by artists such as Italian composers Rossini and Verdi, and Serbian music by renowned composer Stevan Hristic. World War II bombings destroyed much of the building in 1941, which underwent several restorations over the next 50 years in order to return the venue to its former glory. This time a completely new building of very modern architecture was added, an imposing structure of steel and dark glass which now houses the technological part of the Theatre. Thus reconstructed, the National Theatre represents a union of old and modern architecture, and technically speaking, is one of the most modern theatres in the world. Today the Belgrade Opera possesses considerable and varied repertoire, thanks to the musical leadership of prominent composers, directors and soloists who perform successfully on stage here and abroad.

TICKETING

Price Range: Tickets generally range from YUM 100.00 to YUM 800.00.

Concessions: There are discounts available for children and students which vary according to the performances.

Box Office

Tickets cannot be booked in advance other than at the venue itself, where tickets are issued on the day.

PERFORMANCES

Events take place from October to June.

Programmes: Programmes are available for most performances. Most programmes are bilingual in both English and Serbian.

Resident Groups: The Serbian National Opera

SEATING

Capacity: The main hall has a capacity of 559.

Organization: There are two halls at the Narodno Pozoriste, the Grand Hall on three levels and the smaller single level Raša Plaovic. The main halls have six categories of seats which are arranged by price and viewing position.

Best Seats: The 245 seats in the first category, (floor and first gallery) provide audiences with the best views.

Good Seats on a Budget: The seats located in the second gallery provide visitors with a perfect view at a reasonable price.

Seats to Avoid: The sixth category seats, standing on the third gallery provide the cheapest seats, although the view is not impaired.

FACILITIES

Dining

The Boemi Restaurant, located in the basement of the venue, provide visitors with a range of food and refreshments. In addition, a bit of star-spotting can be found at Teatar. Located on the fourth floor, artists can sometimes be seen grabbing a bite from this alternative café/restaurant.

Services

Disabled access.

HOW TO GET THERE

Overground: The building is situated on the Main Square in Belgrade, so visitors can easily gain access to the venue via almost all modes of transport.

The Belgrade Philharmonic Hall

Founded in 1923 by the eminent composer and conductor Stevan Hristic, the Belgrade Philharmonic Hall has a history which has seen it play host to some of the most eminent artists from around the world in this relatively small but prominent concert hall. Over the years, the Belgrade Philharmonic Hall has seen artists such as Rafael Kubelik, Malcolm Sargent, Andre Navarra, Arthur Rubinstein, Julian Rachlin, Valery Afanasiev and Nigel Kennedy performing on its stage. Continuing to attract world-class musicians, it is also keen to harness the talent of the future, and today boasts a relatively young orchestra with an average age of 28. This in turn has attracted younger audiences to the venue, spawning a mini-revival of classical music in Belgrade. The BPO concert hall holds 201 seats and offers ideal conditions for audio and video recordings. Most concerts of the Belgrade Philharmonic Orchestra traditionally take place in the Kolarac Foundation Hall, while the smaller concert hall is used for special events and chamber concerts.

TICKETING

Price Range: Tickets generally range from YUM 500.00 to YUM 1,000.00.

Concessions: There are no concessions available.

Box Office

The Box Office is open Monday to Friday, 9.00 a.m.–4.00 p.m.
Tel: +381 (0)11 328 2977

Studentski trg 11
Belgrade
11000
Serbia
Tel: +381 (0)11 3282 977
Fax: +381 (0)11 187 533
www.bgf.co.yu

PERFORMANCES

Programmes: Programmes can be collected from the Hall Box Office and are provided free of charge with a ticket. Available in Serbian only.

Resident Groups: The Belgrade Philharmonic Orchestra

SEATING

Capacity: 201

Best Seats: Rows 10 and 11 provide the best seats.

Seats to Avoid: Seats in the gallery may have limited views of the stage.

FACILITIES

Services

♿ Disabled access.

HOW TO GET THERE

Bus: From Belgrade Train Station take the bus route 31 to the Philharmonic Hall, or tram lines 11 and 2. Bus and tram tickets cost YUM 20.00 on bus and YUM 12.00 if bought in kiosks to be validated on board.

SLOVAKIA

BRATISLAVA

Slovak National Theatre

Located behind Victor Tilgner's famous 1888 Ganymede's Fountain, what is referred to as the Slovak National Theatre's 'Historical Building' stands on the site occupied by the municipal theatre built at the request of Count György Csáky in 1776. The present building was designed in a Neo-Renaissance style by Ferdinand Fellner and Hermann Helmer, and opened in 1886 with a performance of Erkel's 'Bánk bán', presented by the Budapest National Theatre Company. The building has been housing the Slovak National Theatre ensembles since 1920, today home to just the opera and ballet ensembles. It was restored between 1969 and 1972, when a new modern technical building was added behind the old building. It features a unique lustre, containing 2,532 bulbs enabling producers to create millions of combinations of light pictures based on a selected programme. The venue continues to stage the best classical performances, featuring the work of the greats and continuing a traditional repertoire of the best in classical music.

Pribinova 4
Bratislava
SK-815 86
Slovakia
Tel: +421 (0)25 778 2110
Fax: +421 (0)25 443 0419
www.snd.sk

TICKETING

Price Range: Tickets generally range from €1.50 to €30.00.

Concessions: There is a 50% discount available for children, disabled visitors and their carers.

Box Office

In addition to the Box Office located at the concert hall, there is also a direct sales office in Komenského Square. The Box Office is open Monday to Friday, 8.00 a.m.–7.00 p.m.; Saturday, 9.00 a.m.–1.00 p.m. In addition, the Box Office is open on weekends from an hour before the performance commences. Tickets must be collected from the Box Office at least 30 minutes before the performance.
Tel: +421 (0)254 433 764
Fax: +421 (0) 5443 3890
There is no online booking service, but visitors can email opera.balet@snd.sk in order to reserve tickets.

PERFORMANCES

Resident Groups: The Slovakian National Opera

SEATING

Capacity: 611

Organization: The auditorium is arranged into stalls, a mezzanine section, a dress circle and an upper circle.

Best Seats: The best seats are located in the central stalls.

Seats to Avoid: No seats have restricted views.

FACILITIES

Dining

There is a bar in the Hall which serves drinks and snacks.

Services

Guide dogs welcome.

Wheelchair access is available with designated spaces located in front of the stage.

HOW TO GET THERE

Overground: Tram number 14 from the Main Central Station. Tickets cost from SKK 14.00 (for short journeys). One day travel pass costs SKK 90.00.

The Reduta

A former Baroque granary built in accordance with an order of Maria Theresa in 1773, the Slovak National Philharmonic is a body of international reputation, already in its 58th season. Between 1913–19, the building which houses this orchestra was transformed into a Neo-Baroque style with Rococco and Art Nouveau elements. Local handicraft was put to good use, with many Slovak and foreign craftsmen participating in the decoration of the façade and interiors. Refined stuccowork and other interior wall decorations, stained glass forming various compositions, and precious windowpanes with ornament-etched glass make the most remarkable embellishment of the building. The Reduta became the home of the Slovak Philharmonic in the early 1950s and continues to offer to the wide public a rich concert life and performances of artists and their ensembles from all over the world.

Hviezdoslavovo Square
Bratislava
Slovakia
Tel: +421 (0)25 443 3351
Fax: +421 (0)25 443 3352
www.filharm.sk

TICKETING

Advance Sales: Tickets generally go on sale from three months in advance, although this can vary.

Price Range: Tickets generally range from SKK 90.00 to SKK 450.00.

Concessions: There are discounts available for children and students which vary according to performances.

Box Office

The Box Office is open Monday, Tuesday, Thursday, Friday, 1.00 p.m.–7.00 p.m. and Wednesday, 8.00 a.m.–2.00 p.m. and from one hour before the concert commences.
Tel: +421 (0)25 920 8233 or +421 (0)25 920 8211 (direct).
Fax: +421 (0)25 443 5956
www.ticketportal.sk or at www.eventim.sk

PERFORMANCES

Times: Evening performances generally start at 7.00 p.m.

Resident Groups: The Slovak National Philharmonic Orchestra, the Slovak Philharmonic

Choir and Slovak Chamber Orchestra.

SEATING

Capacity: The Main Hall seats 700 people.

Organization: The Main Hall is arranged into stalls and a balcony.

Best Seats: The best seats are located in the balcony.

SLOVENIA

LJUBLJANA

Cankarjev Dom

Dedicated to the famous Slovenian writer and poet Ivan Cankar, the Cankarjev Dom stands today as a multi-purpose arts centre which hosts a wide range of events throughout the year. The building was originally constructed as an addition to the original Trg Republike Square designed by architect Edvard Ravnikar in 1960, who was charged with the construction of both buildings. In order to prevent it from being too tall, most of the halls were built underground. The above-ground part of the Cankarjev Dom building consists of three wings, the taller one in the middle and the two lower ones at the sides. The façade is covered in white stone and ornamented with decorative folds at the sides. Located in front of the building is a monument by the sculptor Slavko Tihec, shaped in the form of a multi-layer metal cube featuring the face of Ivan Cankar.

Prešernova 10
Ljubljana
SLO-1000
Slovenia
Tel: +386 (0)12 417 100
Fax: +386 (0)12 417 295
www.cd-cc.si

The building of Cankarjev Dom was a drawn out process stretched over seven years due to funding problems. It finally fully opened in 1984. The site now consists of four concert halls, the biggest being Gallus Hall for symphonic works and opera or ballet. Linhart Hall is roughly half the size and caters to similar events, while the smaller Kosovel Hall and Stih Hall are suitable for chamber music and recitals.

TICKETING

Price Range: Tickets generally range from SIT 4,000.00 to SIT 15,000.00. (Both old Tolar and equivalent € prices are also displayed as Slovenia converted to the Euro on 01/01/2007).

Concessions: Children, students, senior citizens and disabled visitors receive a 10% ticket discount.

Box Office

The Box Office is open Monday to Friday, 9.00 a.m.–8.00 p.m.; Saturday, 11.00 a.m.–1.00 p.m.
Tel: +386 (0)12 417 199
Tickets can be bought using the 'Moneta' online system at www.cd-cc.si/siti.

PERFORMANCES

Resident Groups: The Slovenian National Theatre of Opera and Ballet. In addition, the Slovenian Philharmonic plays at the venue regularly.

SEATING

Capacity: Gallus Hall – 1,545; Linhart Hall – 616; Stih Hall – 253; Kosovel Hall – 212.

Best Seats: The best seats are located in the balcony.

Seats to Avoid: Seats very close to the stage may have a slightly limited view.

EDUCATION

Guided Tours

A tour can be arranged with the venue in advance. Visitors are advised to phone the venue to obtain further information and pricing. Tel: +386 (0)12 417 100

FACILITIES

Dining

There is a restaurant at Cankarjev Dom which serves a range of hot and cold food.

Services

HOW TO GET THERE

Bus: From the railway station, bus 9 to the 'Drama' stop, where bus nos. 1, 3, 6 and 19 also stop. Not far away there is also bus stop 'Kongresni trg', where bus nos. 2, 10, 11, 13, 17, 20, 21 stop. Bus no. 14 also goes near Cankarjev Dom to Prešeren Street. A single ticket costs €0.79 (approximately). Day ticket costs €3.75.

Car Parking: Parking is available at Cankarjev Dom after 7.00 p.m.

Slovenian Philharmonic Hall

'*Receat, mentique perennia monstrat*' ('It entertains, and reveals eternal things to the mind'); the motto engraved on the Academia Philharmonicorum's seal, one of the first academies founded in 1701 to perform symphonic compositions of European and particularly Italian Baroque masters to the town's aristocracy. By the end of the eighteenth century the association ceased to exist, and was replaced by the Philharmonic Society (Philharmonische Gesellschaft), founded in 1794, as one of the first establishments of this kind within the Habsburg monarchy. The Society's orchestra was completed with professional and well versed musicians and the repertoire was enriched with works by the most significant composers in Europe such as Haydn, Mozart and Beethoven; Schubert, Schumann, Brahms and Liszt. In 1947, a resolution was passed on the formation of the Slovenian Philharmonic and the first concert of the new Slovenian Philharmonic Orchestra, led by the Spanish conductor Salvador Bacarisse, took place on 13 January 1948. Today, far from being exclusive to only the richest of visitors as was the intention in the eighteenth century, the Slovenian Philharmonic Hall welcomes visitors and performers alike from around the world, with concerts on native and foreign stages and a programme consisting of a vast selection of works, maintaining the high level of quality in its performances that it has always been renowned for.

TICKETING

Price Range: Tickets generally range from SIT 1,200.00 to SIT 6,600.00. (Both old Tolar and equivalent € prices are also displayed as Slovenia converted to the Euro on 01/01/2007).

Concessions: Children, students and senior citizens are admitted at a price SIT 1,000.00. Carers of disabled visitors are eligible for a free ticket.

Box Office

The Box Office is open Monday to Friday,
1.00 p.m.–8.00 p.m.
Tel: +386 (0)12 410 800

PERFORMANCES

Resident Groups: The Slovenian Philharmonic

SEATING

Seat Capacity: 507

Organization: The Great Hall has stalls and one large balcony. The Small Hall has one level.

Kongresni trg 10
Ljubljana
SLO-1000
Slovenia
Tel: +386 (0)12 410 800
Fax: +386 (0)12 410 900
www.filharmonija.si

Best Seats: The best seats are located in the first seven rows of the balcony.

Good Seats on a Budget: The seats at the back of the balcony are cheap with good views.

Seats to Avoid: No seats have restricted views.

EDUCATION

Guided Tours

Free guided tours of the venue can be arranged on request. Contact the venue to arrange. Tel: +386 (0)12 410 800

FACILITIES

Dining

There is a bar at the Hall, serving a range of drinks and light snacks.

Services

Disabled access.

HOW TO GET THERE

Bus: No. 9 runs from the station to the theatre. A single ticket costs €0.79 (approximately). Day ticket costs €3.75.

SPAIN

BARCELONA

Gran Teatro del Liceo

Founded in 1847 and financed by a share trading scheme (in contrast to the majority of opera houses which were financed by royal patronage), the Gran Teatro del Liceo was designed by Miquel Garriga i Roca and Josep Oriol Mestres as a showcase for the power of the bourgeois. However, the venue's philosophy was not free from scrutiny, as was demonstrated when the venue was attacked by an anarchist bomber in 1893. By 1980 the share trading system was no longer seen as viable, and its ownership was transferred to the Consorci del Gran Teatre del Liceu. A large part of it was destroyed in 1994 by a fire, which saw its ownership being transferred to public administrators. Its rebuilding was faithful to the original design but now featured state-of-the-art technology. Today, its programmes reflect the aims of the institution – to attract great opera as an indication of Barcelona's cultural wealth and social significance.

51-59 La Rambla
Barcelona
ES-08002
Spain
Tel: +34 (0)93 485 9900
Fax: +34 (0)93 485 9918
www.liceubarcelona.com

TICKETING

Advance Sales: Tickets can be booked from the beginning of the season.

Price Range: Tickets generally range from €6.75 to €174.00.

Concessions: A 30% discount is offered for tickets brought on the day of performance for those under 26, senior citizens, disabled visitors and their carers. Other discounts (of up to 70%) are available for specific performances, varying by season.

Box Office

The Box Office is open Monday to Friday, 2.00 p.m.–8.30 p.m.; although times can vary during July. The Box Office is closed from 5 to 20 August. During weekends, it only opens one hour before the show commences. There is a €1.20 per ticket transaction charge for remote bookings. Tel: +34 (0)93 274 6411 (international); or +34 (0)93 485 9913 (national)

Lines are open Monday to Friday, 10.00 a.m.–10.00 p.m.
Fax: +34 (0)93 485 9928
www.liceubarcelona.com/liceu directe.asp

PERFORMANCES

Events take place from September to July.

Times: Performance times vary, usually 8.30 p.m.; matinees and morning performances are also available.

Resident Groups: The Symphony Orchestra of the Gran Teatre del Liceu and the Chorus of the Gran Teatre del Liceu

SEATING

Capacity: 2,292

Organization: The auditorium is shaped like a horseshoe around the centre stage, and arranged across six floors.

Best Seats: The best seats are located in Zone 2.

Good Seats on a Budget: Tickets in Zone 6 are fairly cheap and provide reasonable views.

Seats to Avoid: Zone 8 has no vision of the stage, with Zone 7 and some seats in other zones having restricted views.

EDUCATION

Guided Tours

The Gran Teatre del Liceu offers the possibility of daily tours of its most representative spaces, including the auditorium, the Mirrored Salon and foyer. In addition, visitors can experience the Cercle del Liceu, a private club which shares the building with the theatre, providing a stunning example of Catalan Modernism with exceptional pictorial and decorative works of art and a collection of paintings by Ramon Casas. For visitors wishing to gain an insight into what goes on backstage at the Liceo, a special tour introduces them to the various rooms and workings of the theatre. There are limited spaces and places for this tour, therefore, must be reserved in advance. Tel: +34 (0)93 485 9914, email: visites@liceubarcelona.com or see the website for further information or to book tickets.

Times: Public areas guided: 10.00 a.m.; Unguided: 11.30 a.m., noon, 12.30 p.m. and 1.00 p.m.; Backstage tours are conducted at 9.30 a.m.

Cost: Public area tours cost €8.50; €4.00 per person for unguided tours; A backstage tour costs €10.00 per person.

Concessions: €5.00

FACILITIES

Dining

The Gran Teatro del Liceo contains a coffee shop which serves a variety of food and refreshments.

Services

Disabled access throughout the building. Contact in advance for further information.

Guide dogs welcome.

Signed performances are offered on occasion. Contact the venue for further details.

HOW TO GET THERE

Underground: The Liceo Metro stop is located opposite the concert hall. Single ticket costs €1.20. Day ticket costs from €5.00.

Bus: 14, 59

Palau de la Música Catalana

Designed in the Catalan modernisme style by the architect Lluís Domènech i Montaner, the Palau de la Música Catalana was constructed between 1905 and 1908 as a permanent home for the Orfeó Català (Catalan Choral Society), which for many years had moved between various sites in the old quarter of Barcelona. Its musical activities flourished almost immediately with a special set of concerts, the centre-piece of which was the opening of a venue by the Berlin Philharmonic and Richard Strauss. This strong classical music theme continues to this day. Inside, the Palau de la Música Catalana includes the only auditorium in Europe illuminated solely during daylight hours by natural light. The walls on two sides consist primarily of stained glass panes set in magnificent arches, and overhead is an enormous skylight of stained

C/ Sant Francesc de Paula 2
Barcelona
ES-08003
Spain
Tel: +34 (0)93 295 7200
Fax: +34 (0)93 295 7210
www.palaumusica.org

glass designed by Antoni Rigalt, whose centrepiece is an inverted dome in shades of gold surrounded by blue which evokes the sun and the sky. Its cultural significance meant that in 1997 the Palau de la Música Catalana was declared a UNESCO World Heritage Site. Today, more than half a million people a year attend musical performances in the Palau, which ranges from jazz to Cançó (Catalan song), whilst never forgetting its roots in classical music and world-class performances.

TICKETING

Advance Sales: Tickets can be booked from the beginning of the season.

Price Range: Tickets generally range from €9.00 to €175.00.

Concessions: Children 3 and under go free. Typically, the cheapest seats are given to the disabled.

Box Office

The Box Office is open Monday to Saturday, 10.00 a.m.–9.00 p.m.; on Sundays, the Box Office opens from one hour before the concert begins.
Tel: +34 (0)902 442 882
Fax: +34 (0)93 295 7208
www.telentrada.com

PERFORMANCES

Events take place all year round.

Times: Performance times vary, usually 9.00 p.m.; matinees are also available.

SEATING

Capacity: 2,138

Organization: The auditorium is divided into stalls and two balconies. Tickets are priced in zones. Ask at the Box Office for further information.

Best Seats: Seats located on the ground and first floors provide the best views.

Good Seats on a Budget: Seats located on the top of second balcony provide adequate views for a good price.

Seats to Avoid: Some zones have a restricted view.

EDUCATION

Guided Tours

Visitors are invited to join a tour of the Palau de la Música Catalana which is conducted daily at various times throughout the day. Tickets may be purchased on the day, although large groups are advised to purchase their tickets in advance. Tel: +34 (0)902 442 882, email: taquilles@palaumusica.org or see the website for further information or to book a ticket.

Times: 10.00 a.m.–3.30 p.m., tours start every half hour and last approximately 50 minutes.

Cost: €10.00

Concessions: €9.00

FACILITIES

Dining

El Mirador Restaurant is open to visitors during normal business hours, and provides visitors with a pleasant and contemporary atmosphere to enjoy their meals.

Services

Disabled access.

HOW TO GET THERE

Underground: Metro lines I and IV to Urquinaona. Single ticket costs €1.20. Day ticket costs from €5.00.

Bus: 17, 19, 40 and 45

Car Parking: Car parking is available at Plaza de Urquinaona, Av. de la Catedral, Ortigosa 7.

BILBAO

Euskalduna Palace

A triumph of modernist architecture, equipped with excellent acoustics, a magnificent organ and Europe's second largest stage, the Euskalduna Palace opened in 1999 beside the Estuary of Bilbao in the area that was formerly occupied by the Euskalduna shipyards. The venue was designed as a multi-purpose centre, with opera and ballet performances held under the same roof as corporate conferences. Opera soprano, Montserrat Caballé, once stated that never before had she sung at such a stunning venue, and today, visitors can experience the unique and diverse atmosphere that saw the complex win the International Congress Palace Association as the world's best Congress Centre in 2003.

Avenida Abandoibarra
Bilbao
Euskadi
ES-48011
Spain
Tel: +34 (0)94 403 5000
Fax: +34 (0)94 403 5001
www.euskalduna.net

TICKETING

Box Office

Together with the regular Box Office, in the building there are also multi-service teller machines in the foyer from which visitors can collect tickets purchased online or by phone.
Tel: +34 (0)94 431 0310
www.generaltickets.com/bbk

PERFORMANCES

Resident Groups: Bilbao Symphony Orchestra

SEATING

Capacity: Auditorium–2,164; Theatre Hall–613

EDUCATION

Guided Tours

The Euskalduna Palace offers both tours catering for individuals and groups. Group tours are conducted daily by arrangement. A guided tour of the Conference Centre for individuals is held every Saturday. Tickets for individuals can be purchased from the guide of the Euskalduna Centre, group visits should be arranged in advance. Tel: +34 (0)94 403 5000 to book tickets or see the website for further information.

Times: Group tours to be arranged; tours of the Conference Centre on Saturday take place at noon.

Cost: €2.00 for tours of Conference Centre; other tours cost €4.00, with the possibility of group discount.

Concessions: Tours of the Conference Centre cost €1.00 for children and pensioners.

FACILITIES

Dining

The Jauregia and Extanobe restaurants located on-site provide visitors with everything from light refreshments to a range of meals. The latter boasts Antonio Canales as its head chef, one of the most renowned Basque chefs.

HOW TO GET THERE

Underground: San Mames Station. Single ticket costs from €1.20. Day ticket costs €3.00.

Car Parking: There are 475 car parking spaces located on-site.

Teatro Arriaga

Culture in Bilbao had been flourishing for some years before the first formal theatre was constructed in 1799, although sadly the building was destroyed by a fire in 1816. However, the city's hunger for a replacement venue led to construction of two venues on the same site within a century, and on 31 May 1890, the curtain was raised on the inaugural performance of the Arriaga Theatre with Amilcare Ponchielli's 'La Gioconda'. The Theatre provided a perfect combination of classical decoration and the latest technological advances of its time, and the night it opened, the electric lighting impressed the audience more than the performance. In addition, those who wished could even follow the show over the telephone, an option that costs 15 pesetas. Tragedy was to strike a second time when in 1914, a second fire burnt the venue almost to destruction. Architect Federico de Ugalde was charged with the task of rebuilding the Arriaga Theatre. He renewed the building's entire structure, making it larger and safer. The Theatre reopened in 1919 to Giuseppe Verdi's 'Don Carlo', performed by the Ercole Casali Company. Currently, the Arriaga Theatre is owned entirely by the municipality and is managed by a private limited company that was incorporated on 3 October 1986. During this new phase, the Theatre has welcomed first class artists and performances. Many productions continue to debut here, with the venue producing shows which have travelled to cities all over the world.

Plaza Arriaga S/N
Bilbao
ES-48005
Spain
Tel: +34 (0)94 479 2036
Fax: +34 (0)94 41612
www.teatroarriaga.com

TICKETING

Advance Sales: Tickets can be booked from the beginning of the season.

Price Range: Tickets generally range from €4.80 to €42.00.

Concessions: There is a 25% discount available for visitors under 30 and over 65.

Box Office

> The Box Office is open Saturday, Sunday, Monday, and Tuesday, 11.30 a.m.–2.00 p.m. and 5.00 p.m.–7.00 p.m.; Wednesday, Thursday, and Friday, 11.30 a.m.–2.00 p.m. and 5.00 p.m.–8.30 p.m.
> Tel: +34 (0)94 431 0310
> www.generaltickets.com/bbk

PERFORMANCES

Events take place from September to May.

Times: Performances vary; typically starts at 8.00 p.m.

SEATING

Capacity: 1,200

Organization: The auditorium is arranged into stalls and four balconies, arranged in a horseshoe formation.

EDUCATION

Guided Tours

Tours of the venue can be arranged in advance, with visits taking place on weekday mornings provided they fit in with the Theatre's schedule. Tel: +34 (0)94 479 2036 to arrange a tour.

FACILITIES

Services

Disabled access.

HOW TO GET THERE

Underground: The Cascoviejo Station is located two minutes from the venue. Single ticket costs from €1.20. Day ticket costs €3.00.

> The Guggenheim in Bilbao is a museum filled with twists and turns. Frank Gehry's creation is one of the most celebrated buildings of the 90s. Inside, the Museum exhibits some of the best in modern and contemporary art, with Pop Art, Minimalism, Arte Povera, Conceptual Art and Abstract Expressionism. For more information: www.guggenheim-bilbao.es

LAS PALMAS

Auditorio Alfredo Kraus

Opened on 5 December 1997, and named after the tenor of the same name, the Auditorio Alfredo Kraus is a truly majestic building whose geometric shapes and sheer height give it an appearance of real volume. It stands very much apart from its surroundings, being designed as a majestic fortress. However, it is still clearly integrated its local environment, seated on the volcanic rock of the surrounding beach. The Symphonic and the Chamber Hall form the backdrop for frequent concerts, both classical and modern. At the beginning of each year some of the world's foremost orchestras and soloists assemble here for the Canary Islands' Music Festival, and throughout the year the auditorium runs its own programme of concerts, as well as those of the Las Palmas Philharmonic Society and the Annual Jazz and Guitar Festivals, providing more than 100 concerts of music of all varieties. Alfredo Kraus Trujillo himself was a Spanish tenor of Austrian descent, and is considered amongst the legendary tenors of the twentieth century like Plácido Domingo, José Carreras, Jon Vickers and Luciano Pavarotti, with his best known performance probably being his title role in Massenet's 'Werther'.

TICKETING

Advance Sales: Tickets can be booked a month in advance.

Price Range: Tickets generally range from €10.00 to €95.00.

Box Office

The Box Office is open Monday to Friday, 10.00 a.m.–2.00 p.m. and 4.30 p.m.–8.30 p.m.; Saturday, 10.00 a.m.–2.00 p.m.
Tel: +34 (0)92 849 1770
Fax: +34 (0)92 849 1773
www.auditorio-alfredokraus.com

Av. Principe de Asturias, S/N
Las Palmas de Gran Canaria
ES-35010
Canary Islands
Tel: +34 (0)92 849 1770
Fax: +34 (0)92 849 1853
www.auditorio-alfredokraus.com

PERFORMANCES

Events take place from September to July.

Times: Performance times vary, typically starting at 8.30 p.m.

Resident Groups: Las Palmas Philharmonic Society

Annual Festivals/Special Events: Festival de Canarias takes place from January to March. The Canarias Festival of Jazz is held every summer, from June to July.

SEATING

Organization: There are two halls in the venue, the Symphonic Hall and the Chamber Hall. The Symphonic Hall is set up in slopes, giving each seat an excellent view and acoustics; the Chamber Hall is arranged in a semicircle.

Best Seats: The best seats are located in the dress circle and stalls.

EDUCATION

Guided Tours

Tours of the auditorium and the venue, which provide visitors with an insight into the daily running of the Auditorio Alfredo Kraus, take place from Monday to Friday, and every Sunday. See the website for further details.

Times: Monday to Friday, noon; Sunday, 11.30 a.m., coinciding with organ concerts.

Cost: €3.00

Concessions: €1.80

FACILITIES

Services

Disabled access.

HOW TO GET THERE

Bus: 17, 25, 31, 35, 101, 102, 103, 105, 116, 117, 127, 201, 202, 204, 206, 210, 234 and 371

Car Parking: There are 500 car parking spaces located on-site.

MADRID

Teatro de la Zarzuela

As the name may suggest, the Teatro de la Zarzuela was designed by Jerónimo de la Gándara and José María Guallarty Sánchez in 1856 to hold performances of Zarzuela Theatre, a Spanish lyric-dramatic genre that alternates between spoken and sung scenes, with the latter incorporating dance. However, the development of the zarzuela form is itself intimately connected with this theatre, not only in the form itself, but also in its many regional variations. The opening, held on the birthday of Queen Isabella II, featured works by many famous composers of the time, including Arrieta, Asenjo Barbieri, Carnicer, Gaztambide and Hernando. The original decoration of the building was commissioned to the painters Francisco Hernández Tomé and Manuel Castellanos,

Jovellanos 4
Madrid
ES-28014
Spain
Tel: +34 (0)91 524 5400
Fax: +34 (0)91 523 3059
http://teatrodelazarzuela.mcu.es

who carried out a magnificent project which was displayed mainly on the ceiling of the hall. Their paintings, however, eventually disappeared as a result of several refurbishment works and reforms. Sadly, the theatre was destroyed by fire in 1909, but was later reconstructed by Cesáreo Iradier. It was again restored in 1956 by Antonio Vallejo and Fernando R Dampierre, and has since grown from strength to strength, celebrating its 150th birthday in 2006, set to delight audiences for many years to come with its fine opera and dramatic performances.

TICKETING

Price Range: Tickets generally range from €3.00 to €648.00

Concessions: Children and students are eligible for a 30% discount. Senior citizens and the unemployed qualify for up to a 50% discount on the ticket price.

SEATING

Organization: The auditorium is organized into stalls and three balconies.

Box Office

The general Box Office (in the foyer) is part of the INAEM theatre network, allowing tickets to be purchased at the Auditorio, Teatro María Guerrero, Teatro de la Zarzuela or Teatro Pavón. See the website for further details

HOW TO GET THERE

Underground: Banco de España – Sevilla is a two minute walk from the venue. Single ticket costs from €1.00. Day tourist ticket costs from €3.80.

Bus: 1, 2, 5, 9, 10, 14, 15, 20, 27, 34, 37, 45, 51, 52, 53, 74, 146 and 150.

15 May marks the start of the celebrations surrounding the month-long Fiestas de San Isidro, honouring the patron saint of Madrid, and are the most lively and popular festivities in the city. Traditional Castizo dress is worn, and the typical barquillos (rolled wafers), buñuelos (fritters) and rosquillas (doughnuts) are offered for sale.

Teatro Real

Inaugurated in 1850 with a performance of Donizetti's 'La Favorite', the Teatro Real is one of the world's finest stages and acoustic settings for opera. The construction of the Real was ordered by Queen Isabel II and executed by architect Antonio López Aguado, who unfortunately did not live to see its completion. The most successful years of the Theatre were from its construction in 1850 to 1925, during which time composers such as Giuseppe Verdi debuted his new opera, 'La Forza del Destino'. The theatre was forced to close shortly after this time, due to the damage that the construction of the new Metro de Madrid had caused to the building. The Teatro Real reopened in 1966 as a concert theatre until the middle of the 1990s, when it was remodelled to host opera again. Since 1997, the theatre has recouped the fame and the excellence that it possessed during

Plaza Isabel II s/n
Madrid
ES-28013
Spain
Tel: +34 (0)91 516 0600
Fax: +34 (0)91 516 0651
www.teatro-real.com

the nineteenth century, providing visitors with a truly magical experience at the heart of Madrid.

TICKETING

Advance Sales: Generally, tickets can be purchased from one month in advance.

Price Range: Tickets generally range from €7.50 to €235.00, although prices are as low as €3.00 for young people.

Concessions: Young people under the age of 26 qualify for a 60% discount on available seats for any show and on any season tickets for the theatre's G area.

Box Office

The Box Office is open Monday to Saturday, 10.00 a.m.–8.00 p.m. There is a €1.20 per ticket transaction charge for telephone and fax bookings and a €2.40 per ticket charge for online bookings.
Tel: +34 (0)90 224 4848
Lines are open Monday to Saturday, 10.00 a.m.–1.30 p.m. and 5.30 p.m.–8.00 p.m.
Fax: +34 (0)91 516 0621
www.generaltickets.com/teatro-real

PERFORMANCES

Events take place from October to July.

Times: Performances typically start at 8.00 p.m.; matinees and morning performances are also available.

Resident Groups: Orquesta Sinfónica de Madrid

SEATING

Capacity: 1,748–1,854

Organization: The auditorium is arranged into stalls, four balconies, and a tribuna, all with boxes.

Best Seats: The best seats are located in the stalls, first and second balconies and their boxes.

Seats to Avoid: Some seats have partial or no views of the stage.

EDUCATION

Guided Tours

Visitors are invited to join a Historical Tour of the Noble Area of Teatro Real, which takes them through the building and its history. Tours are conducted everyday except Tuesdays. Tel: +34 (0)91 516 0696 or email: info@teatro-real.com for further information or to make a booking enquiry.

Times: Mondays, Wednesdays, Thursdays and Fridays, 10.30 a.m.–1.00 p.m.; Saturdays, Sundays and bank holidays, 11.00 a.m.–1.30 p.m. Tours starts every half hour between these times.

Cost: €4.00

Concessions: €2.00 for students and pensioners; children under 7 have free entry.

FACILITIES

Dining

There is a restaurant which serves a range of meals amongst a distinct opera setting, together with a café showing operas on plasma screens.

Services

Guide dogs welcome.

There are six wheelchair accessible seats in the auditorium.

HOW TO GET THERE

Underground: Metro lines 2 and 5 to opera, which is located opposite the venue. Single ticket costs from €1.00. Day tourist ticket costs from €3.80.

Car Parking: Plaza de Oriente Cuesta and Santo Domingo Plaza Mayor both have parking spaces.

Auditorio Nacional de Música

Designed by José M García de Paredes and opened in 1988, the Auditorio Nacional de Música was constructed under the guidance of the National Plan of Auditoriums, which planned to equip Spain with a range of excellent concert halls. Holding up to four concerts a day, the venue runs an active programme of events, with shows designed to cater to all tastes. Currently, the Auditorio is the home of

Príncipe de Vergara 146
Madrid
ES-28002
Spain
Tel: +34 (0)91 337 0140
Fax: +34 (0)91 337 0300
www.auditorionacional.mcu.es

both the Spanish National Orchestra and Choir, as well as actively supporting the musical talent of the future. Used as the provisional base for the Spanish National Youth Orchestra, the Auditorio is keen to harness its youth, whilst always maintaining its high standard of professional performances. Each year, some of the finest orchestras and musicians in the world perform here, in what can only be described as a truly world-class venue.

TICKETING

Advance Sales: Tickets go on sale at various times during the year, check the website for details.

Price Range: Tickets generally range from €3.00 to €155.00.

Box Office

The Box Office is part of the INAEM theatre network, allowing tickets to be purchased at the Auditorio, Teatro María Guerrero, Teatro de la Zarzuela or Teatro Pavón. The Box Office is open Monday, 4.00 p.m.–6.00 p.m.; Tuesday to Friday, 10.00 a.m.–5.00 p.m.; Saturday, 11.00 a.m.–1.00 p.m. There is a €2.00 per ticket transaction charge for remote bookings.
Tel: +34 (0)91 337 0307
www.auditorionacional.mcu.es

PERFORMANCES

Events take place from September to June.

Times: Performances generally begin at 7.30 p.m., although this can vary.

Resident Groups: The Spanish National Orchestra, Spanish National Choir and Spanish National Youth Orchestra

SEATING

Capacity: Symphony Hall – 2,324; Chamber Hall – 692.

Organization: For both halls, most of the audience are seated in front of the stage, with a few side seats.

Best Seats: The best place to sit in the Symphony Hall is the first balcony. In the Chamber Hall, all seats provide good views.

Good Seats on a Budget: Seats in the second balcony provide good value for money.

EDUCATION

Guided Tours

Tours of the venue take place regularly, although guests are advised to contact the venue prior to their visit for latest dates and times. See the website for further details.

FACILITIES

Dining

There are cafeterias located inside the building, serving a range of food and refreshments.

Services

Guide dogs welcome.

There are approximately 20 seats available for disabled guests.

HOW TO GET THERE

Underground: Metro line 9 to Cruz del Rayo, line 4 to Prosperidad. Single ticket costs from €1.00. Day tourist ticket costs from €3.80.

Bus: 1, 9, 16, 19, 29, 51, 52 and 73

Car Parking: Plaza de Rodolfoy Ernesto Halffter and Museo de la Ciudad both have nearby parking facilities.

SAN SEBASTIÁN

Kursaal Palace

Representing the fun-loving and cosmopolitan city of San Sebastián, the original Gran Kursaal building opened in 1921, incorporating a casino which drew crowds from all over Spain. However, just over three years later in 1924, the venue was forced to close as gambling was declared forbidden during Primo de Rivera's dictatorship. In a change of philosophy, the Kursaal served for the next 50 years as a multi-purpose venue, hosting a range of events without any fixed theme. The building was eventually demolished in 1972 and, in

Avenida de la Zurriola
Donostia
San Sebastián
ES-20003
Spain
Tel: +34 (0)943 00 3000
Fax: +34 (0)943 00 30 01
www.kursaal.org

1989, six internationally famous architects, Mario Botta, Norman Foster, Arata Isozaki, Rafael Moneo, Jaun Navarro Baldeweg and Luis Peña Ganchegui were invited to present projects for the site. Rafael Moneo was the eventual winner, and ten years later on 3 June 1999, the first meeting was held in the new venue. On 23 August of that same year, the architectural complex was officially inaugurated with a series of simultaneous concerts featuring the Euskadi Symphony Orchestra and the soprano, Aihnoa Arteta. Today, this spectacular structure of concrete, metal and glass continues its wide and varied programmes, playing host to a range of musical themes, all within an excellent location overlooking Zurriola beach.

TICKETING

Price Range: Ticket prices and concessions depend on the promoter and the company performing.

PERFORMANCES

Events take place all year round.

SEATING

Capacity: The main auditorium has a capacity of 1,806.

EDUCATION

Guided Tours

Tours of the Kursaal Palace are conducted on Fridays, Saturdays, Sundays and holidays, except for days when an event is taking place at the venue. Tours last an hour and provide a unique insight into various aspects of the venue. Visitors wishing to make an enquiry about a tour are invited to complete the online form on the website.

Times: The Ticket Booth is open from noon–1.30 p.m., with the tour commencing at 1.30 p.m.

FACILITIES

Dining

Everything is possible at the Kursaal, which include both a restaurant with an 'à la carte' menu and a coffee shop serving a range of light refreshments.

Services

Disabled access.

HOW TO GET THERE

Underground: Located near Bilbao, a detailed map on the

website shows visitors the different possibilities for getting to San Sebastián.

Car Parking: There is parking on-site for up to 500 vehicles.

SEVILLE

Teatro de la Maestranza

Located by the river on Paseo Colon, the Teatro de la Maestranza combines an eclectic selection of opera, piano concerts, symphony performances and traditional zarzuela to provide audiences with what is truly a world-class venue. The building was designed by the architects Luis Marin de Teran and Aurelio del Pozo and incorporates the original façade of Maestranza de Artilleria (the Royal Artillery Armoury Building). This magnificent hall incorporates one of the largest stages in Europe, with seating for up to 1,800 people. Various subsidies ensure that it can afford world-class artists, virtually guaranteeing performances of invariably excellent quality. A smaller concert hall with a capacity of approximately 400, plus two exhibition halls complete the main facilities, with regular performances by the Royal Symphonic Orchestra ensuring that the best in classical music is kept alive in this beautiful Spanish city.

Teatro de la Maestranza y
Salas del Arenal S A
Paseo Cristóbal Colón 22
Seville
ES-41001
Spain
Tel: +34 (0)95 422 3344
www.teatromaestranza.com

TICKETING

Price Range: Tickets generally range from €7.00 to €84.00.

Box Office

The Box Office is open daily, 10.00 a.m.–2.00 p.m. and 5.30 p.m.–8.30 p.m.
Tel: +34 (0)95 422 3344
www.generaltickets.com

PERFORMANCES

Events take place from December to June.

Resident Groups: Royal Symphonic Orchestra of Seville

FACILITIES

Services

Disabled access.

HOW TO GET THERE

Bus: C 1, C 2, C 3 and C 4

TORRENT

L'auditori de Torrent

Located just outside the city of Valencia, L'auditori de Torrent was inaugurated in 1997 and has gained a reputation as being a building which combines architectural brilliance with an eclectic programme of events. Perhaps not the most famous concert hall in Spain, nevertheless, the venue puts on several hit performances each season, welcoming through its doors both young and old alike to view its performances of dance, opera, symphonic concerts and even jazz.

TICKETING

Price Range: Ticket prices vary according to the event, although there is often only one or two price groups per show depending on whether seats are purchased in the stalls or in the upper amphitheatre.

Concessions: Generally, only holders of specialist cards qualify for discounts.

Box Office

Vicent Pallardó, 25
Torrent
ES-46900
Spain
Tel: +34 (0)96 158 1077
Fax: +34 (0)96 158 0951
www.auditoritorrent.com

The Box Office is open Monday to Friday, 11.00 a.m.–1.00 p.m. and from two hours before the performance commences.
Tel: +34 (0)902 11 55 77
Lines are open daily, Monday to Saturday, 8.00 a.m.–11.00 p.m.
Sunday, 10.00 a.m.–9.00 p.m.
www.auditoritorrent.com

SEATING

Capacity: 606

Organization: The auditorium is arranged into stalls and an amphitheatre.

VALENCIA

Palau de la Música

Built in 1987 as part of Valencia's 'Vanguard Art' movement, the Palau de la Música in Valencia was designed to promote culture in all its forms, including opera, theatre, musicals and conferences. Situated on the old banks of the River Turia, the venue possesses a unique garden where visitors can watch the fountains designed to accompany the rhythms of the music within the Palau's walls. In addition, another distinguishing feature of the building is the glass enclosure which looks out onto the gardens, providing visitors with an altogether different dimension to the site. Today, the Palau de la Música showcases a wide range of classical music from both Spain and the rest of Europe, together with a diverse programme of educational activities

Paseo Alameda 30
Valencia
ES-46023
Spain
Tel: +34 (0)96 337 5020
Fax: +34 (0)96 337 0988
www.palaudevalencia.com

which are conducted alongside literary readings, family events and traditional concert cycles.

PERFORMANCES

Resident Groups: Orquestra de Valencia

SEATING

Capacity: 1,793

Organization: The Main Hall is arranged into stalls, an upper balcony and side seating which flanks the auditorium.

Palau de les Arts

Designed by Valencian architect Santiago Calatrava, the Palau de les Arts was created as a major centre for musical arts, including shows for opera, ballet, musicals and theatre, with a particular emphasis on promoting Valencia's cultural heritage. The building is itself majestic, having an area of 40,000 square metres that reaches 75 metres into the sky. Replete with symbolist sculpture, the building is in the shape of a concrete dome under a cascade of steel; and surrounding the building is no less than 60,000 square metres of gardens and 11,000 square metres of water. With the opening of the Palau de les Arts, the Valencian Council has fulfilled one of its most ambitious commitments in its efforts to recognize, support and promote the musical heritage of Valencia, Spain and the rest of the world. Many talented composers and performers have made an essential contribution to the important place of this musical tradition, with opera in particular gaining special precedence in this unique and captivating venue.

TICKETING

Advance Sales: Tickets can be purchased for all confirmed concerts.

Price Range: Tickets generally range from €5.00 to €160.00.

Concessions: Last minute tickets are available to people aged under 26, students (of any age) and senior citizens (older than 65) can get a 50% discount from two hours before the

Autopista del Saler 1
Valencia
ES-46013
Spain
Tel: +34 (0)96 197 5800
Fax: +34 (0)96 395 2201
www.lesarts.com

performance. In all cases, visitors must provide proof of status.

Box Office

The Box Office is open Monday to Friday, 10.30 a.m.–2.00 p.m. and 5.00 p.m.–8.30 p.m.; Saturday, 10.30 a.m.–2.00 p.m.
Tel: +34 (0)90 210 0032
www.lesarts.com

PERFORMANCES

Events take place from October to May.

Times: Performances usually begin at 8.30 p.m.; matinees are also available.

Resident Groups: The Orquestra de la Comunitat Valenciana

SEATING

Capacity: Main Hall–1,700; Auditorium–1,500; Aula Magistral–400

Organization: The Main Hall is arranged into stalls and four tiers of boxes. The Aula Magistral is organized into an ascending semicircle of seats.

Best Seats: The best seats are located in the stalls and first tier balcony.

Good Seats on a Budget: Zone 4–Zone 6 provide good side views at a reasonable price.

FACILITIES

Dining

Apart from a bar, which opens during the intervals of each performance, a restaurant, Foyer del Turia, opens after each performance. For further information and reservations, please contact: +34 (0)66 650 8237.

HOW TO GET THERE

Underground: Lines 3 and 5 to Alameda.

Bus: Bus no. 95

Overground: The venue can be reached via El Cabañal and Estación del Norte; however a further bus journey is needed.

SWEDEN

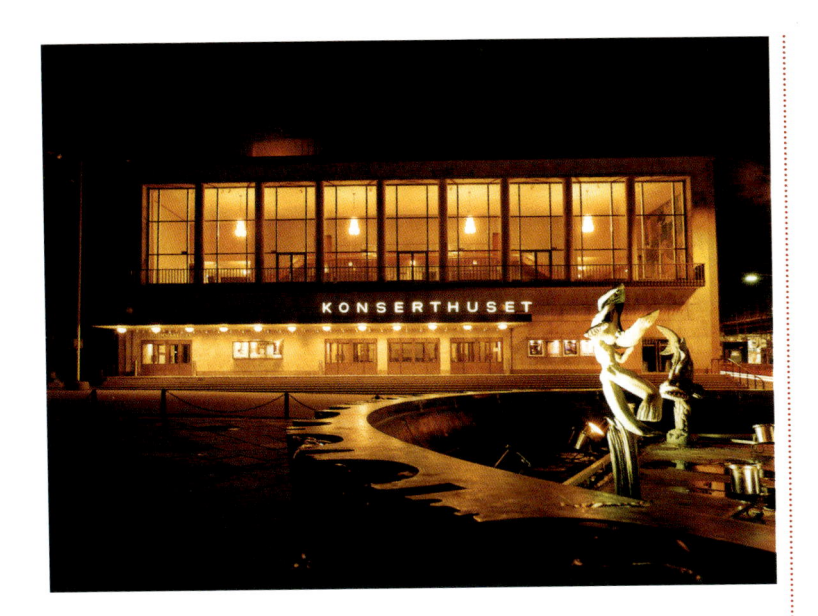

GOTHENBURG

Konserthuset

Home to the Gothenburg Symphony Orchestra, and located conveniently in the city's Götaplatsen Square, the Gothenburg Konserthuset was built in 1935, with the project led by architect Nils Einar Ericsson. The building is designed in a Swedish functionalist style, although the building's façade possesses a Neo-Classical exterior, so as to blend in with the surrounding area. Inside, modern facilities boast superb acoustics, bestowing upon it a reputation which reaches well outside the Swedish borders. The main auditorium's plain shaped walls are clad in yellowish red maple veneer, and are able to hold a capacity of approximately 1,300. There is also a smaller concert hall, Stenhammarsalen, which is designed for chamber concerts. Situated in a prime area for culture and refinement in Gothenburg, visitors can make the most of the

Götaplatsen
Västergötland
Gothenburg
SE-41256
Sweden
Tel: +46 (0)31 726 5300
Fax: +46 (0)31 726 5370
www.gso.se

theatre's superb location, next to the Gothenburg Konstmuseum and City Theatre, all within the watchful eye of the city's grand statue of Poseidon.

TICKETING

Concessions: Under-30s are admitted for SEK 80.00. Carers of disabled visitors are admitted for free. Spare tickets are sold at SEK 170.00 from one hour before each performance.

Box Office

> The Box Office is open Monday to Friday, noon–6.00 p.m.; Saturday, 11.00 a.m.–3.00 p.m. On the day of performance the Box Office is open until the performances begin.
> Tel: +46 (0)31 726 5300
> Fax: +46 (0)31 726 5370
> www.gso.se

PERFORMANCES

Performances take place all year round.

Resident Groups: The Gothenburg Symphonic Orchestra

SEATING

Capacity: 1,286

Organization: The auditorium comprises raked stalls, all of which are the same price. Variations depend only on the performances.

Seats to Avoid: All seats have good views.

EDUCATION

Guided Tours

Guided tours of the venue can be arranged by contacting the concert hall directly. Tel: +46 (0)31 726 5300

Cost: SEK 50.00 per person

Concessions: There are specific tours for younger visitors by arrangement.

FACILITIES

Dining

The Gothenburg Konserthus houses the Kontrabar, where food and drink can be enjoyed whilst sitting by the gigantic windows overlooking Götaplatsen.

Services

🐕 Guide dogs welcome.

♿ There are four designated spaces in the hall for wheelchair users.

HOW TO GET THERE

Overground: Take tram nos. 3, 4 or 5 from the Central Station, approximately a ten minute journey. Single ticket prices cost from SEK 10.00 per coupon/zone valid for an unlimited number of changes (and return journeys) within a 90-minute period. A Red Day Card for use around the Gothenburg area on all forms of public transport (excluding night services) costs SEK 50.00.

The amusement park Liseberg, the largest of its kind in Scandinavia, is situated in the centre of the city. It has entertained millions of people since 1923. Here you can ride roller coasters or see popular artists perform – a great day out for all the family.

STOCKHOLM

Drottningholms Slottsteater

With an interior consisting a unique mix of stucco, papier mâché and paintings, the Drottningholms Slottsteater was built to the design of the theatre architect, Carl Fredrik Adelcrantz, at the request of Queen Lovisa Ulrika. The building was completed in 1766 and rests on the remains of an earlier theatre destroyed by fire in 1762. In 1991 the World Heritage Committee of UNESCO designated the theatre, together with Drottningholm Palace, the Chinese Pavilion and the surrounding park, as being of international cultural heritage significance and listed on the UNESCO's list of world heritage. The Drottningholms Slottsteater specializes in opera and has acquired a growing international reputation as a festival theatre, with a long history of composers such as Haydn,

Box 15417
Stockholm
SE-10465
Sweden
Tel: +46 (0)85 569 3100
Fax: +46 (0)85 569 3101
www.dtm.se

Handel, Gluck and Mozart joined by numerous performances by artists and companies from around the world.

TICKETING

Price Range: Tickets generally range from SEK 165.00 to SEK 410.00.

Box Office

The Drottningholms Slottsteater booking office is open from Monday to Friday, 9.00 a.m.–noon and 2.00 p.m.–4.00 p.m.
Tel:+46 (0)8 660 8225
Ticket: +46 (0)77 170 7070
Fax: +46 (0) 8 556 931 01
www.ticnet.se

PERFORMANCES

Events take place from May to September.

Times: Evening performances commence at 7.30 p.m. Matinee starts at 4.00 p.m.

SEATING

Capacity: 465

Organization: The auditorium is arranged into raked stalls.

Best Seats: The best seats are located in the first four rows.

Good Seats on a Budget: Even the cheapest seats provide unrestricted views.

EDUCATION

Guided Tours

Guided tours at the Drottningholms Slottsteater take place twice every hour throughout the season. Tours are available in Swedish, English, German and French and are conducted alongside a short film showing the unique eighteenth century stage machinery in action, and an exhibition of opera costumes used on stage. Tel: (May to September) +46 (0)8 759 0406; (October to April) +46 (0)85 569 3107 or email: guide@dtm.se (for group bookings)

Times: May: noon–4.30 p.m.; June to August: 11.00 a.m.–4.30 p.m.; September: 1.00 p.m.–3.30 p.m.; The last tour is at 1.30 p.m. on matinee days.

Cost: SEK 60.00

Concessions: Students pay SEK 40.00. Children under 16 years are admitted for free with a paying adult.

FACILITIES

Dining

Visitors are invited to dine at the Drottningholms Wardshus, Tel: +46 (0)8 759 0308 for reservations.

Services

Disabled access.

HOW TO GET THERE

Underground: Take the underground to Brommaplan then change to any of the buses numbered on the 300 route. Single tickets cost from SEK 20.00 (SEK 10.00 for under-20s and over-65s). One day travelcard costs SEK 60.00/SEK 30.00 respectively.

Bus: The theatre bus leaves 15 minutes after the end of the performance and stops at underground stations Fridhemsplan and T-Centralen. Tickets are sold at the cloakrooms of the theatre in connection with performance at the price of SEK 50.00.

Car Parking: There is a parking lot located at the front of the theatre.

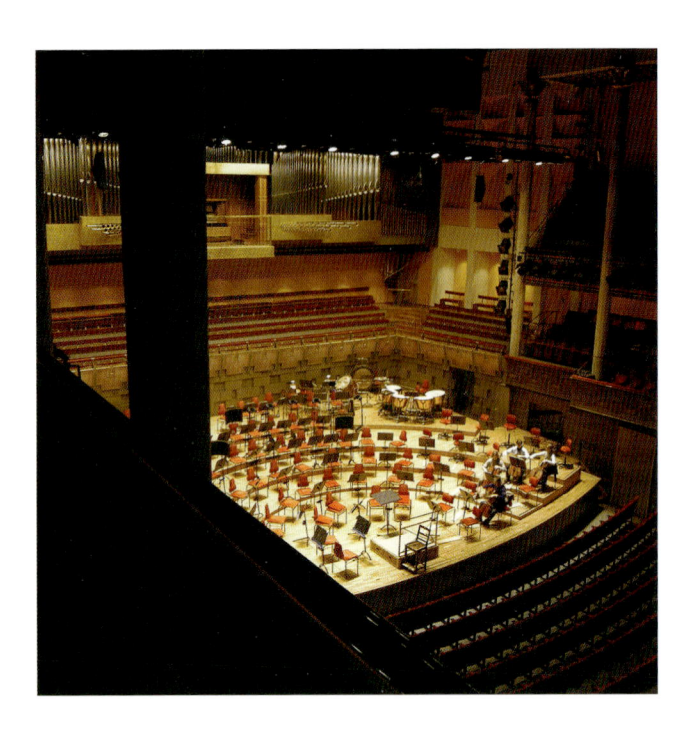

Konserthuset

The Konserthuset in Stockholm is the main hall for orchestral music in the Swedish capital. Designed by Ivar Tengbom and inaugurated in 1926, it is the home to the world-renowned Royal Stockholm Philharmonic Orchestra, which works regularly with well-known composers and soloists. The venue hosts performances by individuals, chamber orchestras, symphonic works and large-scale choral works such as Mozart's 'Requiem'. In front of the building is a statue of Orpheus by Carl Milles, an ancient Thracian king who was considered the greatest musician and poet of Greek mythology, whose songs could charm wild beasts and coax even rocks and trees into movement; now aptly standing outside a venue which

Hotorget 8
Box 7083
Stockholm
SE-10387
Sweden
Tel: +46 (0)8 50 66 77 88 or:
+46 (0)87 86 02 00
www.konserthuset.se

hopes to replicate his musical splendour. Today, apart from hosting a range of classical performances, opera recitals and concerts, the Konserthuset also hosts the Annual Nobel Prize ceremony, a tradition it has maintained since 1926. The nearby City Hall was constructed in this year, and is the venue where winners congregate for the Nobel Banquet.

TICKETING

Price Range: Prices of tickets vary considerably according to individual performances.

Concessions: Young people up to the age of 20 receive a 50% discount if tickets are bought on the day of the concert. Students, senior citizens and the unemployed receive a 10% discount.

Box Office

The Box Office is open Monday to Friday, 11.00 a.m.–6.00 p.m.; Saturday, 11.00 a.m.–3.00 p.m. It also opens an hour before each performance.
www.konserthuset.se
Visitors can also print their own tickets at www.ticnet.se

PERFORMANCES

Resident Groups: The Royal Stockholm Philharmonic Orchestra

SEATING

Best Seats: The best seats are located in the first and second balconies, within the first two or three rows and in front of the stage.

Good Seats on a Budget: Cheap tickets are sold for the choir deck when not in use for a performance.

EDUCATION

Guided Tours

There is a one hour tour often in connection with Saturday concerts. There are also daily tours in the hall's Summer opening period, from mid-July to the end of August.

Cost: SEK 50.00 per person

Concessions: There are specific children's tours in conjunction with children's concerts that cost SEK 20.00 and last 45 minutes.

FACILITIES

Services

Disabled access.

Guide dogs are admitted but not in the auditorium, staff will look after them during the performance.

HOW TO GET THERE

Underground: The Metro Station Hötorget is located directly underneath the concert hall. Single tickets cost from SEK 20.00 (SEK 10.00 for under-20s and over-65s). One day travelcard costs SEK 60.00/SEK 30.00 respectively.

Bus: 1, 52 and 56 serves the concert hall.

Royal Opera – Kungliga Operan

The Kungliga Operan or Royal Swedish Opera is the national stage for opera in Sweden. The building lies in the centre of Stockholm, on the eastern side of Gustav Adolfs torg. The opera company was founded by King Gustav III and its first performance was given on 18 January 1773. The first opera house however, was not opened until 1782. It served for another century before being replaced at the end of the nineteenth century. The old opera was demolished in 1892 to give way to the construction of a new opera by Axel Johan Anderberg and was finished just seven years later. The new opera was inaugurated by Kind Oscar II with a production of Franz Berwald's 'Estrella de Soria'. The new house bears the letters 'Kungl Teatern', literally, 'Royal Theatre' (which caused the later-founded Royal Dramatic Theatre to add the distinction 'dramatic' to its name), and is now simply called the Operan. It is a majestic Neo-Classical building with a magnificent gold foyer and elegant marble grand staircase leading to a three-tiered auditorium somewhat smaller than the old theatre. The Royal Opera Orchestra has 112 members and is Scandinavia's largest orchestra, apart from being one of the oldest in the world, having originated as King Gustaf Wasa's Court Chapel in the sixteenth century.

Gustav Adolfs Torg
Stockholm
SE-11152
Sweden
Tel: +46 (0)8 791 4400
Fax: +46 (0)8 791 4444
www.operan.se

TICKETING

Price Range: Tickets generally range from SEK 40.00 to SEK 590.00 (although for special and some Saturday night performances, these can reach up to SEK 950.00).

Concessions: Concession prices vary.

Box Office

Service charges vary depending on price of tickets purchased and whether tickets are sent via the post or held for collection. Service charges generally range from SEK 10.00–SEK 30.00. Please note that tickets booked through ticnet.se cannot be sent to an overseas address.
Tel: +46 (0)8 791 4400
www.ticnet.se

PERFORMANCES

Events take place from late August to June.

Times: Evening performances generally commence at 7.30 p.m. Weekend matinees start at 3.00 p.m.

Resident Groups: Swedish Royal Opera

SEATING

Capacity: 1,090

EDUCATION

Guided Tours

Every Saturday at 1.00 p.m. from September to May there are public guided tours of the opera house. Visitors can experience the Royal Opera House in a unique way, gaining inside knowledge through looking backstage, having the opportunity to visit the King and Queen's Royal Suite, and visiting some of the opera's many hidden rooms. Contact the venue directly for further information.

Cost: Tickets cost SEK 75.00 and are available at the Royal Opera's Box Office. The number of tickets are limited.

FACILITIES

Dining

The Opera café, downstairs from the main entrance, opens approximately one hour before the appointed time of the performance and serves a range of refreshments and snacks. There are also cafés on the stalls and tier levels. These open approximately 30 minutes before the performance starts. All cafés are open in the intermissions. Visitors are able to place their order before the performance without charge. In the Golden Foyer, a champagne bar is available and opens during intermissions.

Services

- Disabled access.

- The auditorium is equipped with a hearing loop.

HOW TO GET THERE

Underground: Lines 10 and 11 to Kungsträdgården, entrance Gustav Adolfs torg/Operan. Both lines are connected to all other underground lines at Station T-Centralen (the Central Station), only one stop away from Kungsträdgården. Single tickets cost from SEK 20.00 (SEK 10.00 for under- 20s and over-65s). One day travelcard costs SEK 60.00/SEK 30.00 respectively.

Bus: 62 and 65 serve Gustav Adolfs torg, 43 stops at the Jakobsgatan/Regeringsgatan, and 2, 55, 71, 76 stop at Karl XII torg.

Car Parking: Visitors are welcome to use the nearby Galleria garage, which costs only SEK 30.00 when used between 6.00 p.m.–1.00 a.m.

There is a unique tradition at the Kungliga Operan. If the evening's performance is sold out, red lanterns are lit above the main entrance. The lanterns are normally lit at 4.00 p.m. During a matinee performance, the lanterns are lit when the Box Office opens. When a performance is sold out, the tradition differs between ballet and opera performances, since listening seats often become sold out at operas but seldom at ballets. There are often seats left even when the red lantern is lit, but the seats available may only offer restricted viewing.

SWITZERLAND

BASEL

StadtCasino

Situated in the heart of Basel, the StadtCasino combines several concert halls and banqueting rooms to create a versatile and popular cultural meeting place in Basel. The site's Musiksaal has gained a reputation for unique three-dimensional acoustics, making it a popular destination for many international musicians, including touring symphony orchestras. The exterior is modest, perhaps reflecting the fact that it was built in 1939, while the interior is influenced by the eighteenth century and includes an impressive organ. The smaller Hans Huber Hall is good for chamber music and soloists.

TICKETING

Price Range: Tickets generally range from CHF 30.00 to CHF 80.00.

Barfüsserplatz
Basel
CH-4001
Switzerland
Tel: +41 (0)61 225 9393
Fax: +41 (0)61 225 9399
www.casinogesellschaft-basel.ch

Concessions: Concession prices vary.

Box Office

There is a small transaction fee for online booking.
www.ticketcorner.ch

PERFORMANCES

Resident Groups: Sinfonieorchester Basel

SEATING

Capacity: Musiksaal capacity – 1,512; Hans Huber Hall–540; Festsaal–700

Organization: For seating in the Muiksaal, the auditorium is arranged into stalls and balconies at the sides and rear.

Best Seats: The best seats are in the middle of the stalls and at the front of the balconies.

Good Seats on a Budget: Visitors can sit right at the front of the Hall for a mid-range price.

FACILITIES

Dining

The Stadt-Casino offers a choice of four bars and restaurants, details of which can be found on the Stadt-Casino's website.

HOW TO GET THERE

Overground: Take tram no. 1 or 8 to Barfüsserplatz stop from the Hauptbahnhof or tram no. 6 to Barfüsserplatz stop from the Baden Station. Tram fares vary from CHF 1.90–CHF 3.80.

Car Parking: Basel grants its guests a special privilege: all visitors who spend a night at one of Basel City's hotels automatically receive a Mobility Ticket which lets them use all public transport free of charge during their stay. There is no parking near the Stadt-Casino.

GENEVA

Grand Théâtre de Genève

Offering its visitors a wide range of musical performances from classic and contemporary operas to jazz and virtuoso recitals, the Grand Théâtre de Genève faced a much bleaker future during its early days, when the Reformation meant that opera in Geneva was limited by Calvinist orthodoxy. It was not until the 1760s that opera began to reemerge, with the La Grange aux Extrangers and its successor theatre, the Teatre de Neuve, providing visitors with a venue located just outside the walls of the city. By 1872 a competition was opened up for the creation of a brand new opera house, and, after construction was started in 1874, the house opened on 2 October 1879 with a production of Rossini's 'William Tell'. Fire struck in 1951, all but destroying the house during a rehearsal of 'Die Walküre', better known as 'The Valkyrie', by Richard Wagner, leaving only the walls and foyer in a recoverable state. Verdi's 'Don Carlo' welcomed the Theatre's return to the opera scene in 1962, where it continues to this day to offer an eclectic mixture of classical performances and recitals.

11 Boulevard du Théâtre
Geneva
CH-1211
Switzerland
Tel: +41 (0)22 418 3000
Fax: +41 (0)22 418 3001
www.geneveopera.ch

TICKETING

Advance Sales: Sales usually start six weeks in advance.

Price Range: Tickets generally range from CHF 29.00 to CHF 199.00.

Concessions: Young people under 20 gain entry for CHF 20.00 to each opera, and CHF 15.00 to recitals and ballets in the Large Hall. People under 26 receive 10–30% discount on performances in the large theatre. Tickets for carers of disabled visitors cost CHF 113.00 if they wish to sit within the designated wheelchair space area.

Box Office

The Box Office is open Monday to Friday, 10.00 a.m.–6.00 p.m.; Saturday, 10.00 a.m.–1.00 p.m. There is a CHF 2.00 transaction charge for online booking.
Tel: +41 (0)22 418 3130
Fax: +41 (0) 22.418 3131
www.geneveopera.ch

PERFORMANCES

Times: Performances generally begin at 5.00 p.m. and 8.00 p.m.

Resident Groups: The Chorus of the Grand Theatre and Orchestra of French-Switzerland

SEATING

Capacity: 1,488

Organization: The auditorium is arranged into stalls and balconies.

Best Seats: The best seats are located in the middle of the stalls along with the first rows of the balcony.

Good Seats on a Budget: Seats located in the very front of the stalls provide good value for money.

Seats to Avoid: All seats have unrestricted views.

EDUCATION

Guided Tours

Guided tours are by arrangement only for groups of 10–20 people. Tel: +41 (0)22 418 3000 to arrange a tour.

Cost: CHF 5.00 per person

FACILITIES

Dining

There are bars available at the Theatre serving a range of food, drinks and snacks both before the performance and during the interval.

Services

There are two spaces reserved for wheelchairs, please ask in advance.

HOW TO GET THERE

Bus: Take the bus to the Blazenhoff stop in Geneva. Single ticket CHF 3.00. Day ticket CHF 10.00.

LAUSANNE

Théâtre Municipal de Lausanne – Opéra

The forerunner of the Municipal Theatre in Lausanne, the Italian style casino-theatre or the 'Georgette Room' was inaugurated on 10 May 1871. In 1931 a thorough renovation and re-design took place, and the original Rococo style was replaced by the art deco design which remains

Av. du Théâtre 12
CP 7543
Lausanne.
CH-1002
Switzerland
Tel: +41 (0)21 310 1616
Fax: +41 (0)21 310 1690
www.opera-lausanne.ch

to this day. The resident Lausanne Opera took form in the 1980s. Interestingly, the chorus singers of the Lausanne Opera are mainly semi-professionals with doctors and architects amongst them. The principal singers of the opera company often give short lunchtime recitals of opera extracts as a taster, an extra attraction that accompany the performances of opera, ballet and symphonic works.

TICKETING

Price Range: Tickets generally range from CHF 15.00 to CHF 130.00.

Concessions: 15 minutes before each performance, any spare tickets are offered to students and young people at the price of CHF 15.00.

Box Office

The Box Office is open Monday to Friday, noon –7.00 p.m. During weekends and public holidays, the Box Office opens one hour before performances.
Tel: +41 (0)21 310 1600
www.opera-lausanne.ch

PERFORMANCES

Events take place from September to May.

Times: Evening shows begin at 7.00 p.m.; lunchtime shows begin at 12.15 p.m.

Resident Groups: Opéra de Lausanne

Annual Festivals/Special Events: The International Festival of Dance takes place every November.

SEATING

Capacity: 942

Organization: The hall is divided into stalls, two balconies, four boxes and an amphitheatre area.

Best Seats: The best seats in the auditorium are in the central stalls and in the front of the first balcony.

Seats to Avoid: All seats have unrestricted views.

EDUCATION

Guided Tours

Tours of the venue, allowing visitors a special insight into the daily running of the Opéra de Lausanne can be conducted by prior arrangement.
Tel: +41 (0)21 310 1625 or email: fabienne.hermenjat@lausanne.ch for further details.

Cost: CHF 10.00.

Concessions: There are no concessions for the adult tours, although tours for groups of school children are provided free of charge.

FACILITIES

Dining

The Theatre restaurant is open before and after each performance except on Sundays, where it is only open before.

HOW TO GET THERE

Bus: 1, 2, 4, 5, 8, 9 and 12 serve the venue at the Georgette stop. A single bus trip costs CHF 2.40.

LUCERNE

KKL Luzern (Culture and Congress Centre)

'Inclusion' – the term used to describe Jean Nouvel's magnificent KKL building which lies serenely on Lake Lucerne. The KKL Luzern was designed by the French architect and constructed between 1995 and 2000, ranking today as one of the most spectacular modern buildings in Switzerland. The concert hall itself is lined with wooden panels in a lustrous reddish tone. The curved shape of the outer wall bulges into the angular foyer, rather reminiscent of the case of a string instrument. The KKL Luzern is centrally located in the town of Lucerne, right next to the railway station and only a few hundred yards from the old town centre and Lucerne's distinctive landmark, the Chapel Bridge. Originally Nouvel planned to build the new concert hall in the

Europaplatz 1
Lucerne
CH-6005
Switzerland
Tel: +41 (0)41 226 7070
Fax: +41 (0)41 226 7071
www.kkl-luzern.ch

shape of a ship which went directly into the lake, but for town planning and ecological reasons this idea could not be realized. He reworked the project and decided to channel the water into the building instead, physically inverting the concepts of 'inside' and 'outside', hence the crowning term 'Inclusion'. Jean Nouvel's interpretation of this concept was to use water channels that lead directly into the building and a roof that projects over the lake. Today, the venue plays host to choirs, symphony orchestras, jazz, world music and chamber music, and other world-class performances in this unique classical venue.

TICKETING

Advance Sales: Tickets can be booked up to nine months in advance.

Price Range: Tickets generally range from CHF 25.00 to CHF 155.00.

Box Office

There is a CHF 6.00 booking fee online per order for tickets purchased through the official website. Tickets purchased via Ticket Corner incur a service charge which depends on the method of payment and

whether tickets are dispatched to an address or not.
Tel: +41 (0)41 226 7777
Lines are open daily, 10.00 a.m.–6.00 p.m.
Tickets can be booked via the venue website www.kkl.luzern.ch or via www.ticketcorner.com

PERFORMANCES

Resident Groups: The Lucerne Symphony Orchestra

Annual Festivals/Special Events: The Lucerne Festival and the World Band Festival. The Lucerne Festival splits into the Piano Festival in November, the Summer Festival in August and September and the Easter Festival in March and April.

SEATING

Capacity: Concert hall – 1,892; Lucerne Hall – 1,280; standing – 1,700.

EDUCATION

Guided Tours

The KKL Guest Service offers visitors the opportunity to participate in a range of tours where they are able to take a look behind the scenes at the KKL Luzern and discover its unique architecture, aesthetics and acoustics. Tours are tailored towards individual groups and those wishing to participate in a tour should contact the venue. The advance ticket sales desk is also the meeting point for guided tours.
Tel: +41 (0)41 226 7433 or email: guestservice@kkl-luzern.ch for further information or to book tickets.

FACILITIES

Dining

Visitors to the Centre can choose from the KKL Restaurant RED for elegant dining, KKL World Café for deli and coffee, KKL Seebar for cocktails and wine, KKL Waterfront for barbecue, drinks and a lakeview, and the KKL Concert Bar for champagne and fine wines.

ZURICH

Grosser Tonhallesaal– Gesellschaft Zurich

Johannes Brahms opened the Tonhalle Gesellschaft in 1895 with his presentation of 'Song of Triumph'. Since this crowning performance, the venue has continued to draw audiences from around the world, and is the destination for many internationally renowned soloists. The venue's resident Zurich Tonhalle Orchestra was established in 1868, and soon established a central role in the musical life of Switzerland. From its very beginning, the orchestra has been conducted by noted composers of the day, including Brahms, Wagner and Strauss. The Tonhalle Orchestra owes much of its contemporary fame to its Chief Conductor, David Zinman. Under his able conductorship since 1995, the Tonhalle Orchestra's much acclaimed recording of all the Beethoven symphonies won the coveted German Record Critics' Award in 1999. In addition, Zinman was

Claridenstrasse 7
Zurich
CH-8002
Switzerland
Tel: +41 (0)44 206 3434
Fax: +41 (0)44 206 3469
www.tonhalle-orchester.ch

awarded the title of 'Chevalier de l'Ordre des Arts et des Lettres' (Order of Arts and Literature) by the French Ministry of Culture in May 2000. Under Zinman, the Orchestra now plays and records works of the greats such as Beethoven, Mozart, Schubert, Mahler, whilst also pursuing the 'Swiss Connection', featuring works by composers who were connected with Switzerland in one way or another. Extending his contract in 2005 until July 2010, the Zinman era is set to go down in history as the third-longest tenure of a Chief Conductor of the Tonhalle Zurich Orchestra, making room for many more spectacular performances to come.

TICKETING

Advance Sales: Reservations can be made one month in advance.

Price Range: Tickets generally range from CHF 17.00 to CHF 198.00.

Concessions: For the under-25s there are tickets priced CHF 20.00 on sale in the week before the concert. Admission is free of charge for disabled visitors.

Box Office

The Box Office is open Monday to Friday, 10.00 a.m.–6.00 p.m., or until the performance begins; Saturday, 1.00 p.m.–6.00 p.m., or until the performance begins; Sunday, 10.00 a.m.–6.00 p.m.
Tel: +41 (0)44 206 3434
Fax: +41 (0) 44 206 3469
www.tonhalle.ch

PERFORMANCES

Resident Groups: Zurich Tonhalle Orchestra

SEATING

Capacity: 1,500

Organization: The auditorium is divided into stalls, a gallery and balcony.

Best Seats: The best seats are in the stalls.

FACILITIES

Services

There is wheelchair access with four places available in the Big Tonhalle. There are two suitable entrances.

HOW TO GET THERE

Overground: Tram nos. 6, 7, 8 and 13 run along the road to the North of Tonhalle. Tram nos. 2, 5, 8, 9 and 11 run to the South. Bus nos. 161 and 165 run to the East. Tickets must be bought before boarding from machines or kiosks. Zurich City single ticket costs from CHF 3.80. Day ticket costs from CHF 7.60.

Opernhaus Zurich

Built by the celebrated architects Fellner and Helmer in 1891 to replace the 'Aktientheater' which had burnt down in 1834, the Opernhaus Zurich initially presented a wide range of performing arts, but from the early twentieth century it has focused mainly on opera, concerts and ballet. Cultural highlights have included the first performance of Richard Wagner's 'Parsifal' outside Bayreuth in 1913, the premiere of Alban Berg's 'Lulu' and the first staging of Schöenberg's 'Moses and Aaron'. The building itself is an ornate one, with a Neo-Classical façade of white and grey stone adorned with busts of Weber, Wagner, and Mozart. Additionally, busts of Schiller, Shakespeare, and Goethe are to be found. The auditorium is built in the Rococo style behind a contrasting austere Neo-Classical façade. The Opernhaus Zurich has been home to the Zurich Opera since it opened. Its regular programme of concert cycles, recitals, as well as chamber concert provide a complete, sumptuous and varied programme of classical music.

TICKETING

Advance Sales: Visitors can reserve tickets up to nine months in advance.

Price Range: Tickets generally range from CHF 15.00 to CHF 320.00.

Concessions: Concession tickets for children range from CHF 12.00–CHF 35.00 depending on the seats. Concessions for students range from CHF 13.00–CHF 45.00 depending on the seats and performances.

Falkenstrasse 1
Zurich
CH-8008
Switzerland.
Tel: +41 (0)12 686 400
Fax: +41 (0)12 686 401
www.opernhaus.ch

Box Office

The Box Office is open Monday to Saturday, 11.00 a.m.–6.30 p.m. or up until the performance begins. On Sunday the Box Office opens 90 minutes before the performance. There is no transaction charge if tickets are collected from the Box Office. Otherwise there is a delivery charge of CHF 8.00 per order.
Tel: +41 (0)44 268 6666
www.opernhaus.ch

PERFORMANCES

Events take place from September to July.

Resident Groups: The Zurich Opera

Annual Festivals/Special Events: The Zürcher Festspiele is a festival of opera, ballet, symphonic and chamber music together with literature and fine arts exhibitions which take place every summer between June and July.

SEATING

Capacity: 1,238

Organization: The hall is organized into stalls, galleries and balconies.

Best Seats: The best seats are in the stalls, row 1–16 and the front row of the gallery and balconies.

FACILITIES

Dining

In addition to the Belcanto Restaurant, which provide visitors with scenic views of the lake, the catering facilities at Zurich Opera House include numerous buffet counters for intervals, the Bernhard Theatre Foyer, the Piazza terrace, as well as banqueting and catering services.

Services

HOW TO GET THERE

Bus: The Theatre can be reached directly by tram numbers 2, 4, 11 and 15 to the Opernhaus stop. Tickets must be bought before boarding from machines or kiosks. Zurich City single ticket costs from CHF 3.80. Day ticket costs from CHF 7.60.

Car Parking: Parking spaces on Theaterplatz in front of the opera house are very limited. The Utoquai multi-storey car park at Färberstrasse 6 is only a few minutes walk away. There is a car park under development at the opera house.

TURKEY

ISTANBUL

Cemal Reşit Rey Concert Hall

Named after Cemal Reşit Rey, a famous Turkish twentieth century pianist and composer, the Cemal Reşit Rey Concert Hall was opened in 1989. It was the first building in Turkey built specifically for classical music. Visitors can enjoy traditional Turkish music alongside contemporary and more established classical works as well as performances from touring international musicians.

Harbiye
Istanbul
Turkey
Tel: +90 (0) 212 232 98 30; or
+90 (0) 212 231 5498; or
+90 (0) 212 240 5012
Fax: +90 (0)212 248 5451
www.crrks.org

TICKETING

Box Office

During Ramadan the Box Office is open from 10.00 a.m–9.00 p.m. All other times the office is open from 10.00 a.m–8.00 p.m.
Tel: +90 (0)212 252 9830
www.billetix.com

PERFORMANCES

Events take place from October to May.

Annual Festivals/Special Events: The Mystic Music Festival takes place in November. The Leyla Gencer Voice Competition is held every August.

SEATING

Capacity: 900

FACILITIES

Dining

There are bars on-site that also sell snacks, and there are various restaurants nearby Nişantaşi.

Services

Disabled access.

HOW TO GET THERE

Bus: The nearest bus stop is located in Harbiye. Cemal Reşit Rey Concert Hall is then a five to ten minutes walk straight ahead from the old Maçka Hotel.

Car Parking: There is a free car park located under the Cemal Reşit Rey Concert Hall.

UKRAINE

KYIV

National Opera & Ballet Theatre

The National Academic Theatre of Opera and Ballet is the oldest musical theatre in Ukraine. Founded in 1867, the Theatre was originally called the 'Russian Opera', and in 1919 was renamed the State Opera Houses. In 1934 it was again given the new name 'The Ukrainian Theatre of Opera and Ballet'. In 1994, 'Ukraine' was replaced with, 'National'. The opera company tours extensively and remains today a colourful imposing structure in the centre of Kiev with a grand Baroque interior, offering its visitors a wide repertoire of famous ballet and operas.

TICKETING

Price Range: Tickets generally range from UAH 25.00 to UAH 75.00.

50 Vladimirskaya S
Kyiv
01034
Ukraine
Tel: +380 (0)44 279 1169
www.opera.com.ua

PERFORMANCES

Events take place from September to June.

Times: Evening performances generally begin at 6.00 p.m.

ODESSA

Odessa Opera

The Theatre in Odessa is widely regarded as one of the most beautiful opera houses in the world and after the Potemkin Stairs, the most famous edifice in Odessa. Two famous Viennese architects, Ferdinand Fellner and Herman Helmer, began to construct the current structure in 1883. These two had built 70 theatres throughout Europe, including the La Scala in Milan and the Vienna Opera Theatre. The Theatre was remodelled in the 1960s when the scars of war and age took their toll on the building. Sitting on shifting ground and in danger of collapse, the Theatre's eastern half

Tchaikovsry str. 1
Odessa
Ukraine
Tel: +380 (0)48 29132
www.opera-ballet.tm.odessa.ua

sagged almost seven inches in its first three years. Luckily, the damage was repaired before the venue was lost completely, and today, the niches of its façade boast the busts of famous Odessians such as Mikhail Glinka, Nikolai Gogol, Alexandr Griboyedov and Aleksandr Pushkin. The Large Hall is modelled after the style of Louis LXI and is richly decorated with gilded stucco figures and designs. There are scenes from *Hamlet*, *A Midsummer's Night Dream*, *A Winters Tale* and *As You Like It* depicted on the ceiling, with a chandelier that weighs almost two and a half tons.

PERFORMANCES

Times: Performance times are generally at 6.00 p.m. and 7.00 p.m.

The Potemkin Stairs represent a giant stairway in Odessa, Ukraine. The stairs are considered a formal entrance into the city from the direction of the sea and have come to be its best-known symbol. Originally known as the Boulevard Steps, the Giant Staircase, or the Richelieu Steps, the staircase is 27 metres high, and extends for 142 metres, but are so well designed that they create an optical illusion. A person looking down the stairs sees only the landings, and the steps are invisible, whilst a person looking up sees only steps, with the landings becoming invisible. A must-see for all visitors to Odessa.

PHOTO CREDITS

Groβes Festspielhaus: © Karl Forster

Kleines Festspielhaus: © Karl Forster

Felsenreitschule: © Karl Forster

Mozarteum: © Christian Schneider

Wiener Staatsoper: Wiener Staatsoper GmbH/Axel Zeininger

Wiener Volksoper: © Dimo Dimov/Volksoper Vienna

Wiener Konzerthaus: © Herbert Schwingenschlögl

Hrvatsko Narodno Kazaliste: © Simon Boccanegra

Hrvatsko Narodno Kazaliste: © Sasha Novkovic

Statni Opera Praha : © State Opera Prague

Det Kongelige Teater: © The Royale Danish Theatre

Estonian National Opera: © Harri Rospu

Finlandia Concert Hall: © Eero Venhola

Opéra de Lille: © Frédéric Lovino. Interior: Mikaël Libert

Opéra national de Lyon: © Alain Franchella/Bertrand Stofleth

Théâtre musical du Chatelet: © Marie-Noelle Robert/Théâtre du Châtelet

Salle Pleyel: © Pierre-Emmanuel Rastoin/Salle Pleyel

Cité de la musique: © Cite de la Musique

Théâtre Mogador: © Theatre Mogador

Opéra du Rhin – Municipal Theatre of Strasbourg: © Alain Kaiser

Opéra de Toulon: © Khaldoun Belhatem

Théâtre du Capitole: © Patrice Nin

Deutsche Staatsoper unter den Linden: © BildTeam Berlin

Deutsche Oper: © Bernd Uhlig

Komische Oper: © Hanns Joosten

Konzerthaus Berlin – [Schauspielhaus am Gendarmenmarkt]: © Manfred Brückels

Philharmonie & Kammermusiksaal der Philharmonie: © Berliner Philharmoniker & © Reinhard Friedrich/Berliner Philharmoniker

Beethovenhalle: © M. Sondermann, Stadt Bonn

Kolner Philharmonie: © KölnMusik/Jörg Hejkal

Staatsoper Dresden – Semperoper: © Matthias Creutziger/Semperoper Dresden

Stadtische Buhnen – Frankfurt Oper: © Rui Camilo

Alte Oper Frankfurt: Alte Oper Frankfurt/Abdruck Honorarfrei

Konzerthaus Freiburg: © FWTM/Raach

Hamburgische Staatsoper: © Kurt-Michael Westermann, Abdruck frei bei Nennung des Fotografennamens

Badisches Staatstheater: Jochen Klenk

Leipzig Oper: © Andreas H. Birkigt, Fotograf

Neues Gewandhaus zu Leipzig: © Gewandhaus/Gert Mothes for all pictures

Nationaltheater – Bayerisches Staatsoper: © Wilfried Hösl for all pictures

Staatstheater am Gärtnerplatz: © Johannes Seyerlein

Münchner Philharmonie: © Gasteig München GmbH/Ralph Buchner, Carola Amschler

Symphony Hall: © Symphony Hall/ Mike Gutteridge

Canolfan Mileniwm Cymru: © Kiran Ridley

Glyndebourne Opera: © Mike Hoban

Royal Opera House: © Rob Moore

The Coliseum: ENO' images, Credit: © Richard Haughton. Other image Credit: Grant Smith

Barbican Centre: © Morley Von Sternberg

Royal Albert Hall: © Royal Albert Hall/ Marcus Ginns

Megaron: © Karamanian

Teatro comunale: © Archivio Teatro del Maggio Musicale Fiorentino, photos by New Press – Photo Firenze

Teatro Regio di Parma © Roberto Ricci

Auditorio dell'Accademia di Santa Cecilia: Riccardo Musacchio

Arena di Verona: Photos by Maurizio Brenzoni, authorized by Arena di Verona Foundation. All rights reserved

Calouste-Gulbenkian Foundation Auditorium: © RodrigoCésar

Opera Nationala Bucuresti: © Egyed Ufó Zoltán

Mariinsky Theatre: © Natasha Razina

Palau de la Musica Catalana: © Antoni Bofill

Palau de les Arts: © Palau de leas Arts Reina Sofía

Drottningholms Slottsteater: © Bengt Wanselius/Drottningholms Slottsteater for the interior, and Sofi Sykfont/drottningholms Slottsteater for the exterior photo

Grand Théâtre de Genève: © GTG/Carole Parodi

INDEX BY VENUE

Acropolis – Grand Auditorium Apollon	102
Alte Oper Frankfurt	164
Arena di Verona	304
The Assembly Rooms	193
Ateneul Român	362
Auditorio Alfredo Kraus	406
Auditorio dell'Accademia di Santa Cecilia	291
Auditorio Nacional de Música	412
Auditorium Parco della Musica	293
Badisches Staatstheater	173
Barbican Centre	229
Beethovenhalle	150
Belgrade Cultural Centre	378
The Belgrade Philharmonic Hall	384
Bridgewater Hall	248
Brighton Dome	205
Calouste Gulbenkian Foundation Auditorium	355
Cankarjev Dom	392
Canolfan Mileniwm Cymru	207
Casa da Música	359
Cemal Reşit Rey Concert Hall	449
Cité de la musique	105
The Coliseum	241
Concertgebouw Brugge	30
Cork Opera House	271
De Doelen Concertgebouw	333
Den Norske Opera	340
Der Musikverein	15
Det Kongelige Teater	63
Deutsche Oper	137
Deutsche Staatsoper unter den Linden	139
Drottningholms Slottsteater	425
Edinburgh Festival Theatre	212
Estonian National Opera	72
Euskalduna Palace	402
Felsenreitschule	2
Festspielhaus	135
Festspielhaus Baden-Baden	133
Filharmonia Narodowa	349

Finlandia Concert Hall	77	Koninklijke Vlaamse Opera	38
Gaiety Theatre	272	Konserthuset (Gothenburg)	423
Glinka Maly Zal	368	Konserthuset (Stockholm)	428
Glyndebourne Opera	222	Konzerthaus Berlin [Schauspielhaus am Gendarmenmarkt]	144
Gran Teatro del Liceo	397		
Gran Teatro La Fenice	301		
Grand Théâtre de Bordeaux	84	Konzerthaus Stuttgarter Liederhalle	188
Grand Théâtre de Genève	436	Kursaal Palace	414
Great Guild Hall	307	L'Arsenal	95
Grieghallen	339	L'auditori de Torrent	417
Großes Festspielhaus	4	L'Auditorium Maurice Ravel	88
Grosser Tonhallesaal– Gesellschaft Zurich	443	La Scala	283
The Guildhall	195	Laeiszhalle	171
Hamburgische Staatsoper	169	Linnahall	74
Het Muziektheater – De Nederlandse Opera Concertgebouw	331	Liverpool Philharmonic Hall	225
		Magyar Állami Operaház	262
Hrvatsko Narodno Kazalište (Split)	47	Manoel Theatre	323
		Mariinsky Theatre	369
Hrvatsko Narodno Kazalište (Zagreb)	48	Mayflower Theatre	251
		Megaron	258
The Icelandic Opera	268	Moscow P I Tchaikovsky Conservatory	366
Ilije M Kolarca Foundation	379		
IRCAM	107	Mozarteum	10
Juliusz Slowacki Theatre	347	Münchner Philharmonie	180
KKL Luzern (Culture and Congress Centre)	440	Musikhuset Aarhus	61
		Mussorgsky Opera & Ballet Theatre	371
Kleines Festspielhaus	7		
Kölner Philharmonie	152	Muziekcentrum Vredenburg	336
Komische Oper	142		
Koncertna Dvorana Vatroslav Lisinski	50	Národní Divadlo	53

Narodno Pozorište	381
National Centre for Early Music	254
National Concert Hall	274
National Opera & Ballet Theatre	451
National Philharmonic Hall	318
Nationaltheater – Bayerische Staatsoper	182
Natsionalen Dvorets na Kulturata	43
Neues Gewandhaus zu Leipzig	177
Odense Concert Hall [Nielsen Hall]	68
Odessa Opera	451
Olavshallen	344
Olympia	228
Oper der Stadt Köln	155
Oper Leipzig	175
Opéra - Théâtre	96
Opera & Ballet Theatre	319
Opéra Bastille	109
Opéra Berlioz et Salle Pasteur	98
Opera de Flandre – De Vlaamse Opera	28
Opéra de Lille	86
Opéra de Monte Carlo– Salle Garnier	328
Opéra de Nice	103
Opéra de Toulon	128
Opera House	308
Opéra Municipal	93
Opéra National de Lyon	90
Opera Nationala Bucuresti	362
Opera Royal de Wallonie	40
Opéra-Comédie	99
Operette Balzers	314
Operettenbühne Vaduz	315
Opernhaus Düsseldorf	162
Opernhaus Zurich	445
Palais des Beaux-Arts	33
Palais Garnier	112
Palau de la Música	418
Palau de la Música Catalana	399
Palau de les Arts	419
Pátria Hall	264
Philharmonie & Kammermusiksaal der Philharmonie	147
The Reduta	389
Riga Cathedral	311
Royal Albert Hall	232
Royal Concert Hall	217
The Royal Festival Hall	244
Royal Opera – Kungliga Operan	430
Royal Opera House	234
Rudolfinum	54
Salle Gaveau	115
Salle Pleyel	116
Salurinn	267
Salzburger Marionettentheater	12

Shostakovich Philharmonia	373
Sibeliustalo (Sibelius Hall)	79
Slovak National Theatre	387
Slovenian Philharmonic Hall	393
Sofia National Opera	44
St David's Hall	210
St James Cavalier Centre	325
St John's, Smith Square	238
St Petersburg State Capella	375
Staatsoper Dresden – Semperoper	157
Staatstheater am Gärtnerplatz	185
Staatstheater Stuttgart	190
StadtCasino	435
Städtische Bühnen – Oper Frankfurt	166
Státní Opera Praha	56
Stavanger Concert Hall	342
Stavovské Divadlo	58
Symphony Hall	201
Tchaikovsky Concert Hall	367
Teatr Wielki	351
Teatro Arriaga	404
Teatro Comunale	281
Teatro Comunale di Bologna	280
Teatro de la Maestranza	416
Teatro de la Zarzuela	408
Teatro dell'Opera	296
Teatro di San Carlo	285
Teatro Massimo	287
Teatro Nacional de Sao Carlos	357
Teatro Real	410
Teatro Regio (Turin)	299
Teatro Regio (Parma)	289
Théâtre Royal de la Monnaie – Opera National	35
Théâtre Municipal de Lausanne – Opéra	438
Theater Duisburg	160
Théâtre de l'Opéra Comique – Salle Favart	119
Théâtre des Champs-Elysees	120
Théâtre du Capitole	129
Théâtre Femina	85
Théâtre Graslin	101
Théâtre Mogador	122
Théâtre Municipal – Opéra du Rhin	126
Théâtre Musical du Châtelet	124
Theatre Royal (Glasgow)	219
Theatre Royal (Wexford)	277
Tivoli Concert Hall	65
Ulster Hall	196
Usher Hall	215
Villa Medici	298
Waterfront Hall	199
Wiener Konzerthaus	18
Wiener Staatsoper	21
Wiener Volksoper	24